Ireland's Atlantic Shore

PEOPLE AND PLACES FROM MIZEN TO MALIN

N
NW NE
W E
SW SE
S

Inishtrahull Lighthouse •
• Malin Head
Gortnamullan
& Whitestrand Bay
Fort Dunree •

Arranmore Island • • Burtonport
Rutland Island •
DONEGAL

Rotten Island Lighthouse • • Killybegs

Bundoran •

Céide Fields • Blackrock Lighthouse •
• Rosses Point
Enniscrone •
SLIGO

Blacksod Lighthouse •

Achill Island •
MAYO

Croagh Patrick •

Killary Harbour • • Leenane

Roundstone •
GALWAY

Rossaveal • Salthill •

Murrooghtoohy • • Kinvarra
Inis Oírr •
Cliffs of Moher •
Lahinch •
Spanish Point • CLARE

Kilkee •
Scattery Island •
Loop Head • • Tarbert
Ballybunion •

Banna Strand •
Fenit •
Mount Brandon • • Tralee
Castlegregory •
Cromane • KERRY
Rossbeigh •

Cahersiveen •
Valentia Island •
Ballinskelligs • Sneem •
Skellig Islands • Kenmare •
CORK
Ardgroom • • Glengarriff
Eyeries •
Allihies • Castletownbere •
Cahermore •
Black Ball Head • Sheep's Head •
Barleycove • Goleen • Schull •
Mizen Head • • Baltimore

• Fastnet Rock

Ireland's Atlantic Shore

People and Places from Mizen to Malin

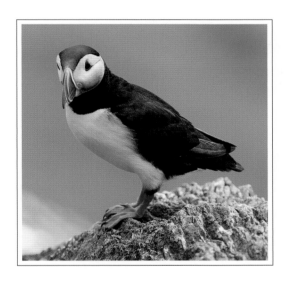

Valerie O'Sullivan

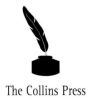

The Collins Press

FIRST PUBLISHED IN 2012 BY

The Collins Press

West Link Park

Doughcloyne

Wilton

Cork

British Library Cataloguing in Publication Data

O'Sullivan, Valerie.
Ireland's Atlantic Shore : People and Places from Mizen to Malin.
1. Atlantic Coast (Ireland) 2. Atlantic Coast (Ireland)—
Social life and customs. 3. Atlantic Coast (Ireland)—
Pictorial works.
1. Title
914.1'5'0946-dc23

ISBN-13: 9781848891586

Design and typesetting by Bright Idea, Killarney
Typeset in Gill Sans
Printed in Italy by Printer Trento

CONTENTS

COUNTY CORK

Baltimore	2	Glengarriff	26
The AK *Ilen* Returns Home from the Falklands	4	Castletownbere	28
The Fastnet Rock	10	MacCarthy's Bar	30
Mizen Head	15	Black Ball Head Signal Tower	32
The Sailmaker	18	Cahermore Harbour	33
ISAF World Team Championships in Schull	19	Casting votes on Dursey Island	34
Barleycove	21	Allihies	36
Sheep's Head Peninsula	22	Eyeries – All the Colours of the Rainbow	38
The Beara Peninsula	26	Ardgroom Stone Circle	39

COUNTY KERRY

Kenmare	41	Dingle Peninsula	79
Mikey Joe Burns, Sneem	43	Mount Brandon	80
Ballinskelligs	44	Power to the Wind	82
Keeper of the Light on Skellig Michael	47	Tralee Golf Club	84
Skellig Michael	52	Castlegregory	85
Valentia Island	64	Fenit	88
Cahersiveen	73	Banna Strand	90
Rossbeigh	76	Ballybunion	92
Cromane	77	Tarbert	93

COUNTY CLARE

Moneypoint	94	Spanish Point	111
Scattery Island	95	Lahinch	113
Diarmuid and Gráinne's Rock, Loop Head	97	The Irish Coast Guard	114
Loop Head Lighthouse	97	The Cliffs of Moher	121
Kilkee	98	Murrooghtoohy The Burren	126
Talty's Sea Vegetables	106		

County Galway

Inis Oírr	128	Johnaí Dubh, The Seaweed Man	143
Páraic Póil, Man of Aran	131	Roundstone	148
Kinvarra	135	The Bodhrán Maker	150
Salthill	138	Killary Harbour	154
Rossaveal	140	Leenane	156

Counties Mayo & Sligo

Croagh Patrick	159	Kilcullen's Edwardian Seaweed Baths, Enniscrone	176
Achill Island	164	Cain Kilcullen, Surfer	178
Blacksod Lighthouse	166	Rosses Point	180
Dominic Keogh – The Man Who Reads Stone	169	Blackrock Lighthouse	182
Fishers of Men – Stephen McHale	171	Prannie Rhatigan: A Gift from the Sea	184
The Céide Fields	174		

County Donegal

Bundoran Beach	187	Fort Dunree	202
Killybegs Harbour	189	Sea Rovers Football Club	206
Rotten Island Lighthouse	192	Peter McAvenue, Malin Head	208
Burtonport	193	Inishtrahull Lighthouse	209
Rutland Island	195	Whitestrand Bay	209
Arranmore RNLI	198	Banba's Crown	212
Mallagh Beacon	201	Malin Head	213

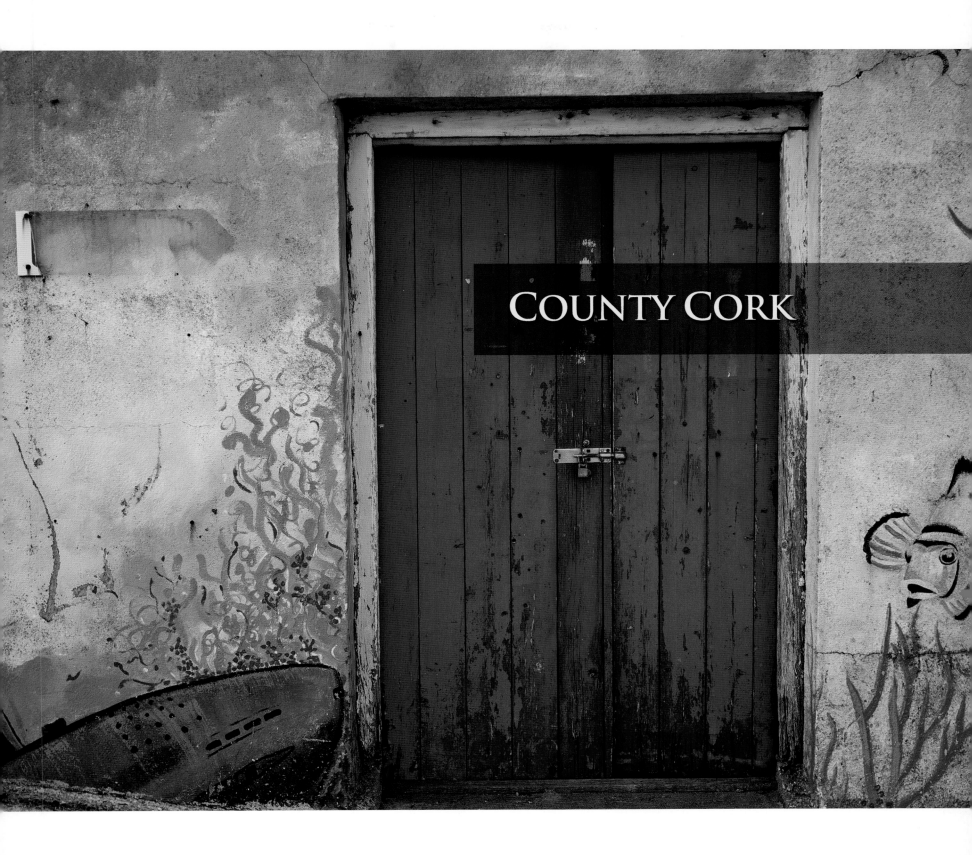

COUNTY CORK

BALTIMORE

THE VILLAGE of Baltimore is an old maritime port, 13km southwest of Skibbereen, steeped in nautical history. In 1631, in what became known as 'the Sack of Baltimore', pirates from Algiers and armed troops of the Ottoman Empire came ashore and carried off every person in the village.

Thankfully, activities are far more benign today. Its west Cork location makes it a centre point for day trips to nearby Sherkin and Cape Clare Islands. It is a very popular destination for the yachting fraternity, kayakers, deep sea divers, whale watchers, anglers, and all manner of holidaymakers, with nearby Roaring Water Bay a beautiful stretch of Atlantic water, a warm Gulf Stream and sheltered harbour.

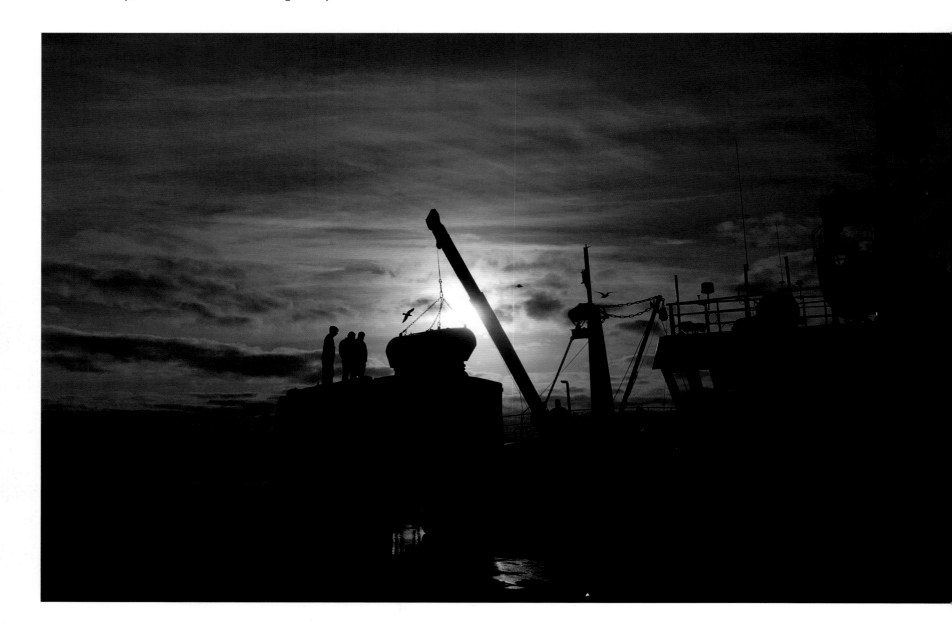

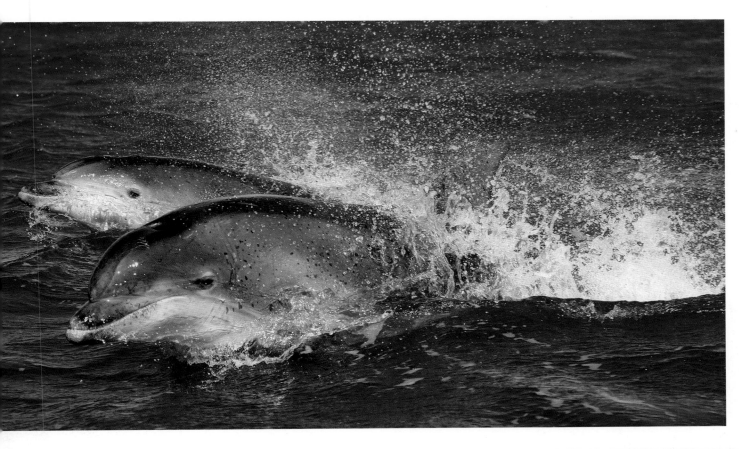

Top: Friendly bottlenose dolphins breezing by on Roaring Water Bay.

Right: This iconic structure, also known as 'Lot's Wife', was built in 1849, a navigational beacon to guide fishermen and sailors back to the entrance of Baltimore Harbour. The conical-shaped white beacon is 15.2m (50ft) high and serves as a popular viewing point.

Opposite: The local fishing industry is still important to the area. Here the day's catch is landed in the harbour.

P. 1: A maritime feel is preserved in this charming village.

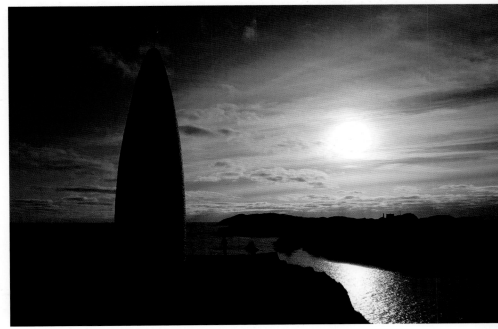

THE AK ILEN RETURNS HOME FROM THE FALKLANDS
THE REAL MARITIME ADVENTURE BEGINS...

By Lorna Siggins, *The Irish Times*

A TALL MAST of Sitka spruce from Vancouver Island, several currachs on frames, and a carvel Kenmare river boat reputedly built for the Lord Justice of Sneem are evidence of more than a hint of activity at the Ilen School of Wooden Boat Building. One of the founders of the school, Gary McMahon, and Liam Hegarty of the Oldcourt Boatyard near Baltimore have been working on restoration of a very special vessel, the ketch *Ilen*, which is 'as significant in Irish maritime history as the *Asgard* or its successor, *Asgard II*,' McMahon says. Designed by Conor O'Brien, the first Irishman to sail around the world in a small boat, it was built in the Fisheries School in Baltimore, west Cork, and named after a local river on its launching in 1926.

Eventually, it found its way to the Southern Ocean, for it was commissioned by the Falkland Islands Company to serve as a trader between the island communities. This it did for over fifty years before McMahon tracked it down and arranged for its return to Ireland in 1998. For him, it represented the 'perfect expression' of an Irish sailing vessel, and so he formed a not-for-profit maritime trust to restore or 'reconstruct' it. It became a social as well as a skill-sharing event, with a number of 'big boat build' workshops hosted in Hegartys' Oldcourt yard near Baltimore. He believes it will return to sea again as a sail-training vessel, filling the vacuum left by the loss of the state's brigantine *Asgard II,* which sank off the French coast in September 2008.

The training now established in Limerick is an extension of the *Ilen* project, and an 'adventure', as McMahon sees it – the 'prize' being the 'cargo of learning and imagination' acquired en route. Shortly after it was set up in 2011, over eighty students from all backgrounds had enlisted in weekly training, beginning with basic carpentry skills and graduating into boat construction.

It isn't the first such initiative, but it may be one of the most ambitious. Padraig Ó Duinnín's Meitheal Mara project in Cork runs courses to encourage young people back into education and training, and has inspired similar projects along the Atlantic seaboard and beyond. One of his former apprentices, Dublin sculptor Mark Redden, transported his passion for traditional craft to Barcelona in Spain.

When Redden finished building the second of two currachs, it was time to row. And so in 2009, Barcelona residents were treated to a St Patrick's Day spectacle that might be more familiar in harbours like Clare's Kilkee or Kerry's Portmagee.

Students who sign up to courses in the Ilen School in Limerick from 2012 will be accredited by Middlesex University's Irish Centre for Work-based Learning. Links have been developed with the USA's Northwest School of Wooden Boatbuilding and Sail Training International. One of the school's mentors, Dr Martin Kay, has also exchanged information with the EU Dorna project, named after the Galician 'dorna' or single-sail keel boat, which aims to preserve the nautical heritage of the northeast Atlantic. Whereas some European projects see this sort of training as an 'end', the Ilen School 'sees it as the beginning', he says.

The Ilen School's emphasis is on 'the engagement between the teacher and the pupil', McMahon explains – an 'irreducible relationship', which nurtures the imagination and facilitates the individual's journey, and goes beyond conventional training. The 'learning infrastructure' is designed for both practical and digital learning methods.

Geometrically intricate lines drawn in pencil on a board on the warehouse floor form the 'map' or chart for the pupils who will learn how to 'take the

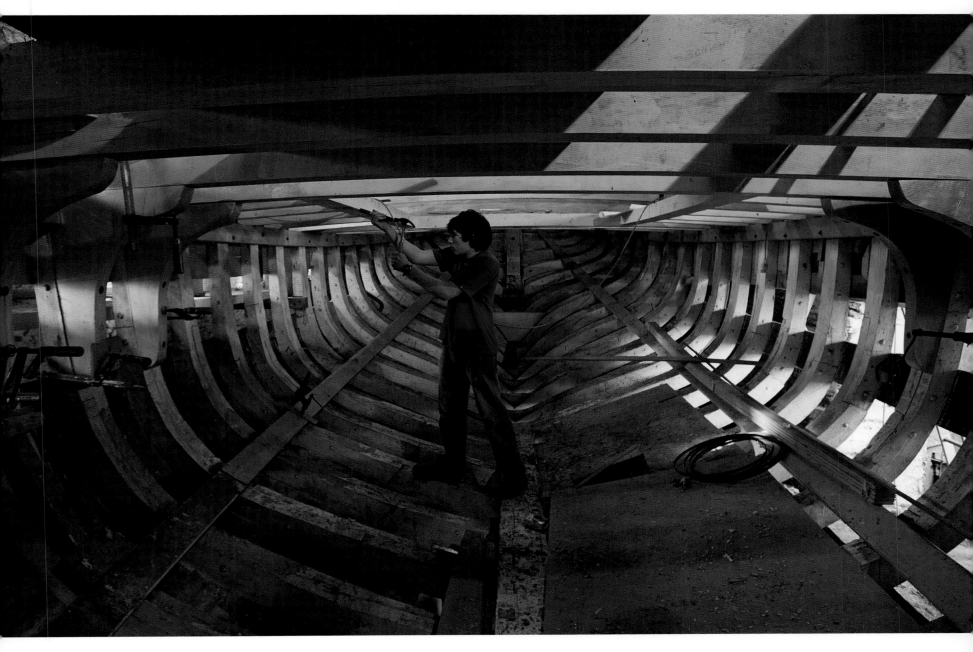

The Auxiliary Ketch (AK) *Ilen* was built in Baltimore, west Cork, in 1926 for service in the Falkland Islands. It was brought back to Ireland in 1998 and is being rebuilt for sail-training and demonstration purposes. The hull is being reconstructed in a traditional boat yard at Oldcourt, near Baltimore, while participants in the Limerick School are working on the masts and fittings. Here Pierce Ryan works on the hull in Hegarty's Boatyard, Baltimore.

lines and apply the dimensions,' explain Jim McInerney of Limerick city and Frank O'Sullivan of Crosshaven, County Cork. They are self-effacing about their own skills. 'You know some of the traditional craftsmen never worked from any plan – they just knew what hull would suit the particular coastal conditions…'

'Turning tacit into explicit skills,' is how Dr Andrew Hodgers, the school's academic director, describes the ethos. 'I don't think we quite anticipated the interest, but there is a great hunger for this out there.' The school hopes to provide a platform for related projects, and to participate in other 'eco-sensitive' learning initiatives identified in the EU Maritime 'Blue Paper'.

'Throughout, the care of boats will remain as important as their creation,' McMahon says. 'The school's sense of stewardship will have extended out into the Celtic Sea and even as far as similar shorelines and like-minded partners.' So while its appeal is in reaching back to the past, it is also 'shining a light forward for those prepared to take that first step.'

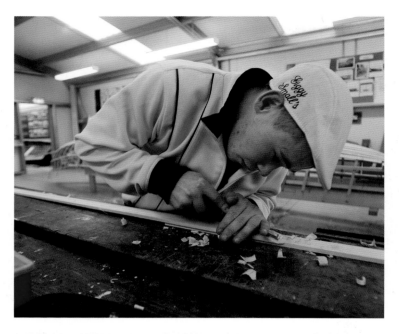

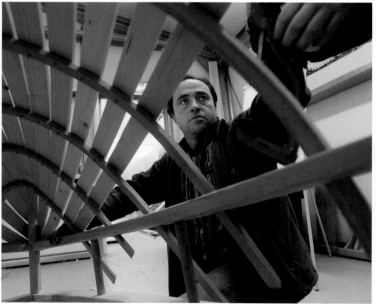

Opposite: Master joiner/turner Jim McInerney puts the finishing touches to the AK *Ilen's* pilot house, at the AK *Ilen* Wooden Boat Building School. Jim is involved in reviving and teaching the traditional skills of wooden boatbuilding to young people.

Above: Ian Waters of Limerick city attending the AK *Ilen* Wooden Boat Building School programme, where young people are taught the use of hand tools, awareness of the attributes of different woods and boat-construction techniques.

Below: James Madigan is an instructor and master craftsmen, teaching the art of currach making to young people at the boatbuilding school in Limerick.

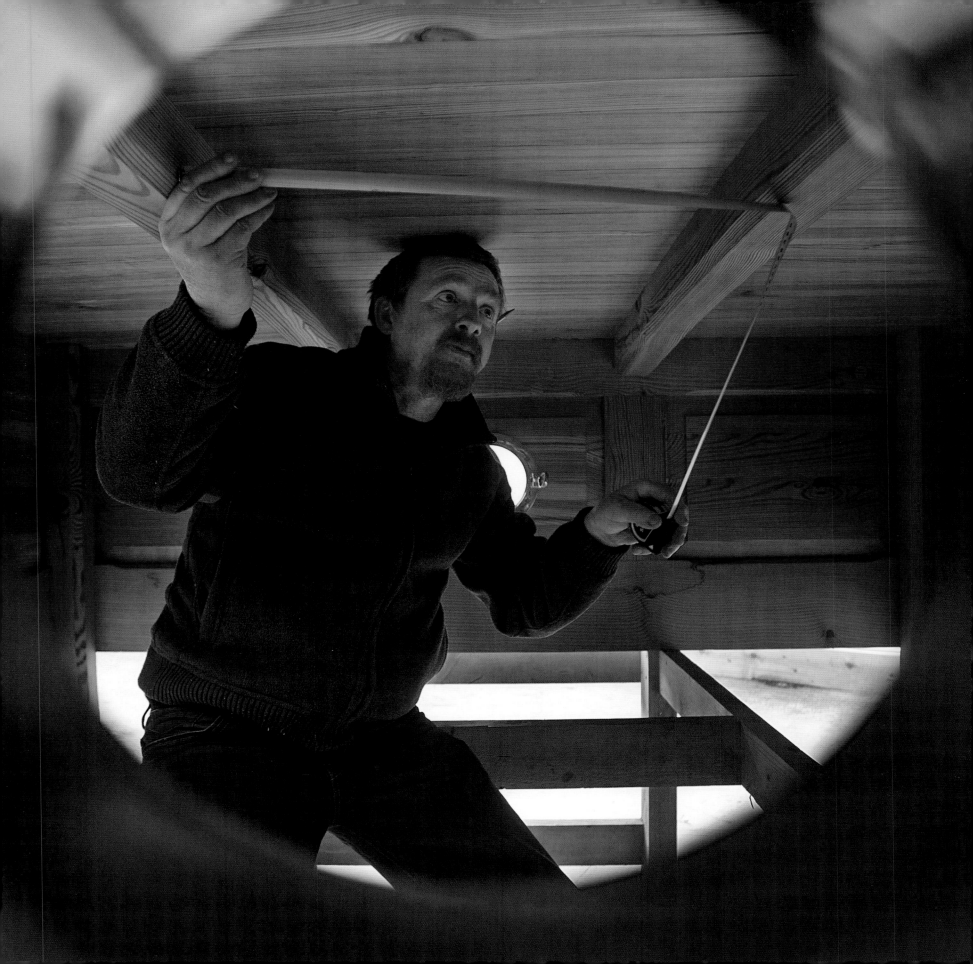

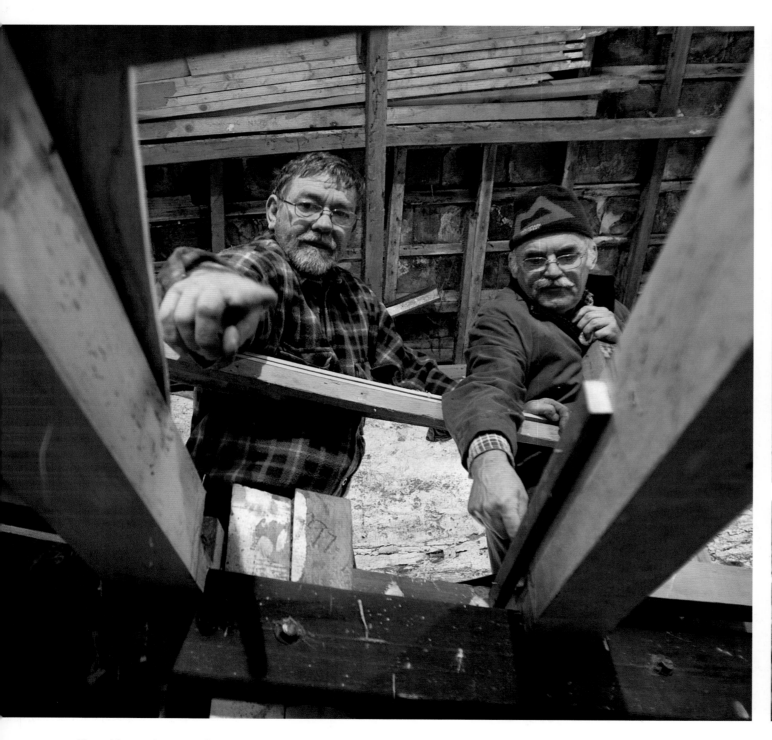
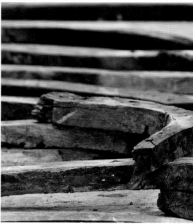
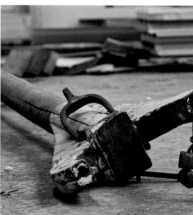
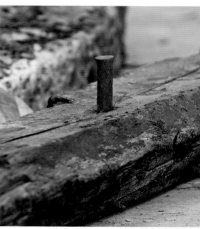

Above: Hegarty's senior shipwright in the project, Fachtna O'Sullivan (left), is a relative of one of *Ilen*'s original builders. With volunteer David Verdett.

Right: Parts of the original mast and fittings from the AK *Ilen*.

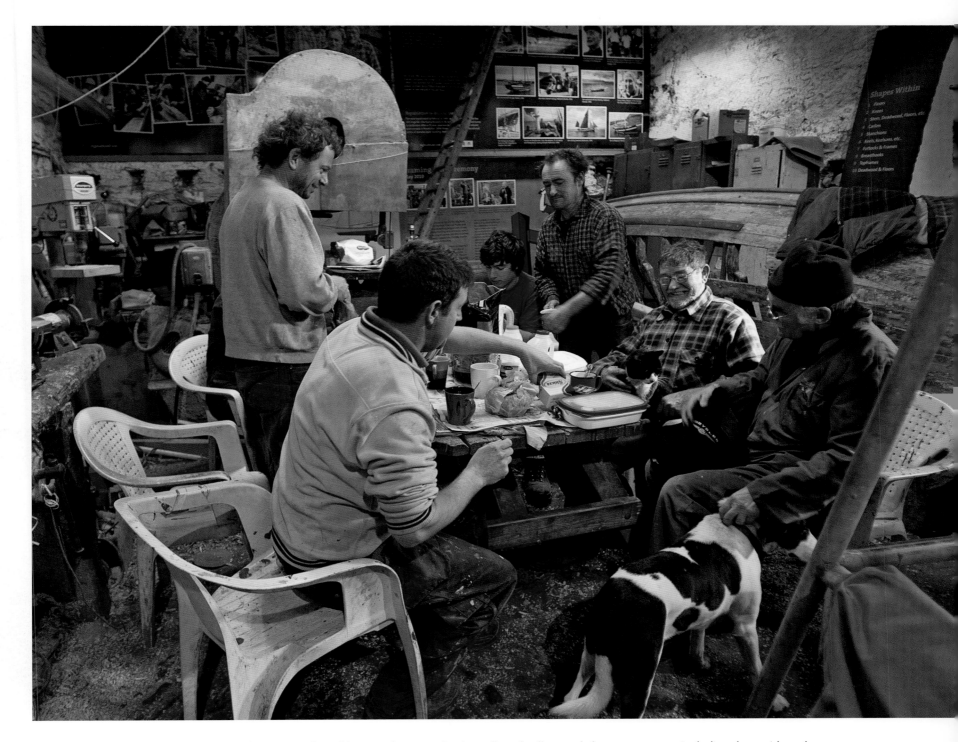

Lunchtime at the Oldcourt Boatyard: volunteers and neighbouring boat mechanics call to the *Ilen* workshop to meet up, including the resident dog, Jasper, and cat, Joe. (l–r): Leo McDermot, Nick Cotter, Pierce Ryan, Brendan Lennox, Fachtna O'Sullivan, shipwright, and David Verdett.

THE FASTNET ROCK

The Fastnet Rock stands firm against the ravaging Atlantic Ocean; locals talk of the lighthouse being submerged entirely by rogue waves. Lying 6.5km southwest of Clear Island, 19km off Baltimore and located southwest of Mizen Head, the Fastnet Rock is the most southerly point of Ireland. Its light is 49m (161ft) above high-water mark, making it the tallest lighthouse in Ireland.

The first lighthouse to be built on the Fastnet was designed by George Halpin and was made of cast iron. In 1865 the unforgiving Atlantic swept away much of the nearby Calf lighthouse and the Commissioners of Irish Lights sanctioned the building of a new tower. In 1896, William Douglas, an engineer with Irish Lights, proposed a granite tower 42ft in diameter and 147ft in height. Granite blocks were shipped from Cornwall to build the new lighthouse. Horrendous weather hampered the workers, and living conditions on the rock were less than comfortable. The foreman in charge of its construction, James Kavanagh, who joined the project in 1896, stayed on the Fastnet until the last granite block was in place. He had personally set every stone on the lighthouse.

The tower is divided into seven rooms with granite floors. On the first floor is the storeroom. It contained the magazine for storing gun cotton for the fog signal. On the second floor was the oil-room and, on the third floor, a spare bedroom for workmen. The fourth floor contained the principal storeroom with a special felt-lined cupboard for storing the detonators for the fog signal charges. The fifth floor served as a kitchen, on the sixth floor were the bedrooms for the lighthouse keepers, while the seventh floor was a service room with a cast iron rainwater tank.

The new light was eventually established on 27 June 1904. The 1854 light was discontinued and the cast iron tower dismantled down to its lower room, which became an oil store. The Commissioners of Irish Lights came to Crookhaven on board the Irish Lights' steamer SS *Alexandra* to inspect the light's beams; with new technology, the intense flash was visible for up to 27 nautical miles.

There were six keepers at the Fastnet Rock – four at a time and two on leave. Reliefs were twice a month when two men were taken off. Each man did four weeks on, two weeks off. One man had to stay on watch during daytime to look out for fog and to signal passing ships. As soon as fog was seen another man was called up to work the fog signal.

Name	Fastnet
Latitude	51°23.358' North
Longitude	009°36.178' West
Character	Fl W 5s. Exhibited by day in conditions of poor visibility
Light Range	27 nautical miles
Height of tower	54m
Height of light above MHWS	49m
Radar beacon	Morse 'G' on vessel's radar display

Technical data courtesy of Commissioners of Irish Lights

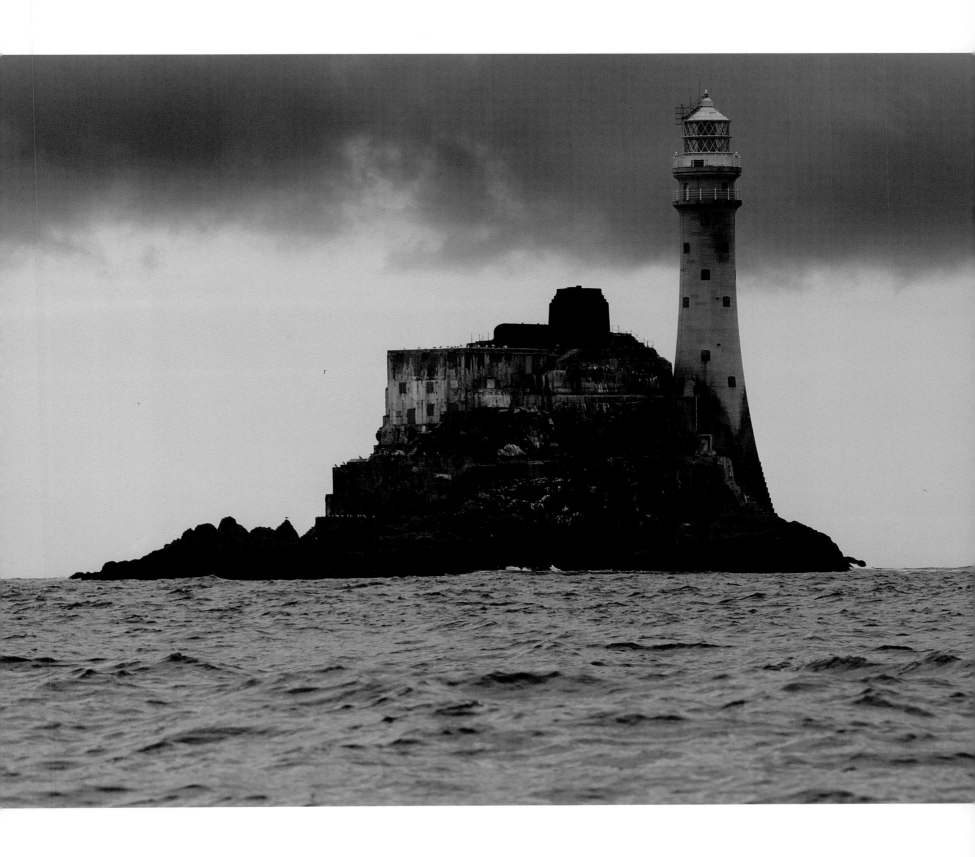

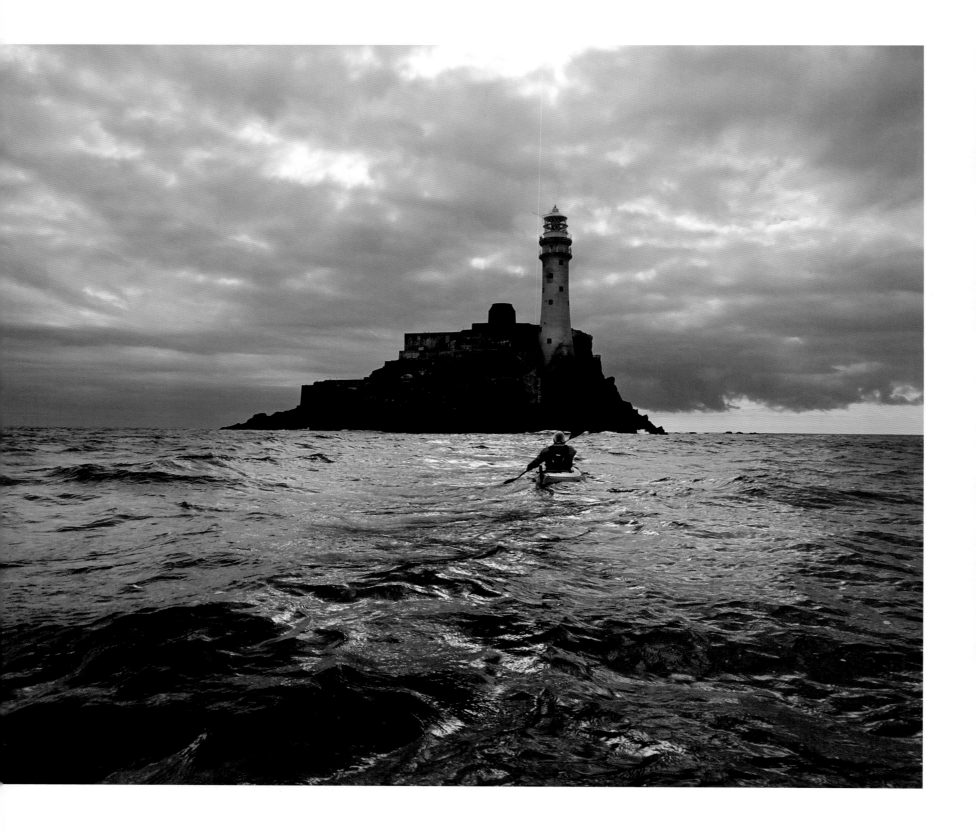

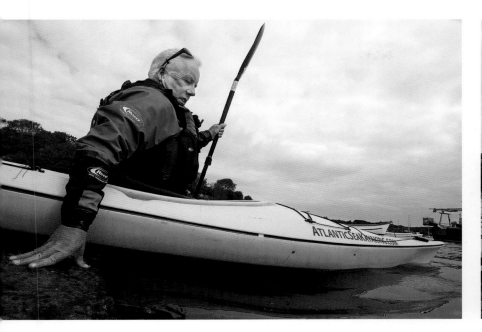
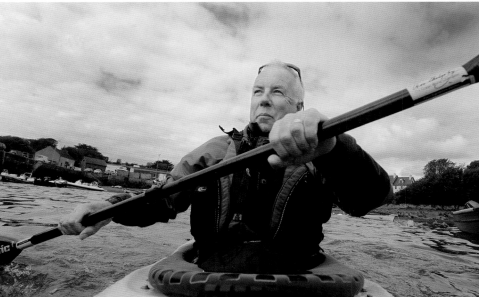
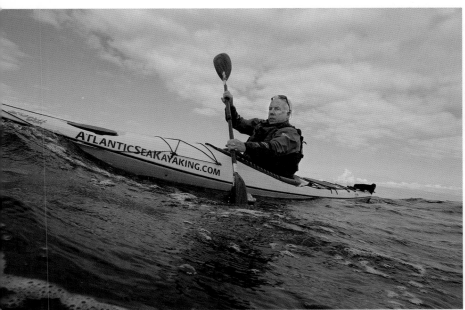
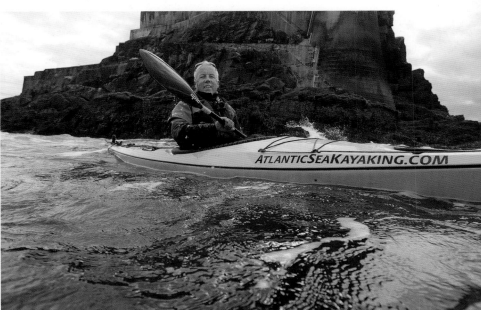

Jim Kennedy owns and runs Atlantic Sea Kayaking, based in Schull, west Cork. A level 5 Irish Canoe Union sea kayak instructor, Jim has raced with the Irish National Kayaking team and has been the Irish and British Sprint and National kayak champion. He won the International Devizes-to-Westminster 126-mile non-stop kayak marathon, and also leads expedition tours in Ireland, Spain, Mexico, Italy and America. Organising a kayaking trip to the iconic Fastnet Rock proved arduous, during what seemed to be the worst year of Atlantic sea swells and unpredictable weather in Ireland in 2010.

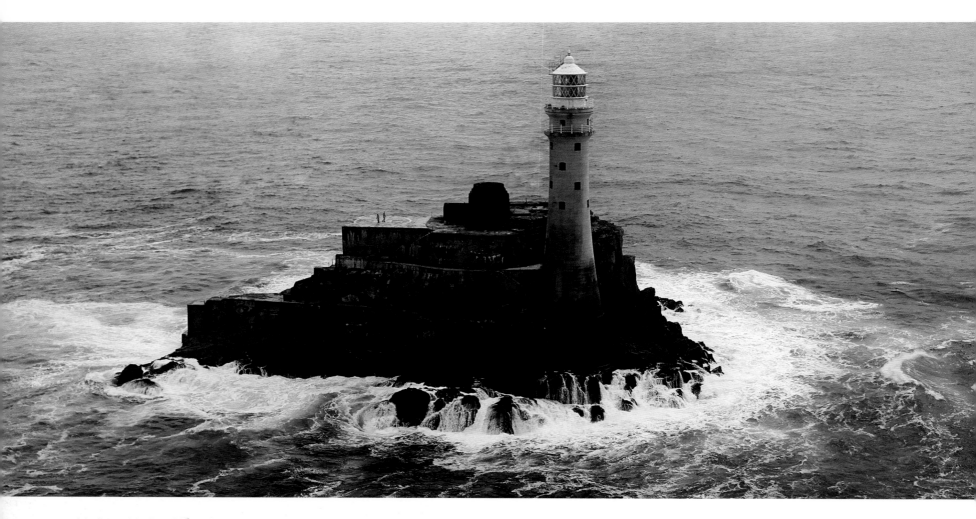

Neilly and Jackie O'Reilly wait for the helicopter to arrive to take them home after three days of maintenance work on the Fastnet.

The Fastnet Lighthouse was automated in March 1989 and, in January 2011 with advanced technology in navigation, the fog signal was permanently discontinued. Now Fastnet is *Carraig Aonair* – 'the lonely rock' – once more, except for lighthouse keeper Neilly O'Reilly, who maintains the lighthouse every three weeks. Often stranded for days at a time because of mountainous seas and seasonal high winds, he has great affection for the rock and his work. Fastnet now guides sailors, and yachtsmen and women home, and is used as a mark for local yacht races in nearby Schull, and also the classic biennial Fastnet Race, from Cowes on the Isle of Wight.

In the 1979 Fastnet Race, one of the worst sailing disasters of modern times occurred. Over 300 vessels were competing when an Atlantic storm struck, capsizing twenty-five boats. Fifteen people lost their lives. The former British Prime Minister Edward Heath survived. The event led to more safety measures for boats, such as more ballast to be carried. Improvements were also made to safety harnesses and radio communications.

In 2011, *Rambler 100* capsized at the Fastnet Rock after losing her keel. This custom-built superyacht was favourite to win The Rolex Fastnet Race that year. All twenty-one crew members were rescued: sixteen were picked up by the RNLI Baltimore lifeboat *Hilda Jarrett*, and five, including the owner/skipper George David, were rescued by Baltimore diving vessel *Wave Chieftain* after spending two and a half hours in the water.

MIZEN HEAD

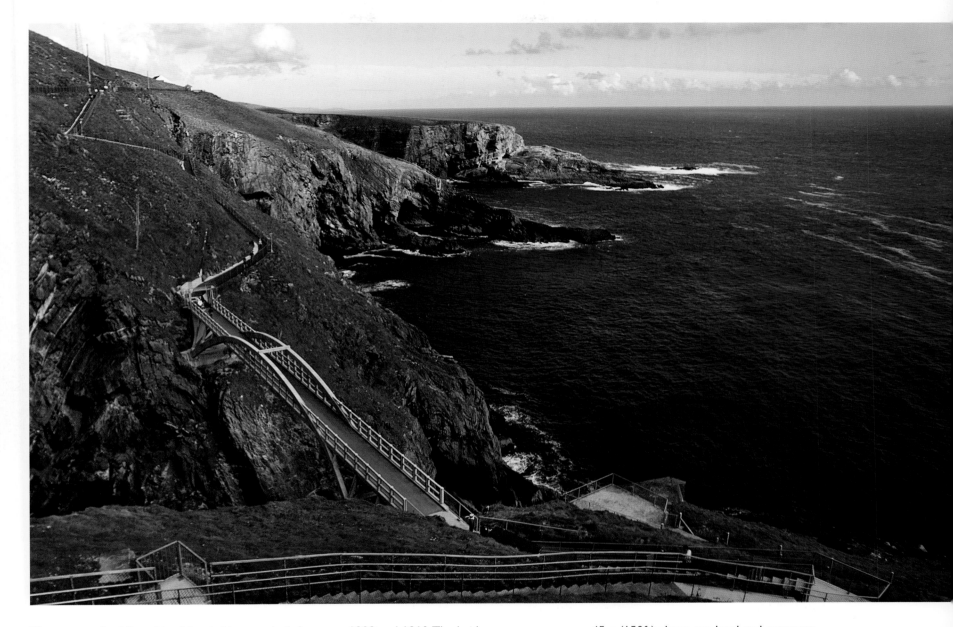

The spectacular Mizen Head footbridge was built between 1908 and 1910. The bridge spans a sea gorge 45m (150ft) above sea level and connects the mainland to Cloghan Island. Its purpose was to provide access for lighthouse keepers and staff of the Commissioners of Irish Lights in the operation and maintenance of the aids to navigation facilities at Mizen Head. The original Victorian bridge stood the test of time but weather conditions caused serious deterioration. In 2010, a replica bridge was built, constructed with reinforced concrete and stainless steel. The €1.8m reconstruction project was funded by Fáilte Ireland, the Commissioners of Irish Lights and Cork County Council. The bridge was opened in June 2011 by Leo Varadkar, Minister for Transport, Tourism & Sport.

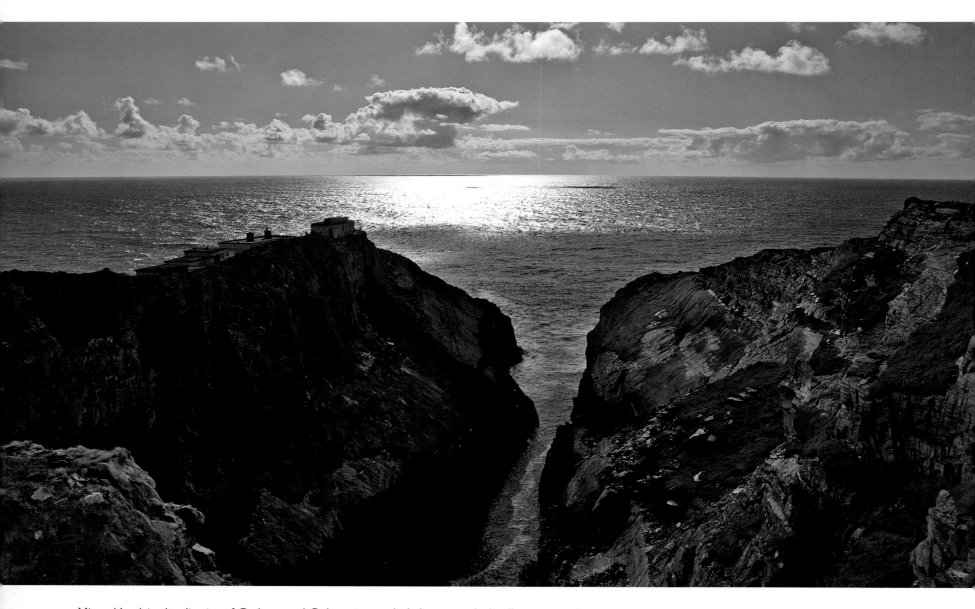

Mizen Head, in the district of Carbery and Goleen, is popularly known as Ireland's most southwesterly point. Even the best of Cork weather cannot soften this daunting seascape and cliff face, rimmed by the wild Atlantic.

The Mizen Head Signal Station was completed in 1909. In 1931, a wireless beacon was installed and in 1959 a light was placed on the rocks at the end of the head at a height of 55m (180ft), with a range of 13 miles in clear weather. The fog signal was discontinued in the 1970s when sonar and satellite navigation (GPS) took over.

In 1993 Mizen Head Signal Station was automated by the Commissioners of Irish Lights. In 1993, with a lease from the Irish Lights and funding from the first LEADER programme of EU funding for rural development, the Goleen community registered a co-operative to develop a visitor attraction here. Now Mizen Head Signal Station is an award-winning Maritime Museum and Heritage Attraction. This authentic all-weather experience documents the maritime history and recreates the golden era of Irish Lights and seafarers.

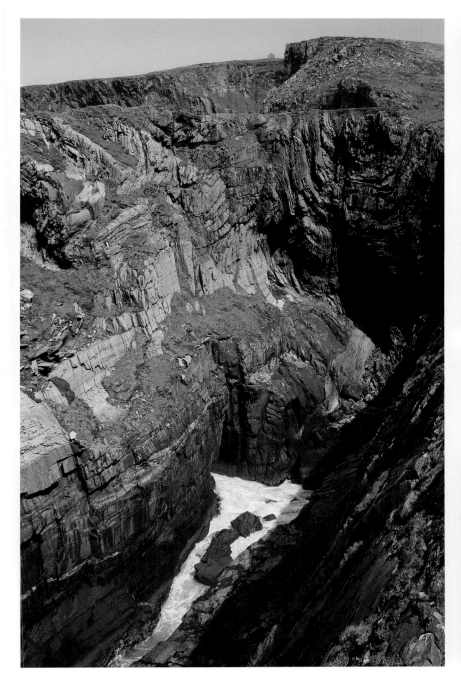

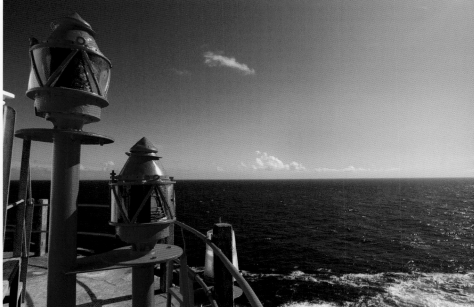

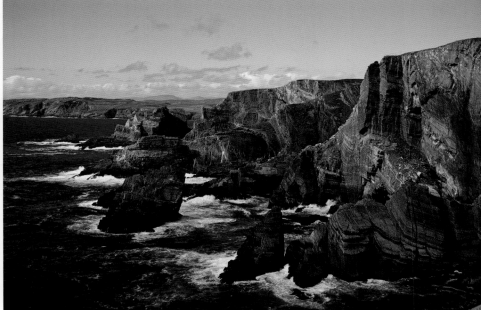

Clockwise from above:

A view from the suspension bridge, 45m (150ft) above sea level, of the gorge below; overlooking the Atlantic Ocean from the signal station;

the dramatic coastline at Mizen Head.

THE SAILMAKER

When French sailor and author Christophe Houdaille moved to west Cork in 2003, he found himself drawn to the beauty, isolation and ideal sailing conditions at Schull Harbour. He established his company, Fastnet Sails, in the former Church of Ireland church in Goleen in 2003. The church provides the perfect space for making sails, which come in many shapes and sizes. The floors are raised 4ft above the original floor to accommodate the sewing machines. Work in winter can be harsh as there is no heating in the church.

Christophe supplies and repairs sails for both leisure yachtsmen and the Irish navy. He exports sails to France, Italy and Argentina, and to transoceanic cruisers. He has worked on various special projects, manufacturing a set of five sails for a 25m (82ft) converted trawler and also supplies dinghy sails for the local sailing school in Schull.

Christophe's love of the sea is evident in his work. He has sailed since he was six years of age, and says he is 'only truly happy when on a boat'. After leaving school, Christophe purchased an 11m (37ft) steel boat and headed for Antarctica where he spent five years trekking and sailing around South Georgia, and the Falkland and Kerguelen Islands. He has written three books about his adventures: *Îles des Quarantièmes, Au vent des Kerguelen* and *Le Chant des Voiles*.

Sailing to Christophe encompasses all his being: 'being on a boat, you're playing with something which is true, if there is a storm, there's nothing to do about it, the storm is not there to upset you, you're not there to observe the storm, you just have to deal with it technically. You need some knowledge, you need some strength, you need some nerves to get you through'.

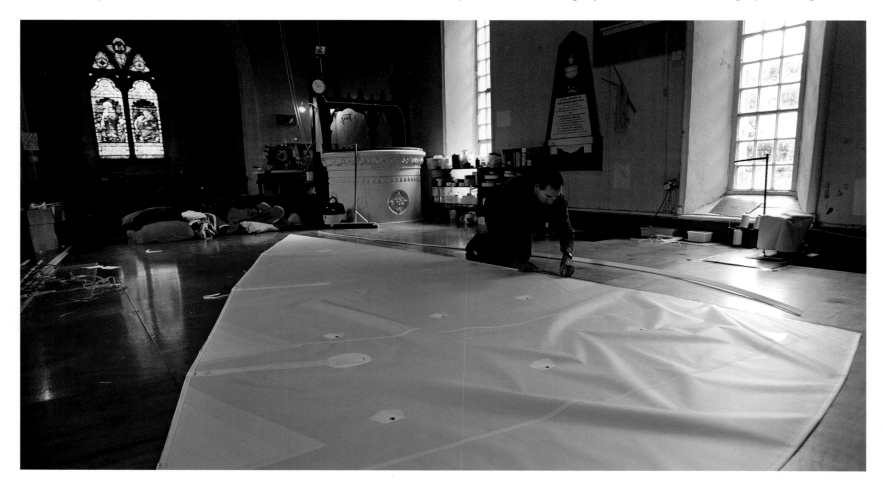

THE INTERNATIONAL SAILING FEDERATION (ISAF) IN SCHULL

Right: Sailing teams from Australia, Japan, the USA, Thailand, Italy, Spain and Ireland descended on the seaside village of Schull in July 2011 to contest the ISAF Team Racing World Championships at both open and youth level. The host country had to provide 25 identical sailing boats for the championships; the hulls were made in Midleton, County Cork, and fitted out in Schull by bosun Mark McCarthy.

Below: Kevin Murray of Fastnet Marine Outdoor Education Centre organised the safety launches, coordinated the jury boats, coxswains and safety RIBs for the event.

Below right: Locals Bridie O'Driscoll and Jean O'Hanlon watch the Parade of Nations, which welcomed the teams competing in the ISAF Championships.

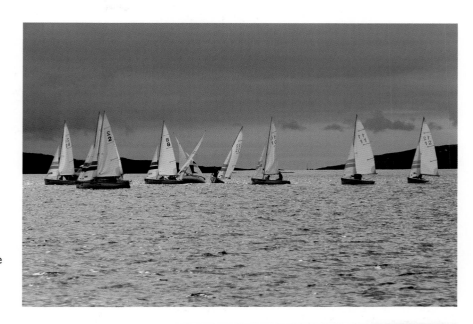

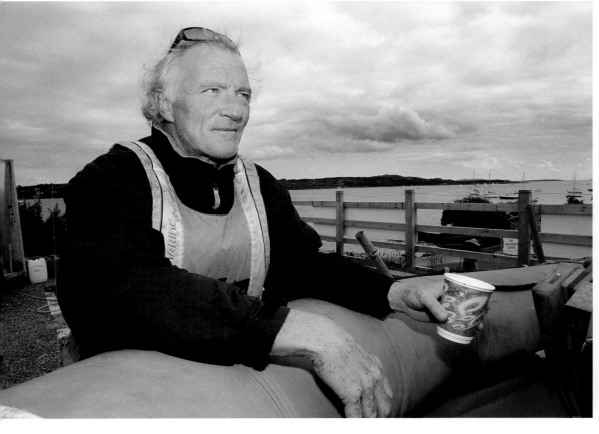

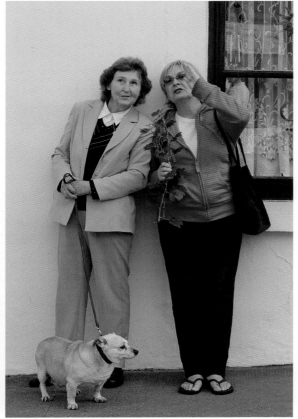

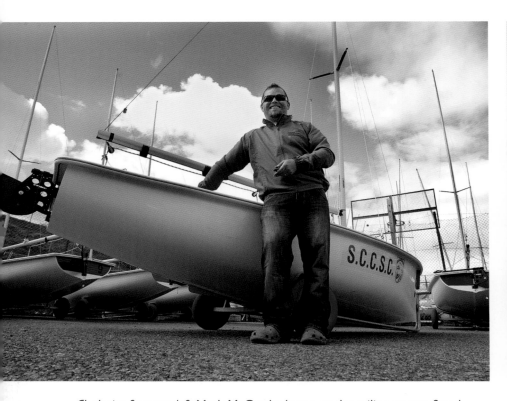

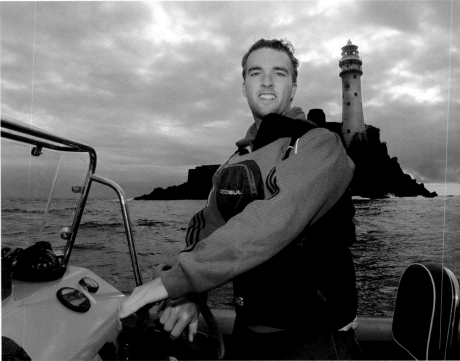

Clockwise from top left: Mark McCarthy, bosun at the sailing centre, fitted out the 25 sailing boats for the ISAF Championships. He has sailed since he was nine years old and his family have a strong association with the sea. His father, Geoff, was lighthouse keeper at the Mizen, Bull and Fastnet lighthouses;

Simon Murray, in front of the iconic Fastnet lighthouse, was one of the many RIB operators volunteering for the ISAF World Team Racing Championships in Schull. Simon is a full-time student and currently working on his Masters degree in medical physics in NUI Galway;

Waiting for the whistle: boys from Ballydehob GAA Club wait to take their place in the Parade of Nations in Schull.

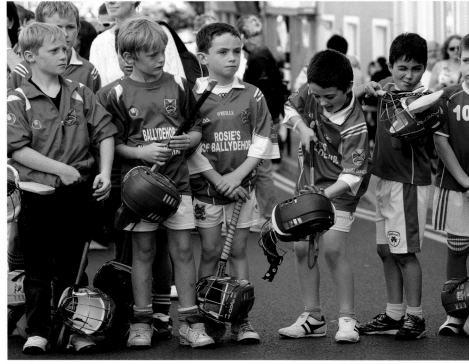

BARLEYCOVE

Barleycove Beach, near Mizen Head, has been designated as a Special Area of Conservation by the EU. Its beautiful sand dunes were deposited in the tidal wave that swept Europe after the Great Lisbon Earthquake in 1755.

John O'Donoghue, poet and philosopher, reflects on the ocean as immense divinity, from his book *The Four Elements*: 'One of the most ancient conversations on the planet is that between the sea and the seashore. This conversation is a sublime metaphor for expectation. The land is trapped where it is. It can never move anywhere. The Zen-like stillness and "thereness" of the land makes it vulnerable, it cannot get out of the way. But the ocean has a fluency, it can travel anywhere, even deeper into its own self.'

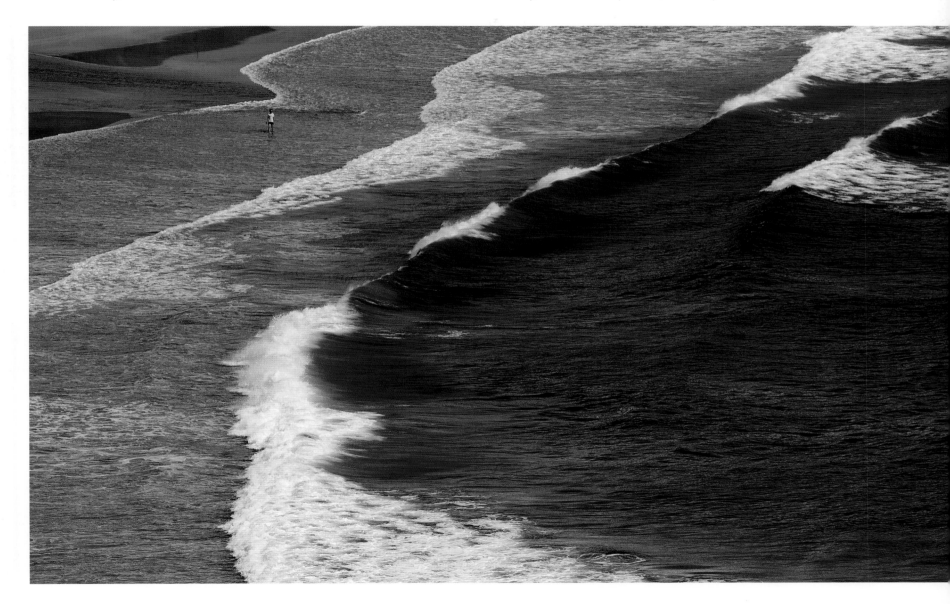

SHEEP'S HEAD PENINSULA

What sets Sheep's Head apart from the three neighbouring peninsulas is its remoteness and rugged landscape. It is reputed to have the mildest climate in Ireland because of its proximity to the Gulf Stream. The highest point on the peninsula is just 345m (1,132ft). The headland is at the end of the peninsula between Bantry Bay and Dunmanus Bay.

The Sheep's Head Way is a long-distance walking route of 88km (55 miles). Following old tracks and roads the route starts and finishes in Bantry and takes you to Sheep's Head at the tip of the peninsula. The walks are clearly defined, along ridges, moors and coastline routes, easy terrain for the holiday walker.

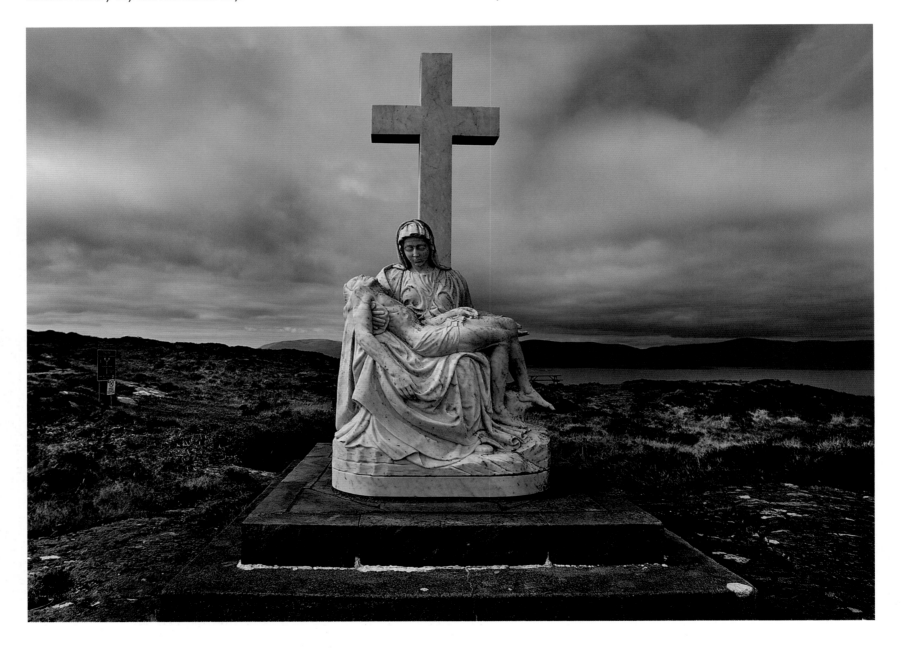

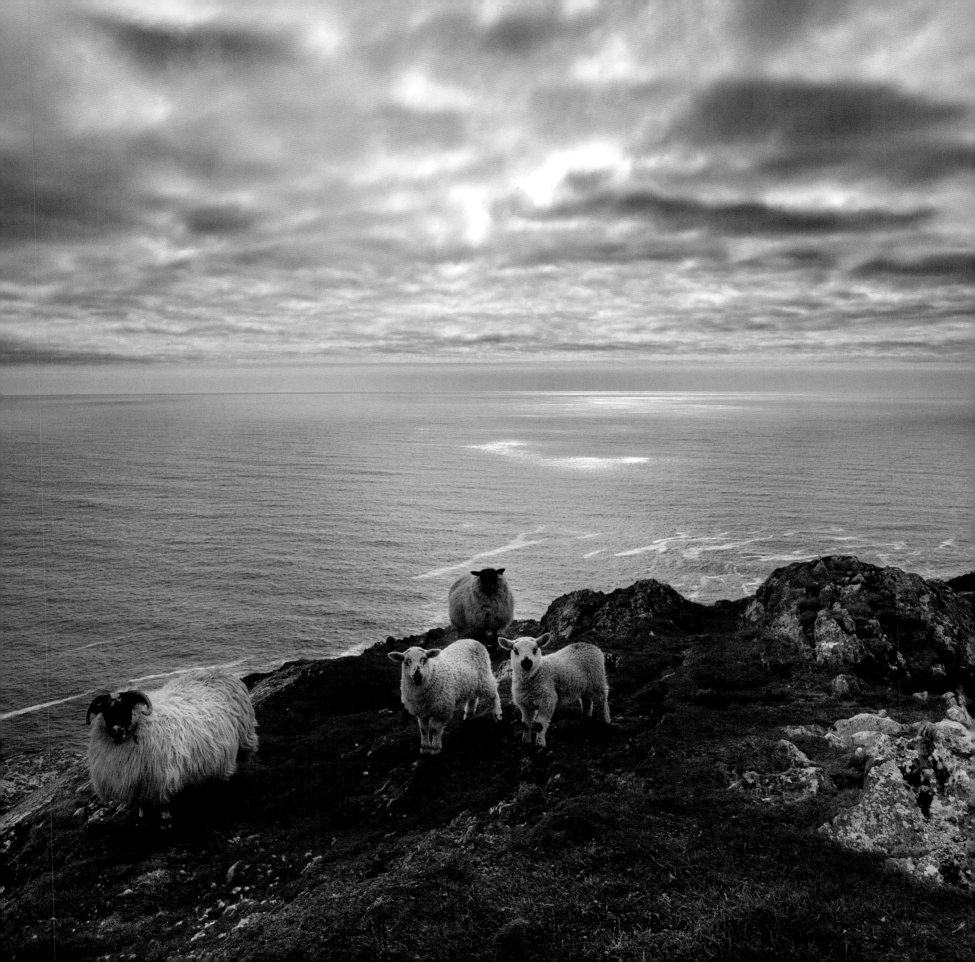

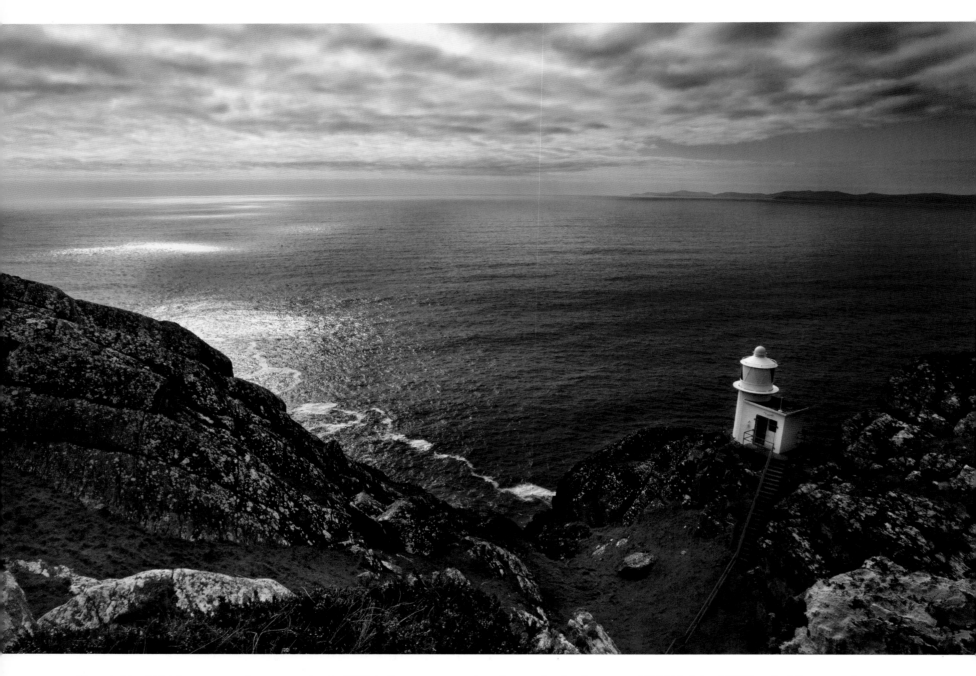

Sheep's Head Lighthouse came into operation in 1968, built to accommodate the nearby development of Whiddy Island Oil Terminal. Because of its distance from the road, much of the equipment and materials used in the construction of the lighthouse had to be airlifted by helicopter. The lighthouse consists of a 7m/23ft-high round tower on a square building. The lantern is 83m (272ft) above sea level.

The lighthouse marks the southern tip of Bantry Bay, and a 2km trail walk leads to the lighthouse with spectacular views of the peninsula.

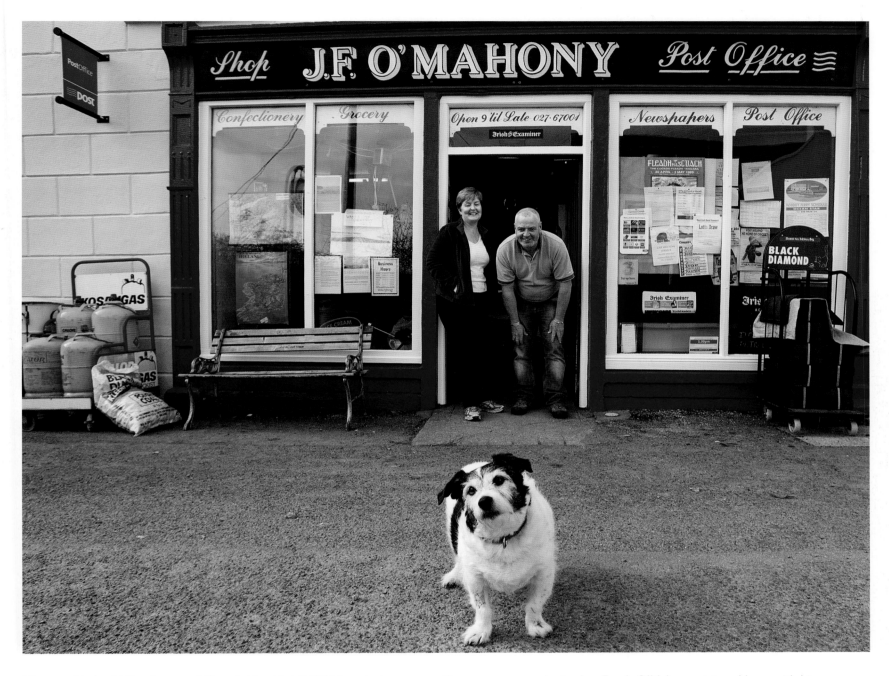

The social hub of Kilcrohane and Sheep's Head is J. F. O'Mahony's shop, post office, restaurant and wine bar. Frank O'Mahony, pictured here with his wife, Maria, and their dog, Flor, is the fifth generation of O'Mahonys to run the family shop, which opened in 1860.

THE BEARA PENINSULA

The Beara Peninsula is dotted with old-world seaside towns and fishing villages, megalithic stone circles and neolithic sites. It is thought to have more archaeological sites than anywhere else in Europe, some of which date from 2500 BC, including standing stones, souterrains and burial grounds. Its mining history dates back to the Bronze Age. It was the seat of power of the O'Sullivan Beare, the last Gaelic chieftain left standing after the Battle of Kinsale in 1602, against Queen Elizabeth I.

Beara is the least frequented of all the peninsulas in the southwest of Ireland. It is dominated by the Caha Mountains, which form the spine of Beara, and the Slieve Miskish Mountains. The windy Healy Pass between Adrigole and Lauragh in County Kerry rises 334m (1,900ft) above sea level, with beautiful glacial lakes, and magnificent views of Kerry and Cork.

The peninsula is also home to the Dzogchen Beara, a Tibetan Buddhist Retreat centre, is situated on the most majestic coastal cliffs on Beara, 8km (5 miles) from Castletownbere.

GLENGARRIFF

Glengarriff – the name means 'rough glen' – is nestled between Bantry Bay and the Caha Mountains. It has been an important tourist destination since 1700, and in Victorian times it was an important stop on the Prince of Wales Route, which included Killarney and Bantry.

Because of its sheltered location and the warming influence of the Gulf Stream, its almost subtropical climate is favourable to the growth of ornamental plants from many parts of the world. Its numerous natural attractions include Garnish Island, an island garden (known in Victorian times as 'the Madeira of Ireland') and Glengarriff Nature Reserve, which contains some of the oldest and most extensive oak and birch groves left in Ireland and well-marked walking trails.

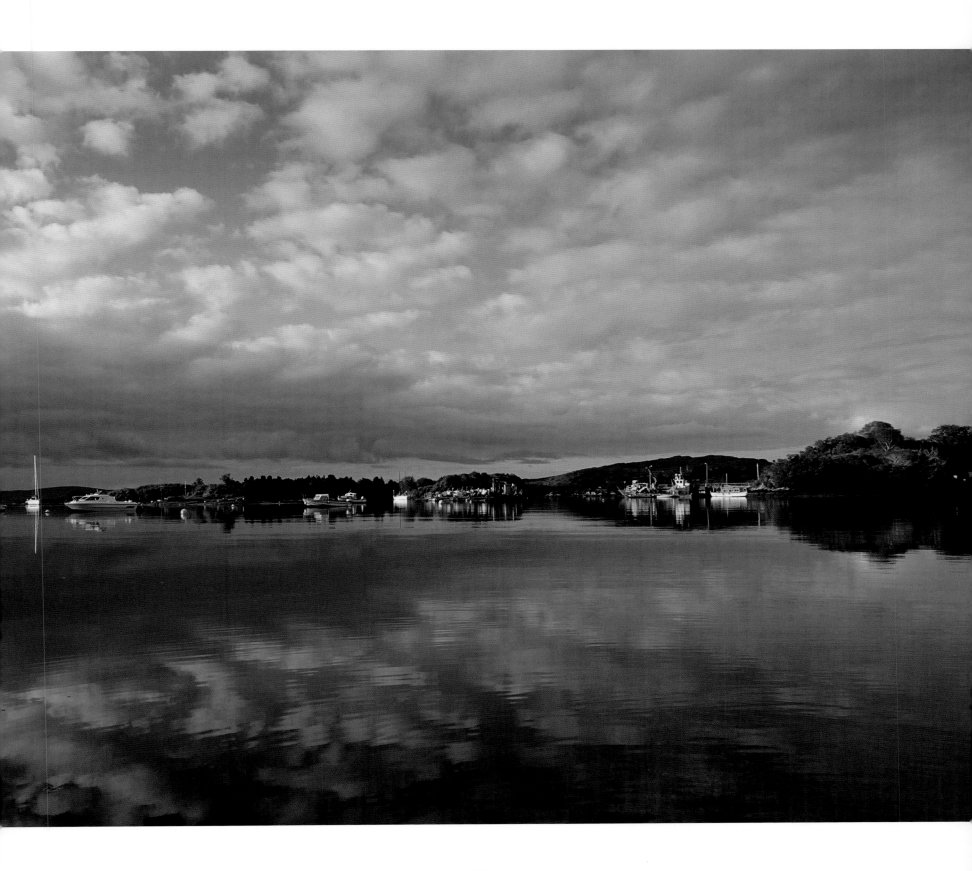

CASTLETOWNBERE

Right: John O'Shea, chairman and founding member of Castletownbere Rowing Club and starter for the annual Castletownbere Gig Regatta.

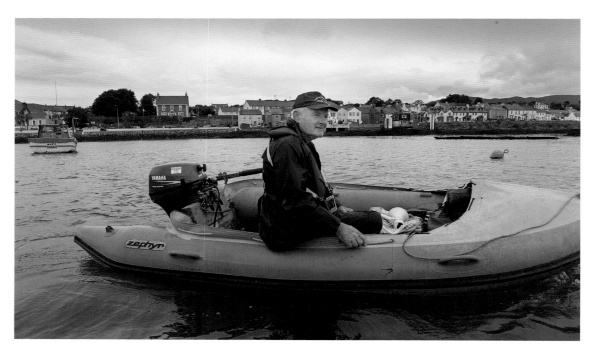

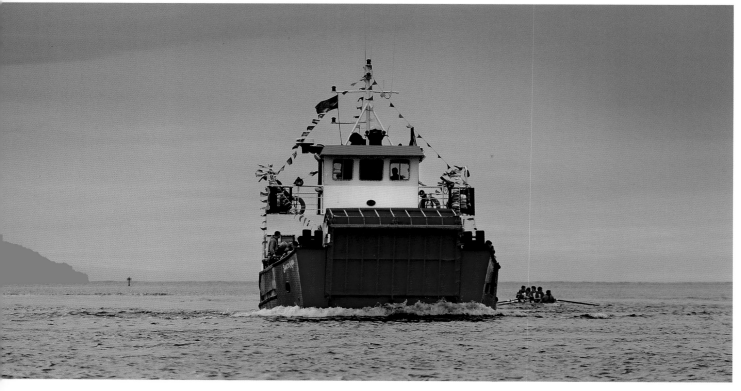

Left: Bere Island ferry *Santa Maria* making its way to the island from the slipway in Castletownbere. Alongside are members of the Kenmare Rowing Club, on their way to the start of the annual regatta, which is held on the August bank holiday.

Right: Castletownbere is the principal town on the Beara Peninsula. Fishing is the chief economic activity in the town – it is the largest whitefish port in Ireland – and it is the second-safest natural harbour in the world.

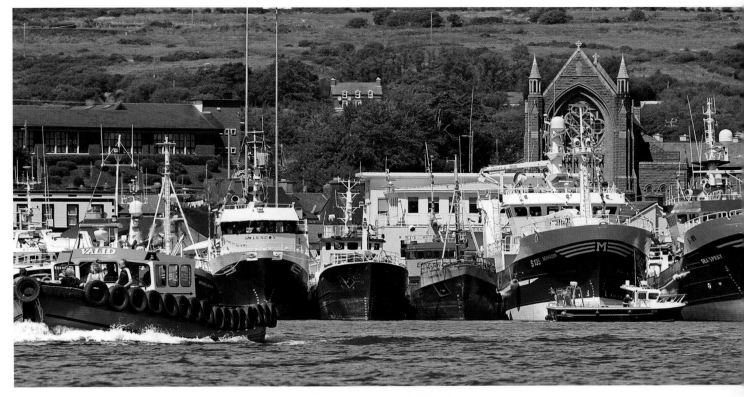

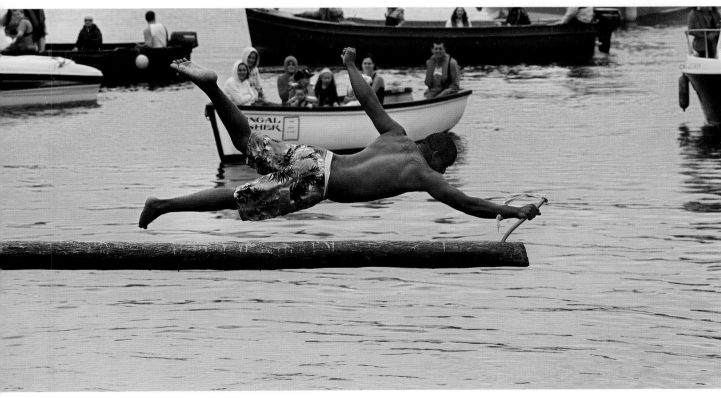

Left: William O'Sullivan, from Bere Island, competing in the greasy pole competition at Castletownbere's annual regatta in August.

MacCarthy's Bar

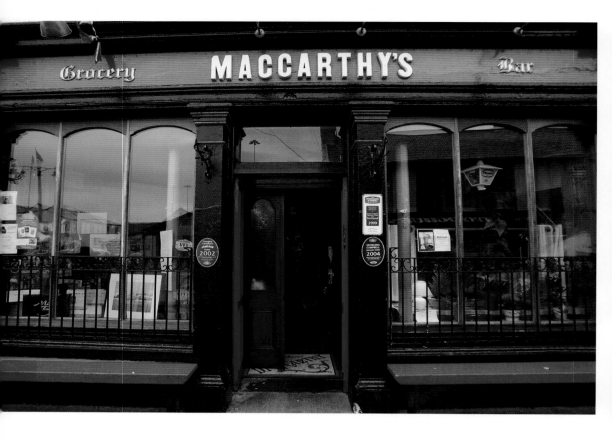

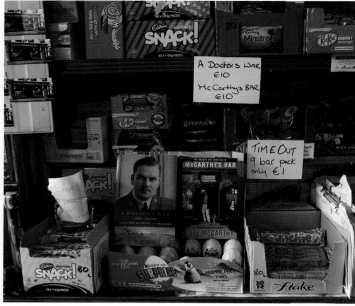

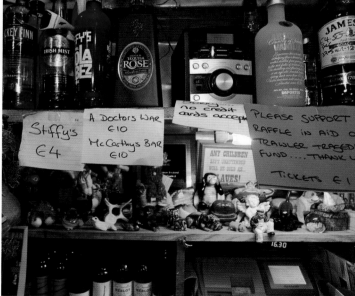

The world-renowned MacCarthy's Bar, in the heart of Castletownbere in west Cork, is an old-world pub and provisions store. It is celebrated in travel writer Pete McCarthy's book *McCarthy's Bar*.

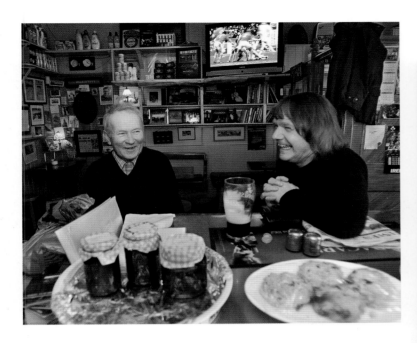

Above: Local men, Michael O'Sullivan (left) and Geoff Ward, enjoying a pint together in MacCarthy's Bar.

Below: The floor tiles at the front door came from the nearby Church of the Sacred Heart, built in 1912.

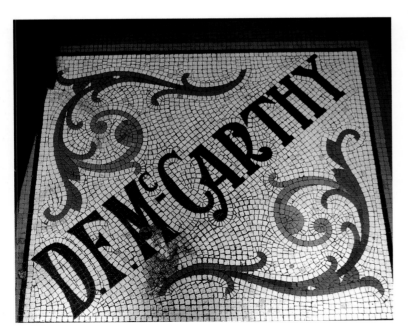

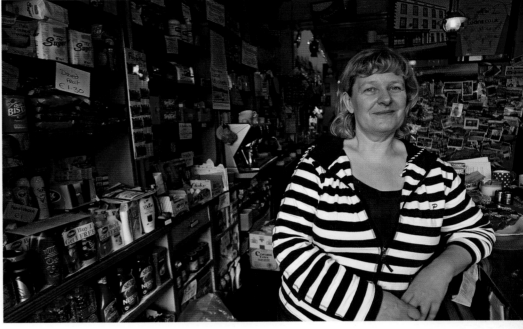

Adrienne MacCarthy took over the pub, over thirty years ago, having led a busy working life in London. She says, 'I came back and I couldn't leave the place.' Her family have owned MacCarthy's for generations, over 150 years in fact, and she has retained the original facade and interior of this landmark pub. Adrienne is a member of the local Irish Coast Guard and is an avid mountaineer, who has trekked to Everest base camp, Morocco and the Inca Trail. Her sister, Niki, runs a restaurant a few doors down from the pub.

Their grandfather was the celebrated Air Commodore Joseph Aidan MacCarthy, GM OBE, (1914–1995), an Irish doctor who served with the Royal Air Force during the Second World War. He showed enormous courage and humanity during his capture by the Japanese in Sumatra, after the USA bombed Hiroshima and Nagasaki in 1945. He was evacuated from Dunkirk, where he attended wounded Allied soldiers while under fire from German aircraft. In 1992 Dr MacCarthy published an account of his horrendous ordeal, the much-celebrated *A Doctor's War*. His medals are proudly displayed and still a great topic of conversation in MacCarthy's Bar.

BLACK BALL HEAD SIGNAL TOWER

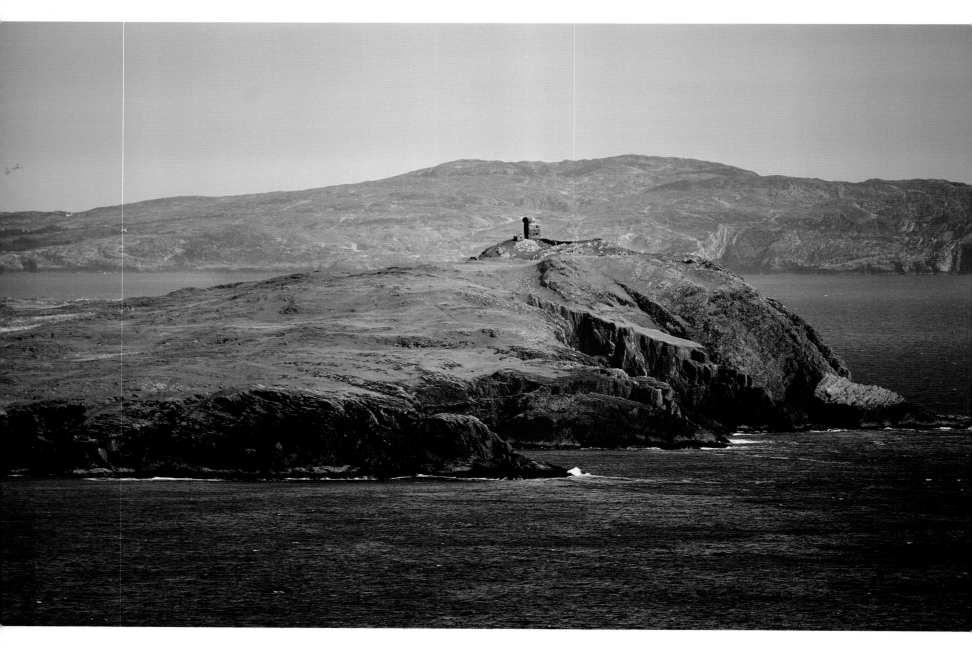

Black Ball Head Signal Tower on the Beara Peninsula is one of several towers built along the coast by the British between 1804 and 1808, as part of their defences against French invasion. This two-storey tower communicated by signal mast. Each tower was built in line of sight of the next, and the next in line to Black Ball Head is Sheep's Head Tower, now a ruin.

CAHERMORE HARBOUR

A day's fishing ends at Cahermore Harbour as two fishermen head for the harbour.

CASTING VOTES ON DURSEY ISLAND

On 25 February the Irish electorate cast their vote in the 2011 general election. Of 2,600 island residents off the Irish coast entitled to vote, nine live on Dursey Island.

Dursey Island, the most westerly of Cork's inhabited islands, at the southern tip of the Beara Peninsula, is a rugged but gentle island. The island is 6.5km long and 1.5km wide and although it has no shops or accommodation it is popular with daytrippers. The island is accessed by cable car at Ballaghboy, as Dursey Sound is often hazardous by boat. This is the only cable car in Europe to travel over the sea.

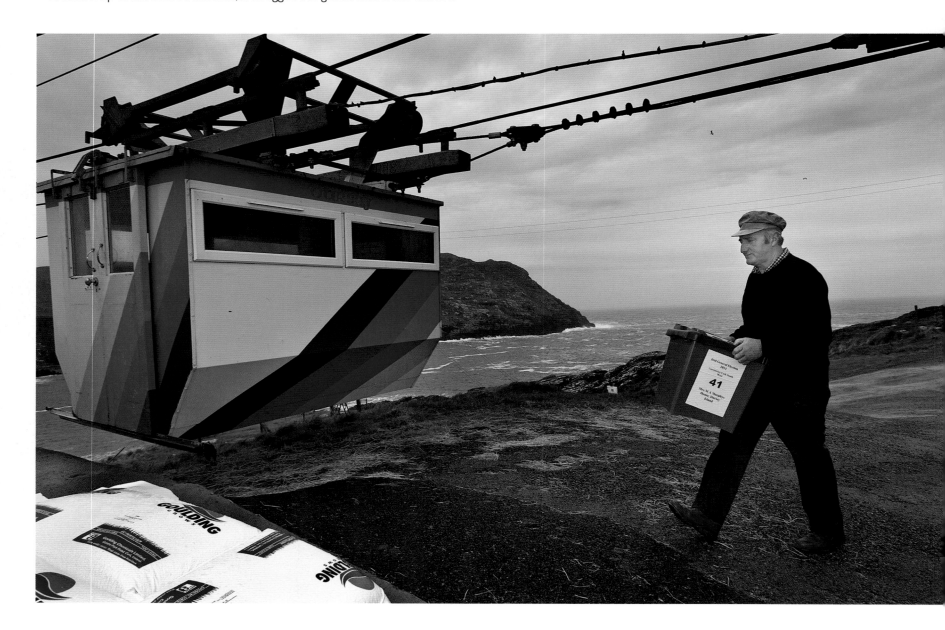

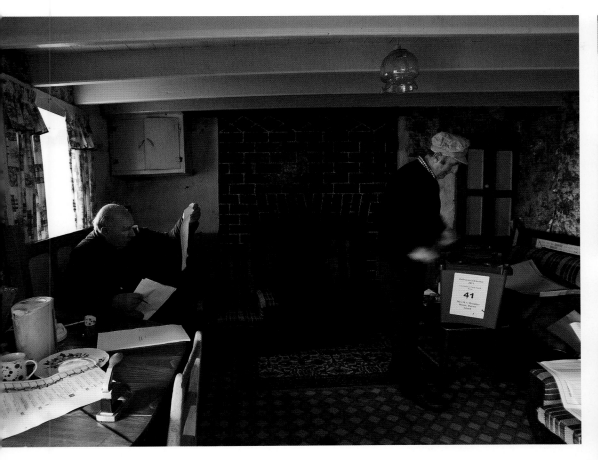

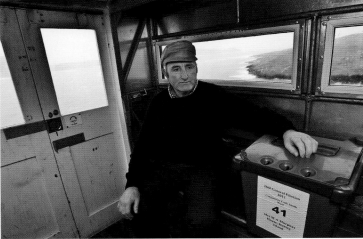

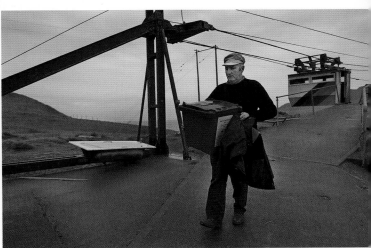

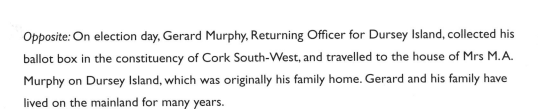

Opposite: On election day, Gerard Murphy, Returning Officer for Dursey Island, collected his ballot box in the constituency of Cork South-West, and travelled to the house of Mrs M.A. Murphy on Dursey Island, which was originally his family home. Gerard and his family have lived on the mainland for many years.

Above: Eddie Sheehan, the polling clerk on Dursey Island, is ready to cast his vote but first goes through all the electoral information and data.

Right from top: Arriving safely on Dursey Island; Gerard Murphy makes the journey by cable car to Dursey Island. The cable car can carry six people or one cow or three sheep; Paddy Sheehan has operated the cable car for twenty years. The cable car runs 365 days a year and the crossing takes approximately ten minutes.

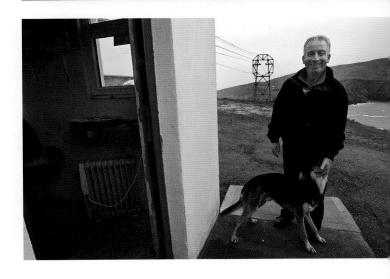

ALLIHIES

Allihies, in Irish *Na hAilichí,* means 'cliff fields'. The area is said to have been mined for copper as early as the Bronze Age. However, its most productive period began in 1812 when a local landlord, John Puxley, identified the large quartz promontory as copper bearing, with its bright malachite staining.

Between 1812 and 1912, over 297,000 tons of ore were exported from Allihies mines through Swansea Port. When the mine closed due to a fall in the price of copper, it led to mass emigration from the area. Both the mountain mine and engine house have been conserved by the Mining Heritage Trust of Ireland. A museum commemorating the mining history was opened in Allihies in 2007, in a chapel built in 1845 by the Cornish miners who worked the mine.

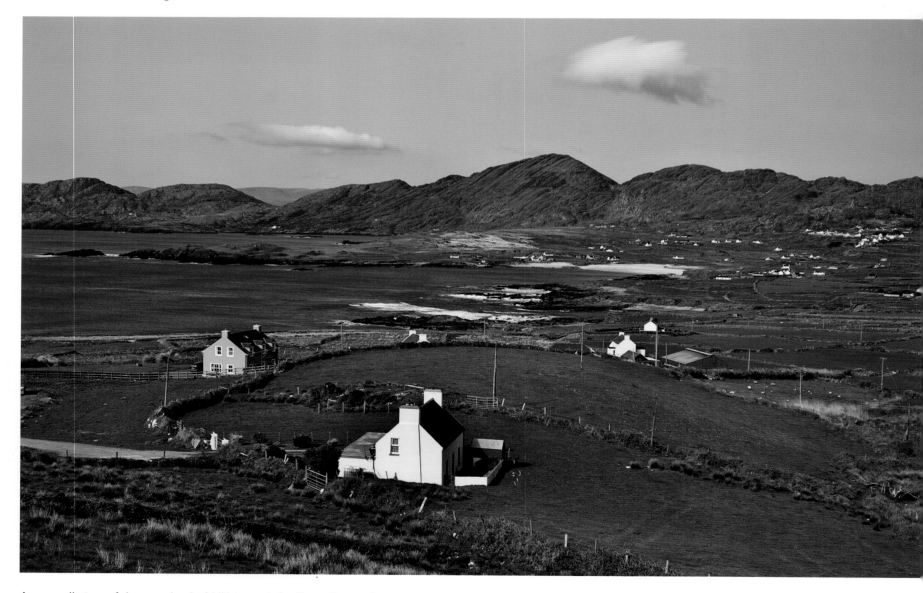

An overall view of the townland of Allihies and the Beara Peninsula overlooking Ballydonegan Bay. The village itself is on the far right.

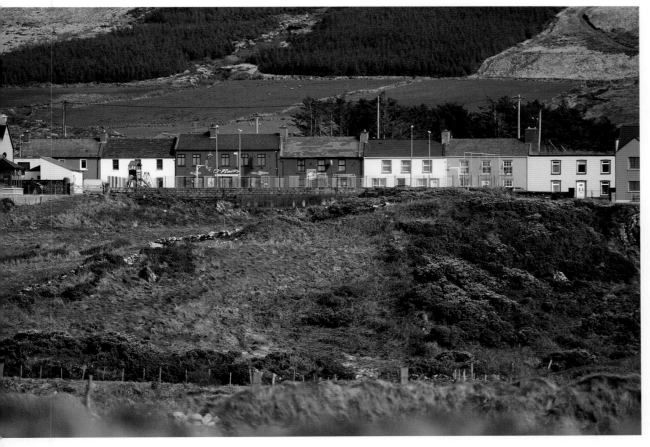

Left: Like their neighbours in Eyeries, Allihies' inhabitants have painted their town in similarly bright colours.

Bottom left: The engine house of the abandoned copper mine has recently been conserved by the Mining Heritage Trust of Ireland. It housed a steam engine that was transported from Cornwall to alleviate flooding problems and pump water from the bottom of the mine.

Bottom right: A remnant of one of the pumping houses.

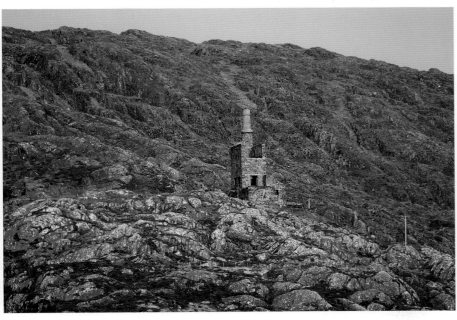

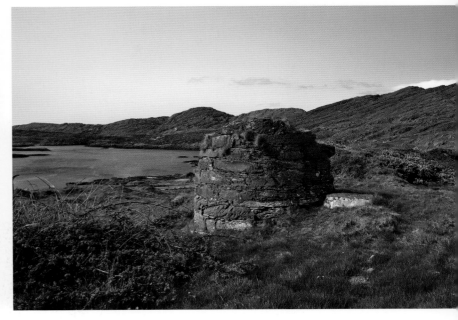

EYERIES – ALL THE COLOURS OF THE RAINBOW

Eyeries, on the Beara Peninsula overlooking Coulagh Bay and Kenmare Bay, is the possibly the most colourful village in Ireland. The colours are bold, brave and creative. No wonder its claim to fame was the shooting of the film *The Purple Taxi* (1977), which starred Fred Astaire and Peter Ustinov, and novelist Deirdre Purcell's 1998 TV series *Falling for a Dancer*.

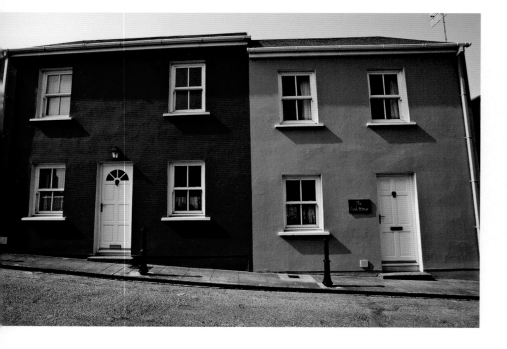

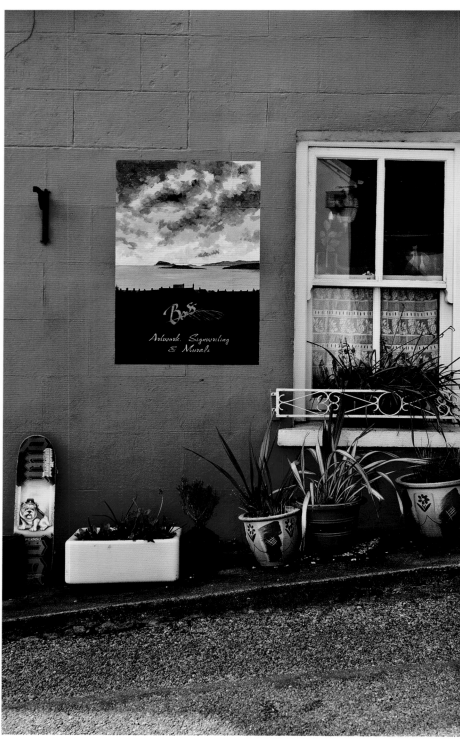

ARDGROOM STONE CIRCLE

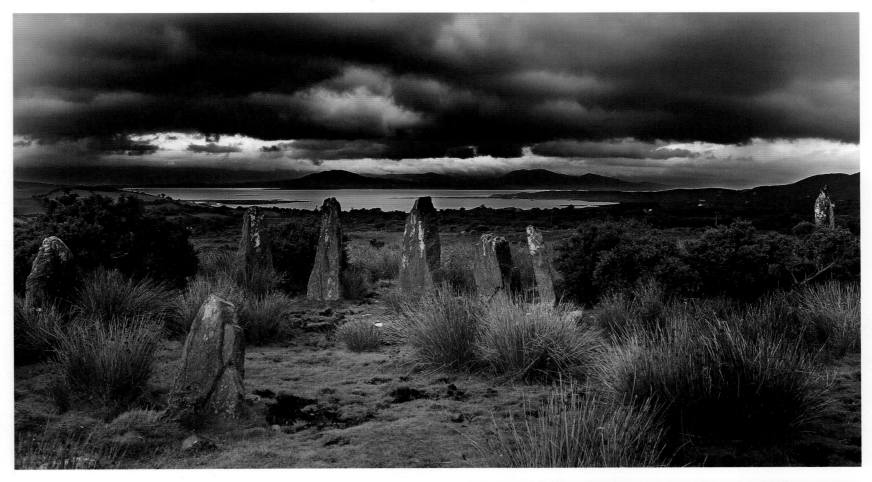

Megalithic monuments are abundant on the Beara Peninsula and one such, Ardgroom stone circle, is located near Ardgroom village. As with other stone circles, it was constructed as a ritual and ceremonial site during the Bronze Age, making it over 3,000 years old. Ardgroom stone circle is 7.25m (23ft) in diameter and once consisted of eleven stones. One stone is missing and one has fallen. A tall standing stone, 6m (20ft) to the east, appears to draw attention to the stone circle. Under the altar stone is a 'cyst', a stone box containing human remains. The workmanship and knowledge of the solar system that the builders displayed continues to mystify each generation.

Right: As happens often with intriguing monuments, people leave coins as a reverence or an offering to the site.

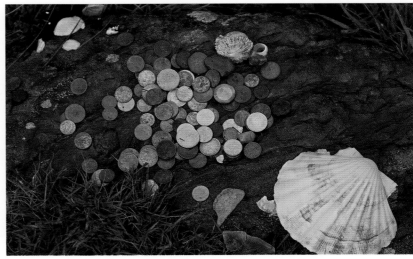

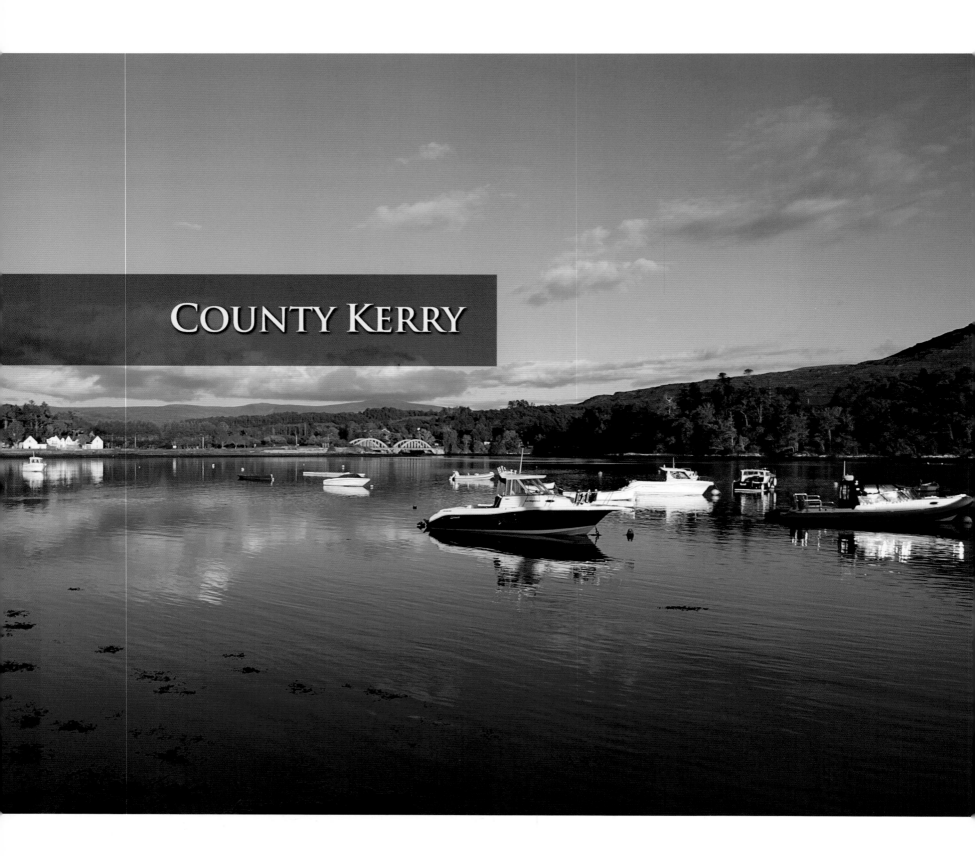

COUNTY KERRY

KENMARE

Our Lady's Bridge. When it was opened in 1841, Kenmare Suspension Bridge over the Kenmare River was claimed to be the first in Ireland. Its construction had cost £7,280. A feat in engineering, it provided a direct link to Bantry and the Beara Peninsula. In 1932 the bridge was declared unsafe with girders becoming warped. Demolition began with the removal of the road metal and railings, to be replaced by Our Lady's Bridge in March 1933.

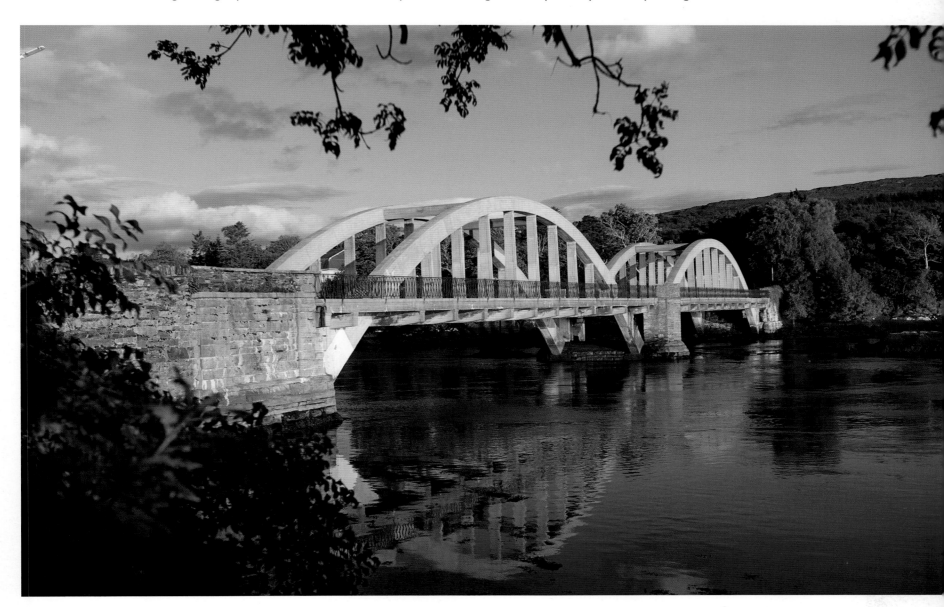

Opposite: Everything about Kenmare Bay is tranquil, natural and unspoiled. Sitting between the Beara and Iveragh Peninsulas, Kenmare is renowned in Ireland as a haven for the finest gourmet restaurants, artisan foods, famous Kenmare Park Hotel and luxury camping holidays.

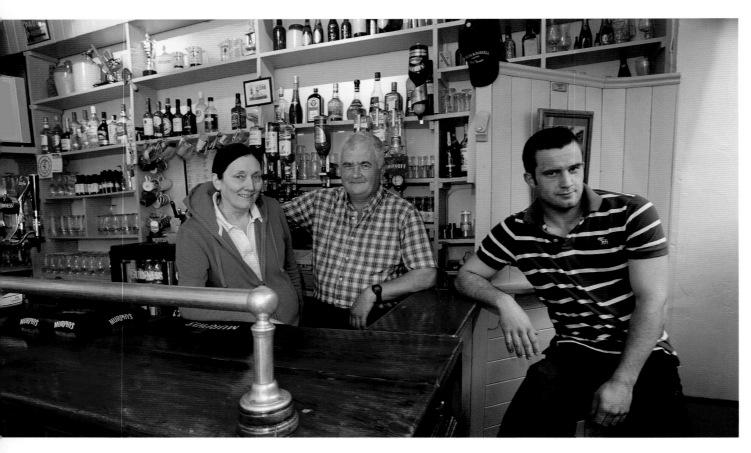

Above: Florry Batt O'Sullivan's traditional bar is located in Henry Street, Kenmare. It was built in the 1860s from surplus chalkstone and local stone from the construction of the nearby parish church. The countertop, shelving and brass fittings give it a distinctive appearance. The present Florry Batt (centre) and his wife, Kathleen (left), took over the running of the pub from his father in 1977, who had run it since 1944. Florry Batt is also a farmer and keeps sheep and cows at his farm in Cappagh, Kenmare. He is involved with Kenmare Rowing Club and Kenmare Rugby Club. He hopes that his son Florry Batt Junior (right) will take over the running of the pub some day.

Right: Conor Brady counts down the seconds before the start of the 'Lost Sheep' Triathlon in Kenmare, which begins with a 1,900m (1.2-mile) swim in Kenmare Bay, an 83km (52-mile) cycle on the Healy and Caha Passes and finishes with an undulating 21km (13-mile) run to Kenmare town.

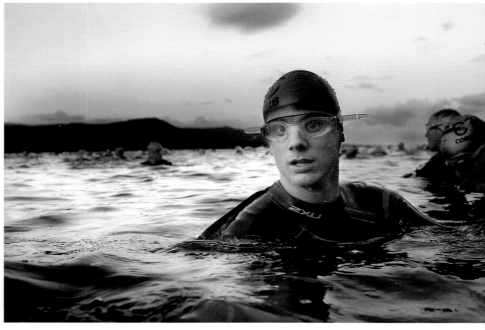

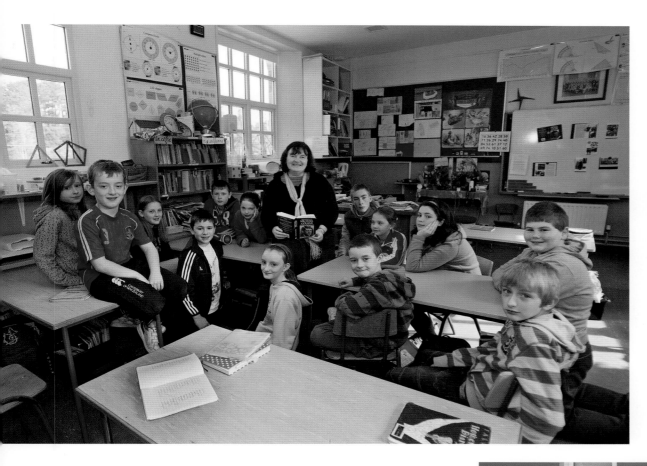

Right: Mary O'Shea, Principal at Lauragh National School on the Beara Peninsula, with fourth, fifth and sixth class pupils as they discuss Irish history. Front row (l–r): Jude O'Neill, Seán O'Shea, Kevin Lowney; middle row (l–r): Laura O'Sullivan, Callum Murphy, Ciara O'Shea, Jake O'Driscoll; back row (l–r): Finbar Lehane, Sarah McCarthy, Kevin Knabe, Caoimhe Smyth, Rachael O'Sullivan, Damian O'Shea.

MIKEY JOE BURNS, SNEEM

Mikey Joe Burns owns and runs the local bike shop in Sneem. His father, Mixie, opened the shop in 1947, and it served as the local grocery, hackney, petrol pump and bike shop. Mikey Joe took over in 1984 and now runs it as a dedicated bicycle shop. He is a master craftsman, working with iron. He is passionate about rowing and Kerry football and is head coach with the Workmen's Rowing Club in Killarney.

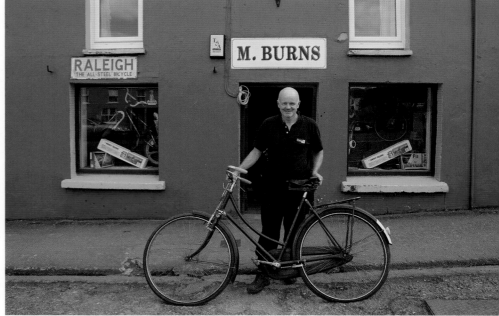

BALLINSKELLIGS

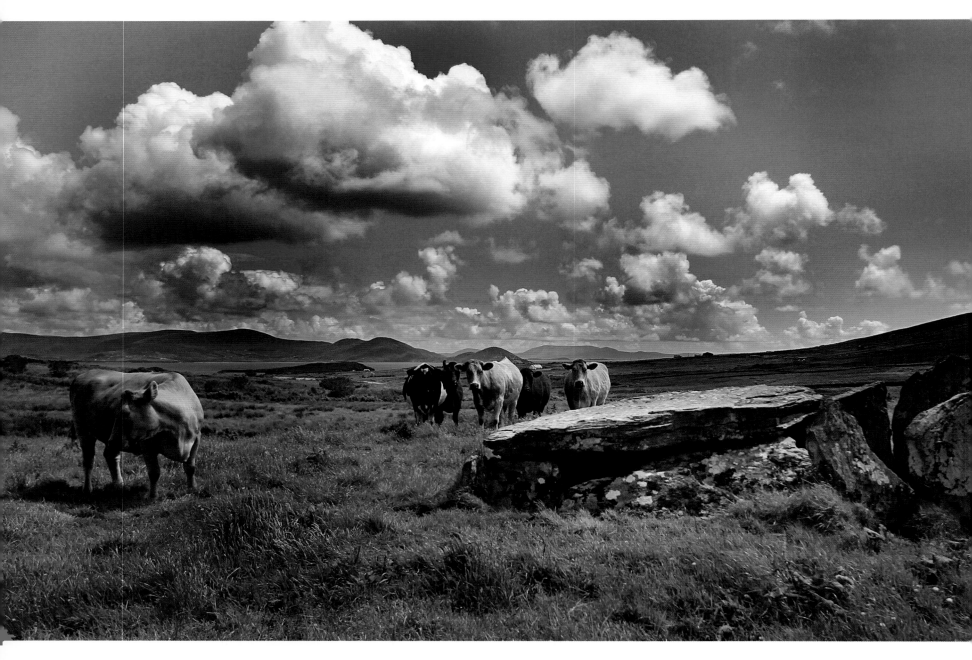

Situated at Coom, Ballinskelligs, the Coom wedge tomb is believed to be associated with the arrival, starting around 2300 BC, of a particular group of people with an advanced knowledge of bronze metallurgy. Hence their arrival marked the beginning of the Bronze Age in Ireland.

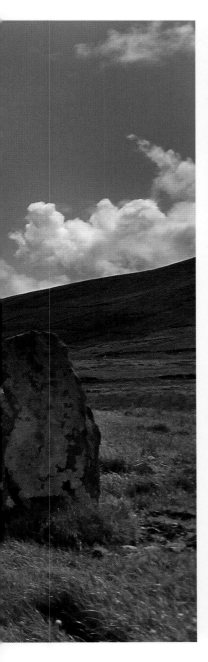

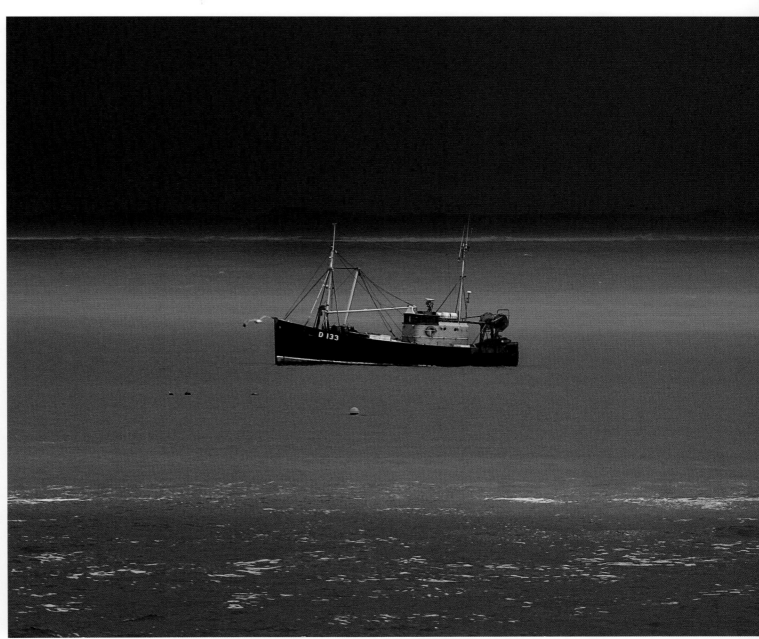

A fishing boat lies anchored at Ballinskelligs, an area with an abundance of monastic antiquities (the name comes from the nearby island of Skellig Michael). The influence of the monks makes the area a magnet for historians and archaeologists: nearby is Cill Rialaig, a sixth-century monastic settlement, St Finan's Bay, Bolus Head, and the remains of beehive huts.

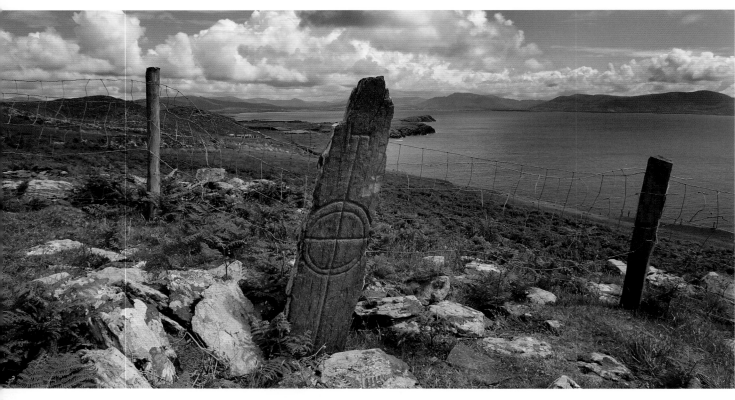

Left: At Cill Rialaig, there is a fine example of a cross-inscribed slab. Found in early Christian monasteries, these slabs are usually flat stones with an inscribed cross, and an inscription asking for a prayer for the person commemorated.

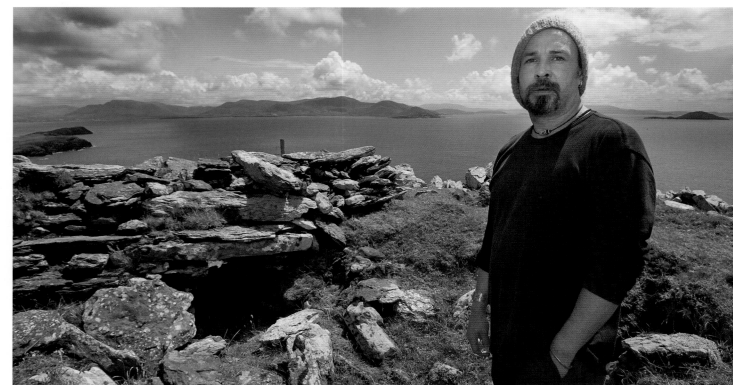

Right: Local archaeologist Dan O'Meara standing at the entrance to the oratory of Cill Rialaig, a sixth-century monastic site at Ballinskelligs.

KEEPER OF THE LIGHT ON SKELLIG MICHAEL

Richard Foran from Valentia Island is the lighthouse keeper on Skellig Michael. The Skellig lighthouse is one of the main sea lights off the southwest coast and is located on the outer and larger of the Skellig Rocks, 12.8km from the nearest mainland point, northeast of Puffin Island. Two lighthouses were established on Skellig Michael in 1826, but only one remains and it was automated in 1987. Richard Foran visits and maintains the lighthouse every third week and often is stranded on the island due to adverse weather conditions.

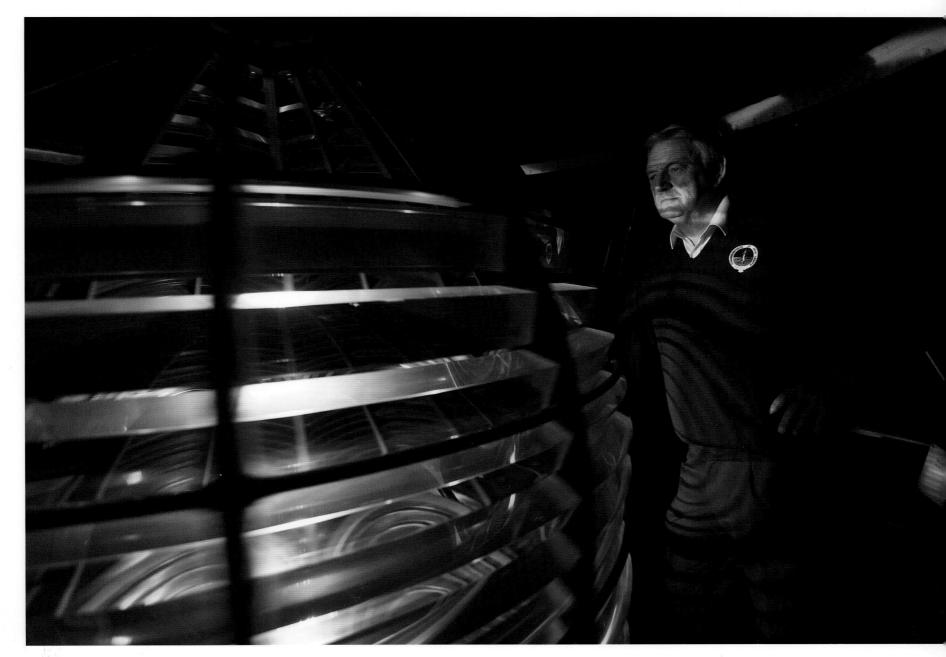

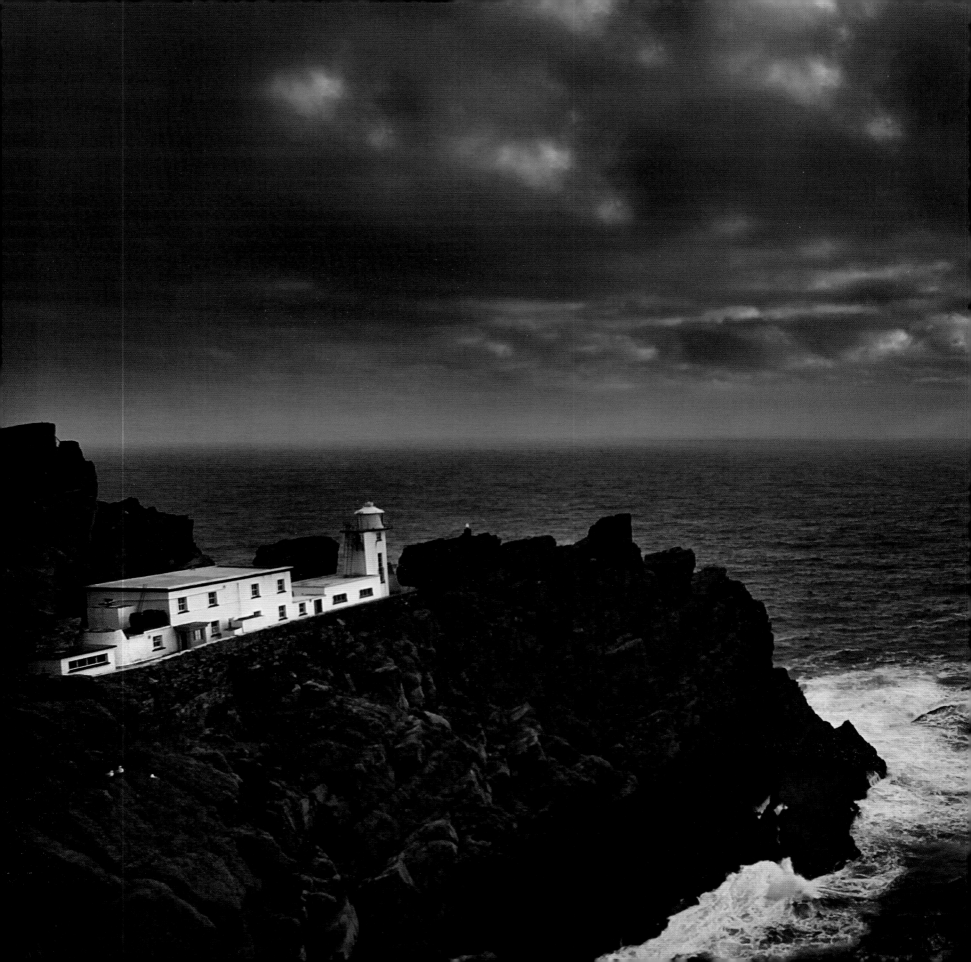

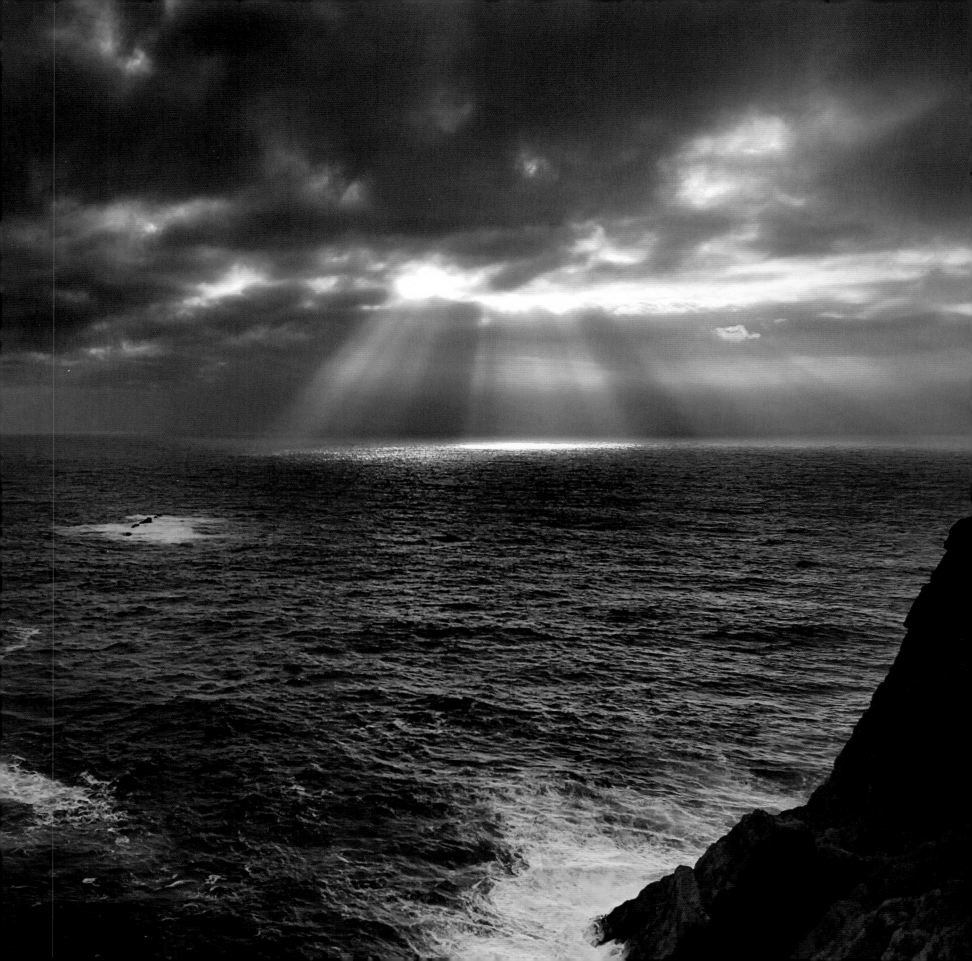

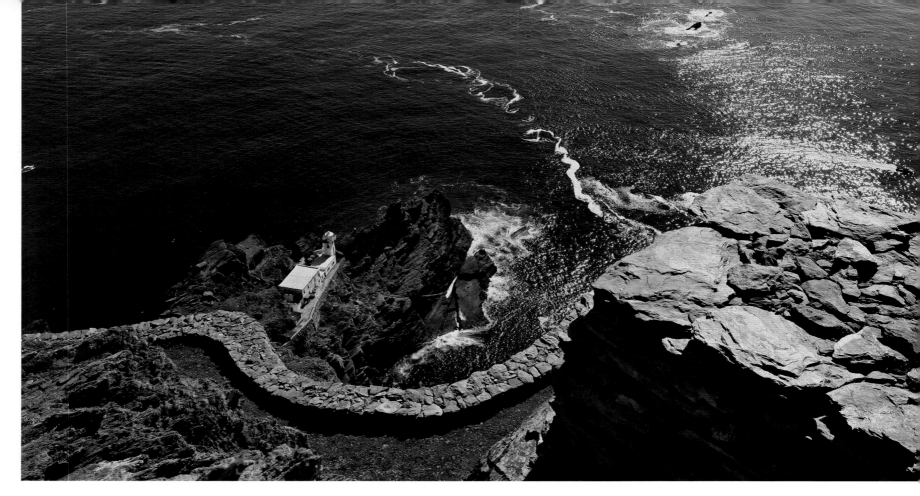

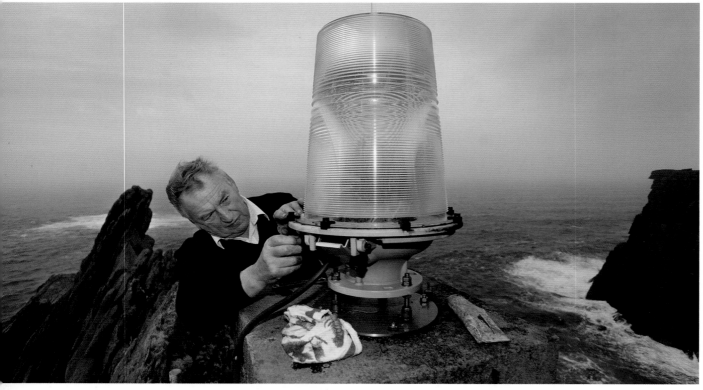

Above: The lighthouse on Skellig Michael is located on the southwestern cliff face of the revered Skellig monastic site, 12km (7 miles) from the south Kerry mainland. Established in 1870 and renovated in 1965, it was automated in 1987.

Left: Lighthouse Keeper Richard Foran carries out essential maintenance on Skellig's emergency beam.

Previous pages: Late evening on Skellig Michael as the brooding clouds close in and Atlantic swells rise up.

Right: Waiting for clearance: Richard Foran waits on Skellig Michael helipad for news from Irish Lights helicopter pilot Colm Martyn on failing weather conditions.

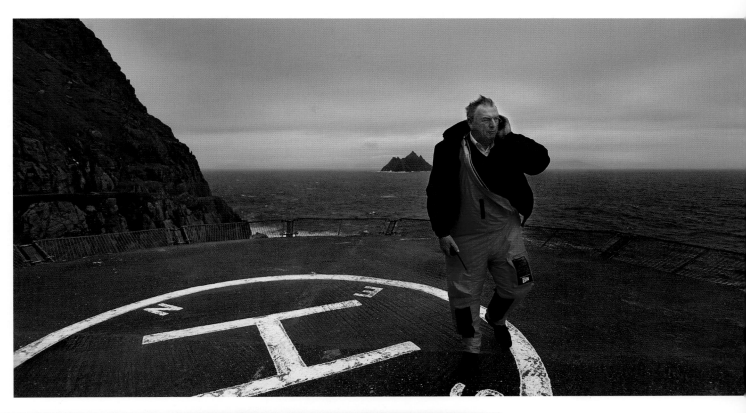

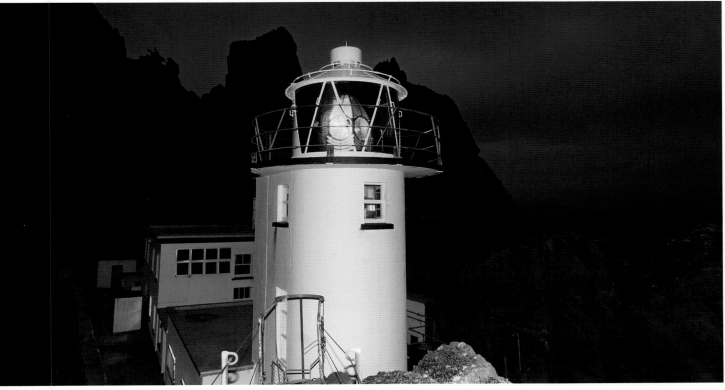

Left: Two lighthouses were established on Skellig Rock in December 1826. The upper lighthouse was discontinued in 1870. The remaining lighthouse was converted to electricity in May 1967. The present optic dates back to 1909. In 2001 it was converted to solar power. The character of the light is flashing (3) white every 15 seconds.

SKELLIG MICHAEL

Skellig Michael is a place between heaven and earth, a spiritual journey like no other, from the extremities of the Atlantic crossing by boat, to the endurance testified by those brave monks who wanted to live out their daily existence as a penance for Christ's suffering on earth.

Both Skellig Rocks – Little Skellig *(Sceilig Bheag)* and Skellig Michael *(Sceilig Mhichíl)* – are renowned for their seabird colonies. Both have thriving populations of gannets and puffins, and are considered one of the most important breeding colonies in Europe. Other seabirds include fulmars, Manx shearwaters, peregrine falcons, guillemots, razorbills and the occasional white-tailed eagle.

Grey seals are commonly seen and sharks, minke whales and dolphins have also been recorded.

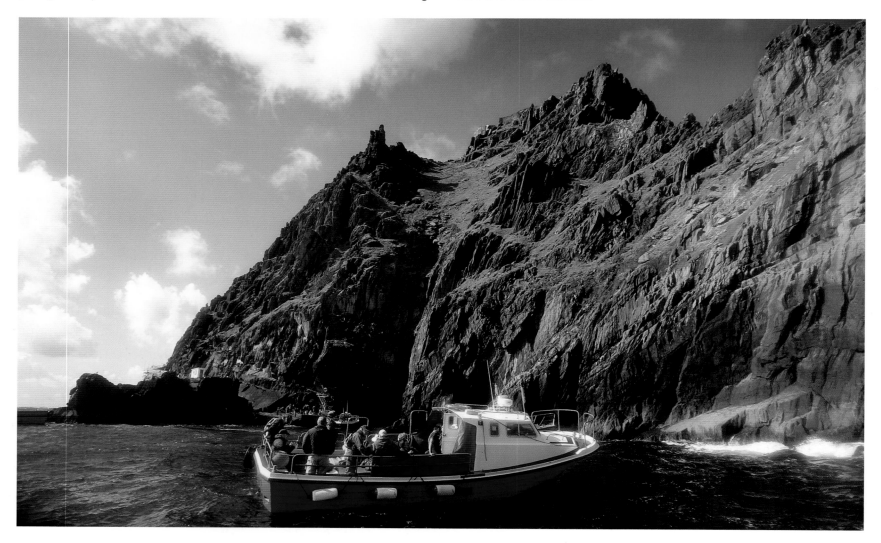

Skellig boats arriving safely after the sea journey to the island.

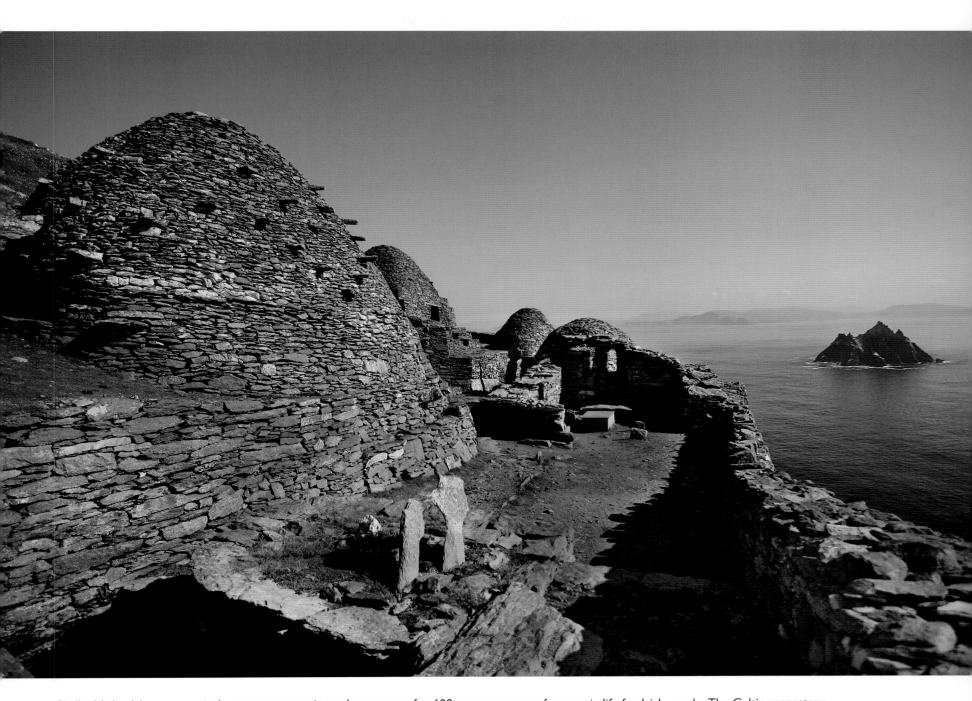

Skellig Michael, home to a sixth-century monastic settlement, was for 600 years a centre of monastic life for Irish monks. The Celtic monastery, which is situated almost at the summit of the 230m-high rock, became a UNESCO World Heritage Site in 1996. It is one of Europe's better known but least accessible monasteries.

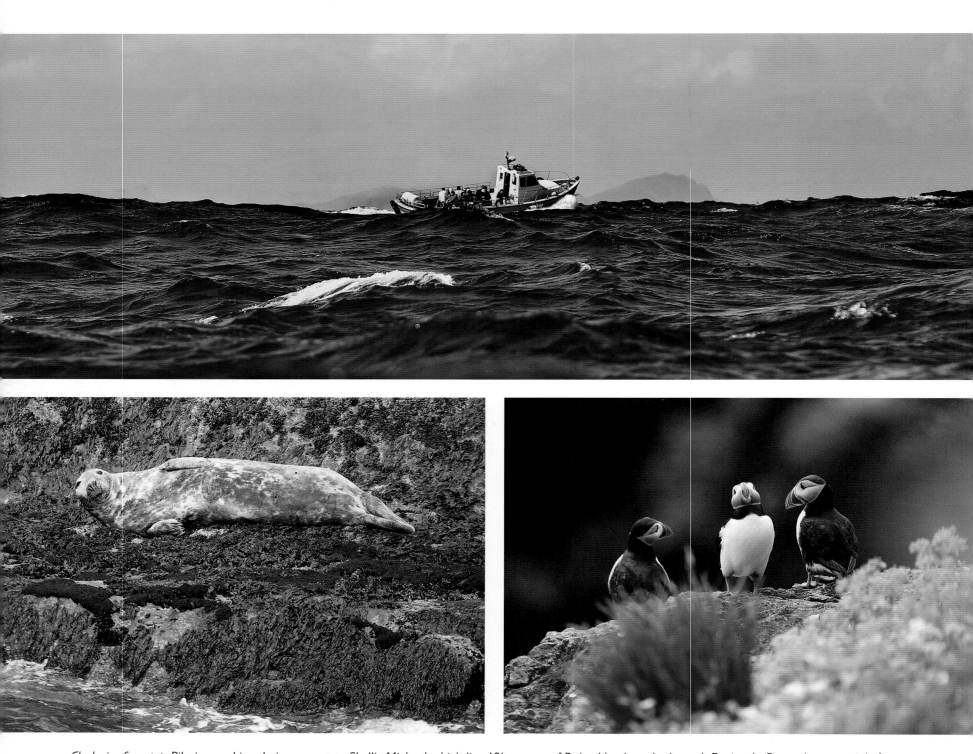

Clockwise from top: Pilgrims making their way out to Skellig Michael which lies 12km west of Bolus Head on the Iveragh Peninsula. Boats depart mainly from Portmagee Pier, weather permitting; On the journey to Skellig Michael, grey seals can be seen lazing on rocks; Skellig Michael is famous for its colourful collection of puffins, which migrate here from June to September. As they live mainly on sea cliffs and remote islands, Skellig Michael is an ideal home.

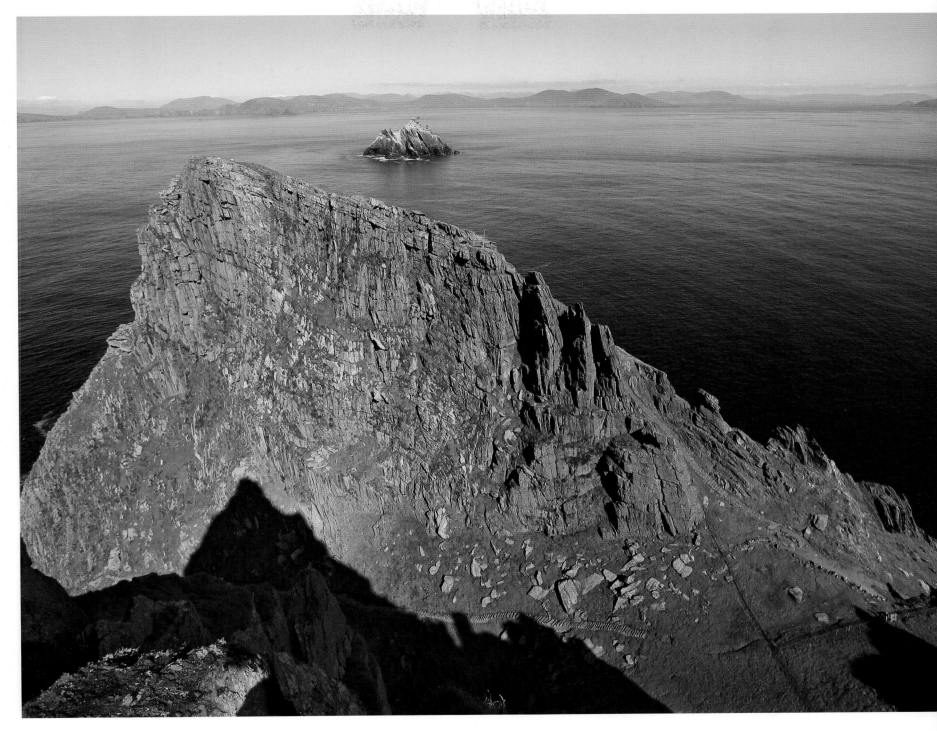

A view from the open monastic huts of Skellig Michael, looking across at Little Skellig and the Kerry coast.

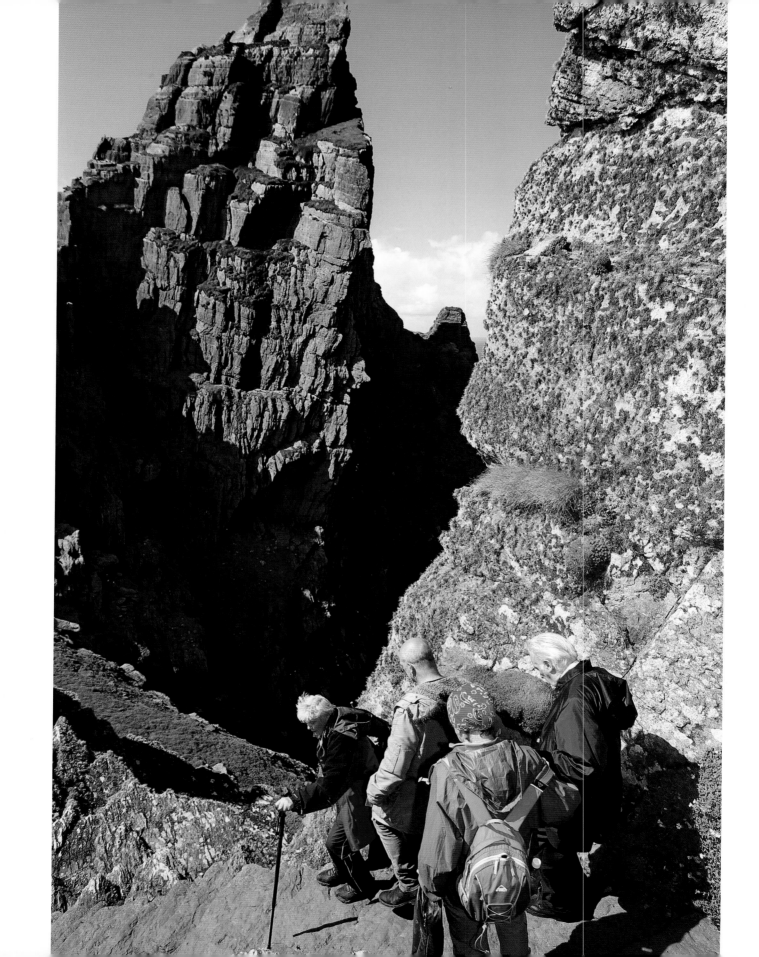

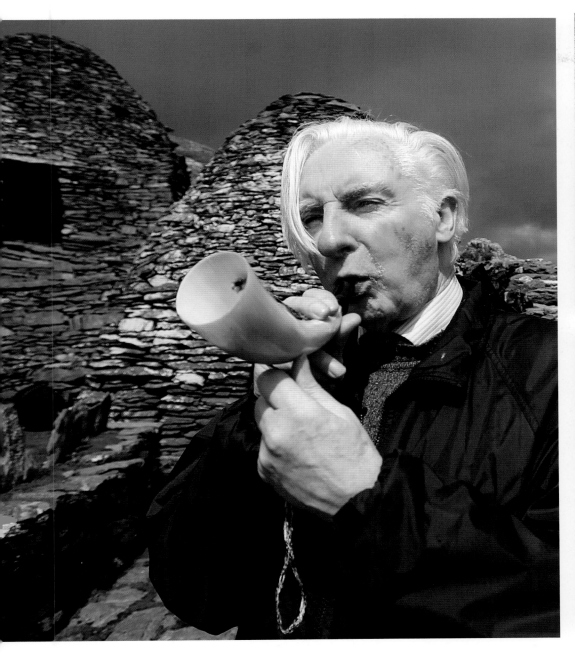
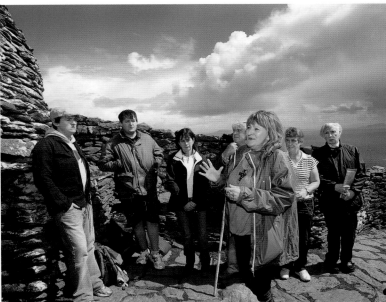
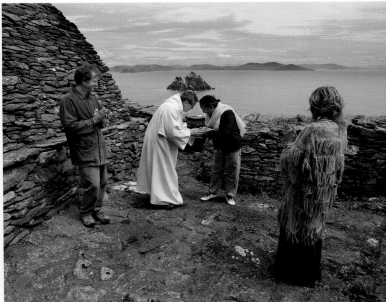

Clockwise from top left: Renowned Celtic scholar Fr Sean O'Duinn OSB, Glenstal Abbey, calls pilgrims to prayer on Skellig Michael as he performs the *'solas na soilse'* ('light of lights') blessing on the island; Irish Celtic spiritual singer Nóirín Ní Riain, with her sons Míchael (left) and Eoin (second from left), chanting as part of the *'solas na soilse'* blessing, with Fr Sean O'Duinn OSB (far right); East meets West: Fr Gregory Collins of Glenstal Abbey exchanges traditional blessings with Dzigar Kongrul, Rinpoche, Tibetan Buddhist lama, as part of an inter-religious ceremony on Skeillig Michael. Also in attendance are philosopher Richard Kearney (left) and singer Nóirín Ní Riain.

Opposite: Pilgrims carefully making their way down from the sixth-century monastery on Skellig Michael.

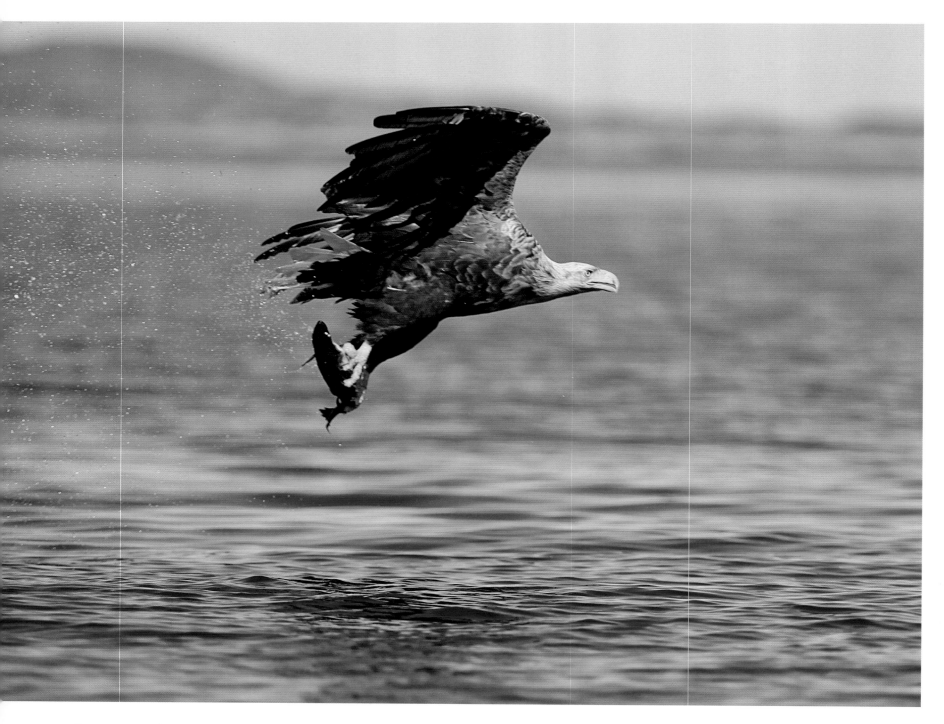

Over seventy white-tailed eagles were reintroduced to Ireland from Norway in 2007 after more than a 100-year absence in the Irish countryside.

The initiative is being managed by the National Parks and Wildlife Service and Golden Eagle Trust. The project's coordinator is Dr Allan Mee.

The eagles' preferred habitat is along coastlines and sea cliffs, feeding mainly on carrion, preying on seabirds and fish.

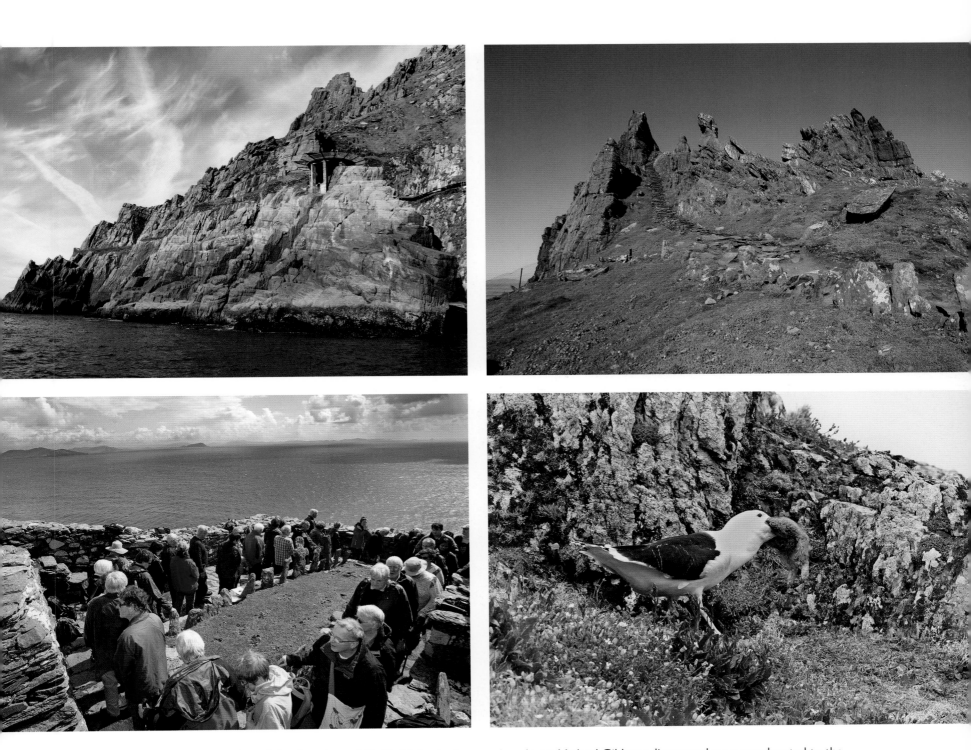

Clockwise from top left: The disused south landing place of Skellig Michael, where archaeologist Michael Gibbons discovered, on a spur located to the left of the outcrop of rock, a stairwell dating back to the ninth century; A view of Christ's Saddle on Skellig Michael, also known as 'Christ's Valley'; Head first: a greater black-backed gull catches a rabbit and tries to eat it whole on Skellig Michael; *Cor Deiseal:* pilgrims walk three times around the monastic graveyard in tune with the cosmic forces in a blessing called *'solas na soilse'* ('light of lights').

'ON A ROCK TOO HIGH FOR ME TO REACH'
(PSALM 61)

By Mark Patrick Hederman

THE SKELLIG ISLANDS appearing out of the Atlantic Ocean about 12km southwest of Valentia Island, County Kerry, in Ireland, are places where I feel near to God. Other places of pilgrimage impose hardship on the seeker as a moral or ascetic obligation whereas this sanctuary, by its geography and nature, demands strenuous and startling effort to reach it and to accommodate yourself to its extremities. Just to be requires stamina. 'On a rock too high for me to reach, set me on high,' King David sang in Psalm 61, and this place is a perfect answer to that prayer. You are placed beyond yourself across a threshold where another world is on display. The journey in a boat, especially if the sea is rough, puts you in elemental contact with water as some wild and unpremeditated baptism. 'Greater than the roar of mighty waters, more glorious than the surgings of the sea, the lord is glorious on high.' The psalms seem to fit this setting, not because they were prayers which sixth-century Irish monks would have chanted on the island, but because in themselves they reach an elemental level in our souls.

These Skelligs Islands are places where Celtic spirituality becomes most manifest, bare rocks where so many have communicated with God. Sometimes people have to wait for days around the port before the sailing conditions are favourable for landing. It is not the weather but the swell of the sea which dictates possibility. You land on the great Skellig in a cove facing east where a monastery was in existence, 600ft above sea level, from the sixth century. The island is only about 4 acres in all but these make up such varieties and extravagances of shape and contrast that they assume archetypal proportion: a mirror of the Celtic psyche measuring contortions of extremism within a tiny span. A compelling geography of land and sea lends itself as map to heights and depths of a spiritual world. Two peaks, one 600ft the other 700ft, meet at 'Christ's saddle' in the middle of the island: centre of gravity with access to every dimension of surrounding space.

The lesser Skellig, hardly possible to reach, but starkly visible from Skellig Michael, is mythic also in shape: an impregnable fortress guarding secrets surrounded by water. The many thousand gulls and gannets forever circling this rock are like the souls of the dead, in a different dimension from ourselves, forming a heavenly chorus. Something happens in this setting as if you reach a centre of gravity within yourself by adjusting to the perspectives outlined in this natural theodolite. You do seem to be at the equipoise of Christ's Saddle, riding before him on a galloping steed. Inside the beehive cells you find yourself in a perfectly rounded stone womb. There is also something about the sea – its vastness and depth and its fullness of dark and murky life – mirroring the immensity of God.

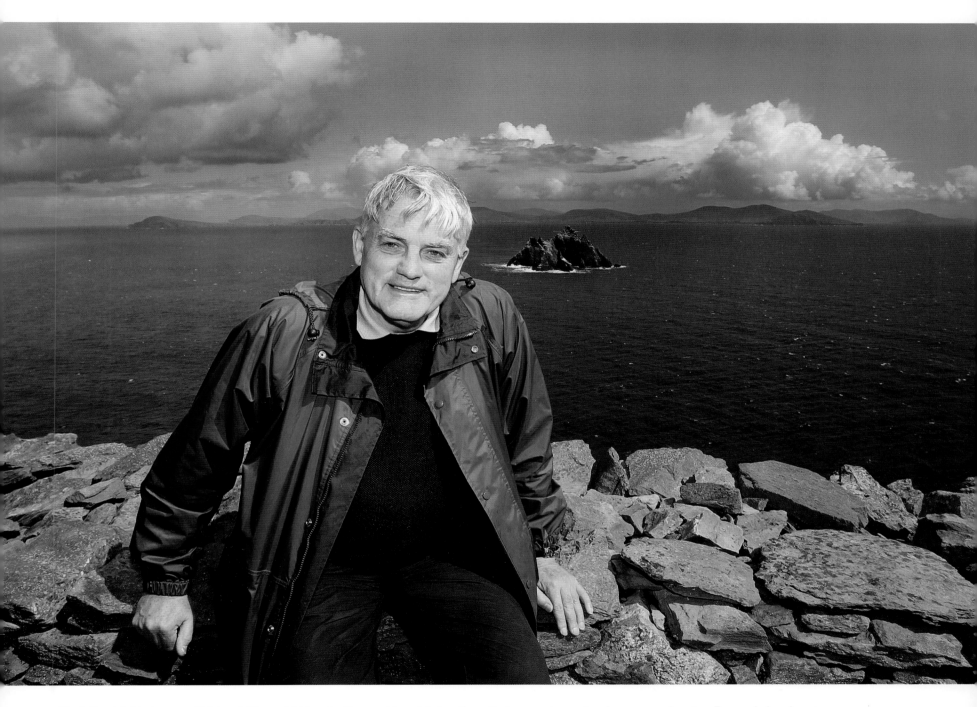

Mark Patrick Hederman, Abbot of Glenstal Abbey in County Limerick, is a Benedictine monk, teacher, lecturer and writer. Formerly headmaster of the school at Glenstal, he was elected fifth abbot in 2009. He has lectured extensively throughout the world, and has published many books.

Following pages: Aerial view of Skellig Michael.

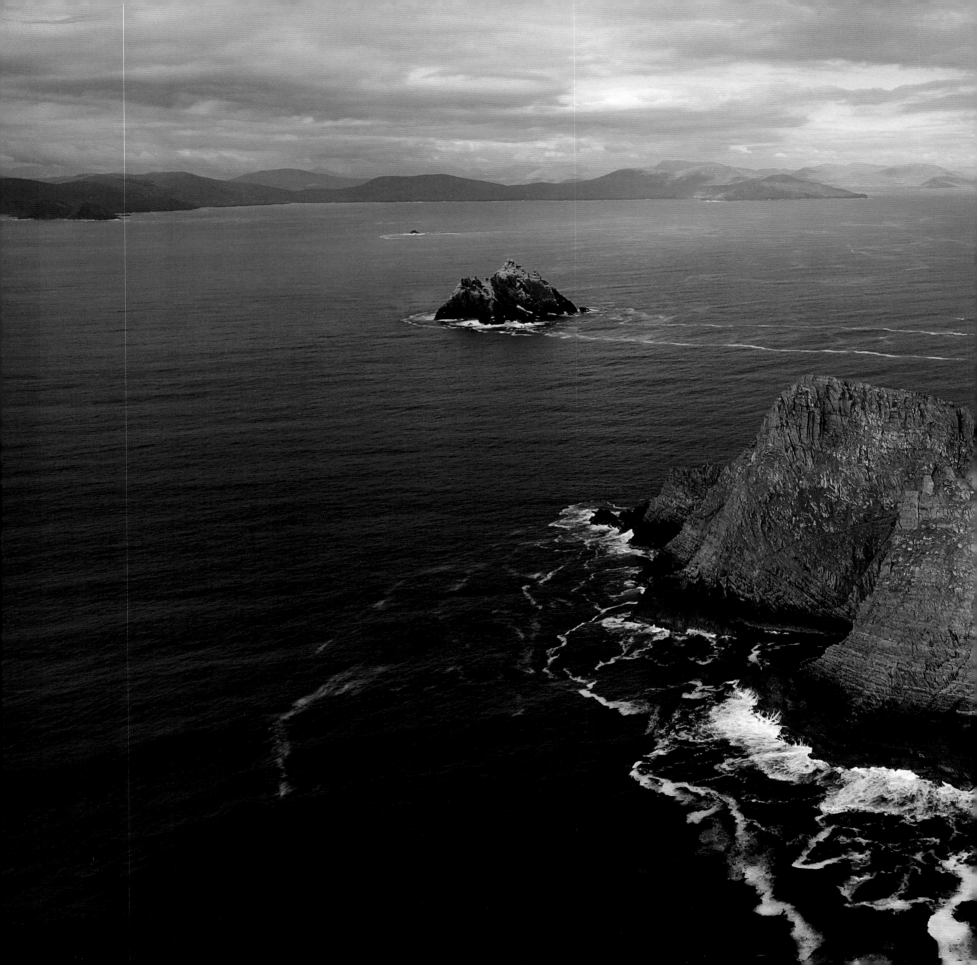

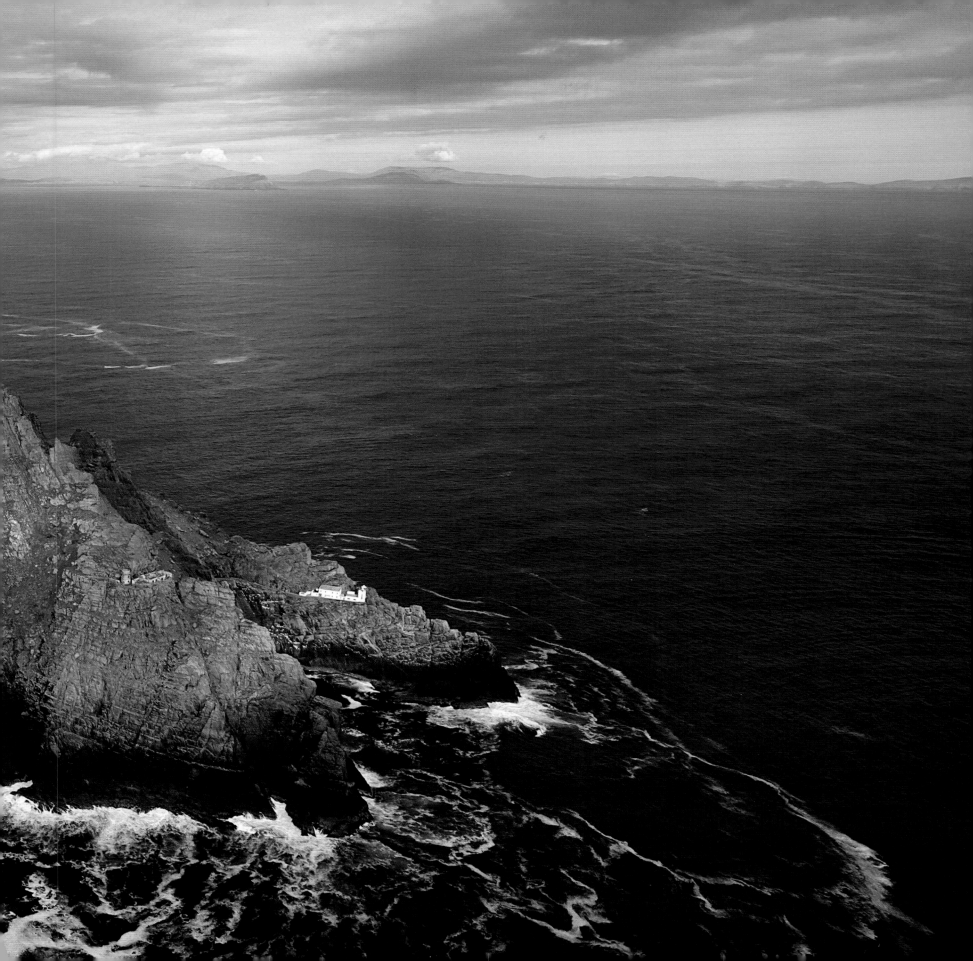

VALENTIA ISLAND

Valentia Island has long had a place on the world stage of history, science, engineering, megalithic remains, meteorological and geodetic data, heritage, and of course sport. It has an exotic history as well as location, being one of Ireland's most westerly points, lying off the Iveragh Peninsula, linked to the mainland by the Maurice O'Connell Memorial Bridge at Portmagee Harbour, and by the seasonal ferry from Renard Point to Knightstown, its largest village.

THE CABLE

One of the most fascinating stories in Valentia's history tells of the first transatlantic telegraph cable, laid between Valentia Island and Heart's Content, Newfoundland. The first attempt to lay the Atlantic cable was in 1857–58, and the first message was sent on 16 August 1858 from Queen Victoria to the American President James Buchanan. A new cable was laid in 1865 by the largest ship of its day, the *Great Eastern*, establishing a permanent electrical communications link that altered for all time personal, commercial and political relations between people across the Atlantic Ocean.

The Western Union International cable station functioned for 100 years until, in 1966, it terminated its cable operation. At the time much of the contents were either sold off or discarded, but now the story of the cable, the expeditions to Newfoundland, the science and engineering involved, are being collected again. An exhibition of the Transatlantic Cable is on display at Valentia Island Heritage Centre, in Knightstown.

THE SLATE QUARRY

Another of Valentia's claims to fame is its slate quarry, which was opened in 1816 by Peter George Fitzgerald, the 19th Knight of Kerry. The quality of the slate was celebrated worldwide and used in the roof of the British House of Commons, London, Leicester and Derby railway stations and in Bahia, South America, in the San Salvador railway stations. A well-known Valentia story is that the Public Record Office in London uses 40.2km (25 miles) of Valentia slate in its shelving.

A rock fall closed the quarry in 1911. In 1998, a number of local businesses forged together and now operate Valentia Slate Ltd.

THE WEATHER

Valentia Observatory is Ireland's oldest weather station, opened in 1860 by Admiral FitzRoy, head of the Meteorological Committee of the British Board of Trade. It was chosen because of its telegraphic link to London and its location on the Atlantic seaboard, which serves as a direct path for almost all weather systems approaching Ireland, Britain and Europe. The British Meteorological Office ran the observatory until September 1937, when it was transferred to the Irish Meteorological Service. The Valentia Observatory now located outside Cahersiveen is highly regarded for its advanced equipment and instrumentation.

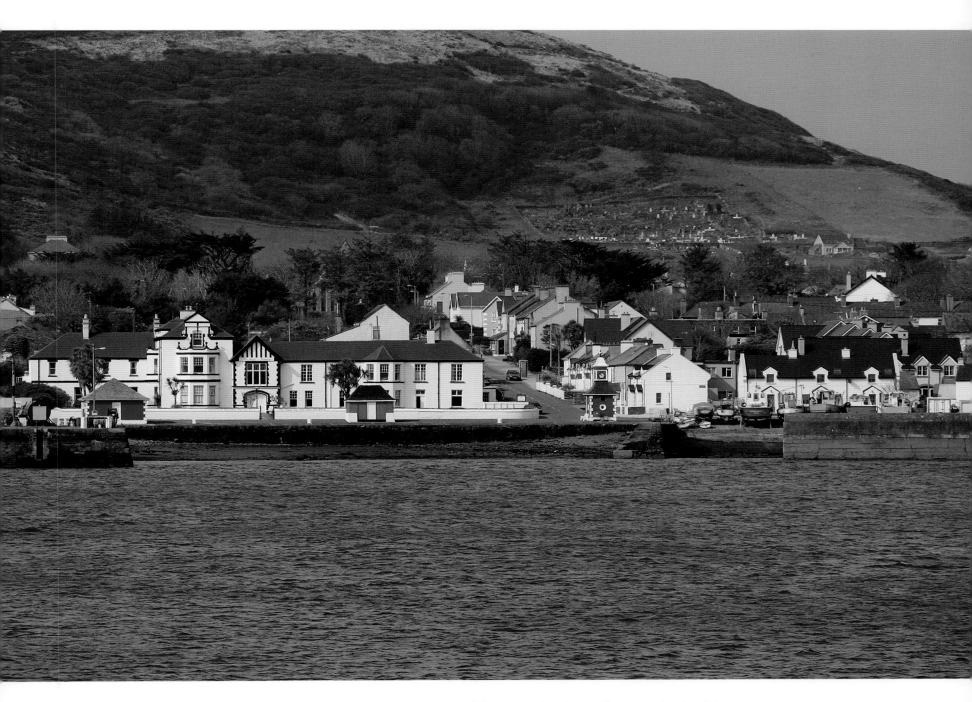

The vibrant village of Knightstown on Valentia Island is the largest on the island. It boasts a hotel, art gallery, juice bar, bookshop, coffee shops, restaurants and pubs.

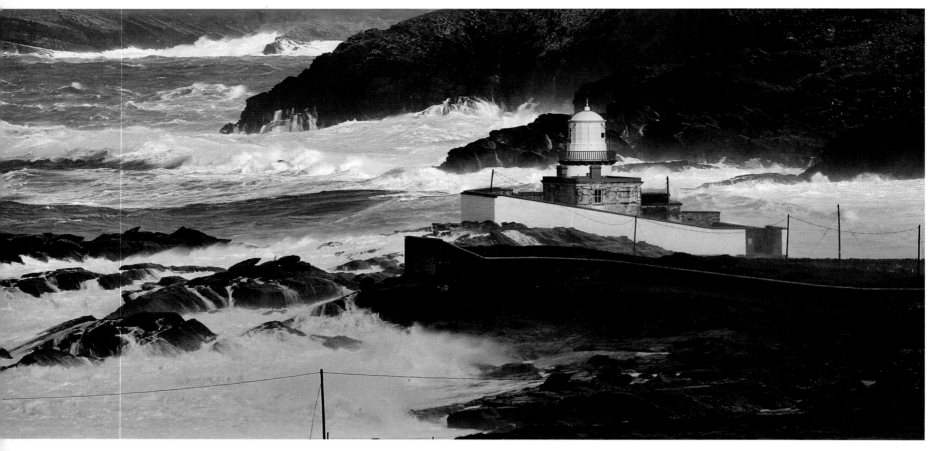

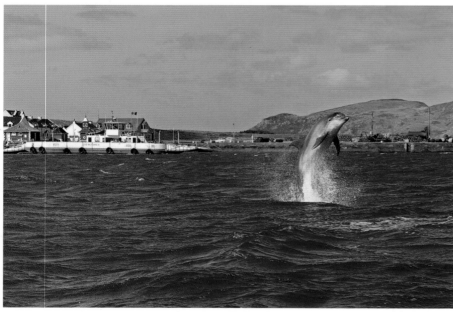

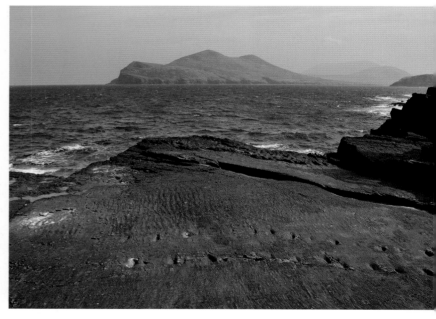

Right: John Patrick Murphy, a volunteer with the Valentia RNLI crew, takes part in a test run emergency plan to Skellig Michael with crew members from the Irish Coast Guard from Shannon and Waterford.

Opposite, clockwise from top: Gale-force winds batter the coastline and Cromwell Point Lighthouse on Valentia Island. The lighthouse was commissioned in 1837, and operated until 1947 when, with the advent of automation, it was discontinued. It fell into severe disrepair but was subsequently taken on as a conservation project by the Irish Landmark Trust who restored it for use as a short-term holiday let. In 2007 the Irish Georgian Society contributed over €2,000 to the repair and conservation of two of the house's sash windows.

In 1992, on the land of farmer Patrick Curran, an undergraduate geology student discovered fossilised tetrapod tracks – footprints in mud preserved in Devonian rocks on the north coast of the island. About 385 million years ago, a primitive vertebrate passed along a muddy shoreline and left prints as if in wet concrete. The prints were preserved by silt overlaying them, and were converted to rock over the ages. The Valentia Island trackways are among the oldest signs of vertebrate life on land.

Bottlenose dolphins are a regular sight around Valentia and will follow the ferry as it plies between Renard Point and Knightstown.

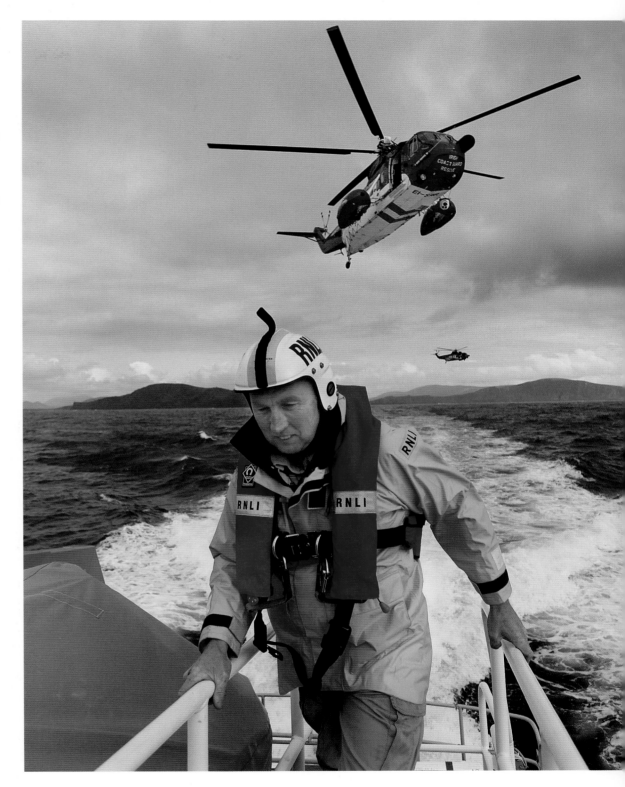

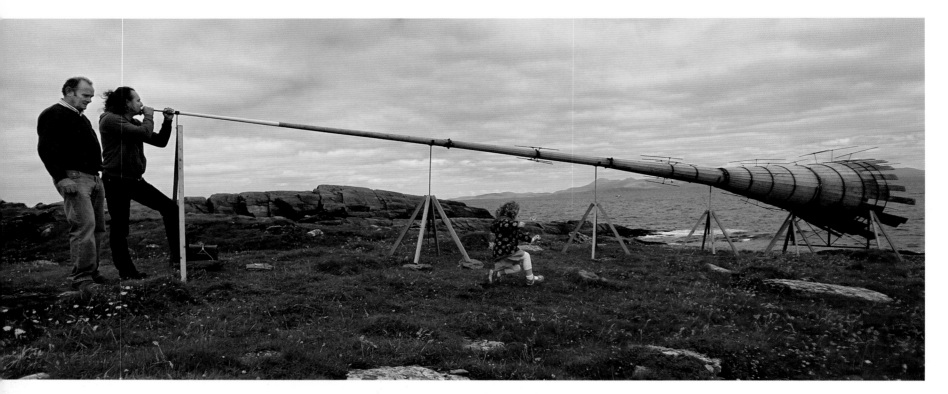

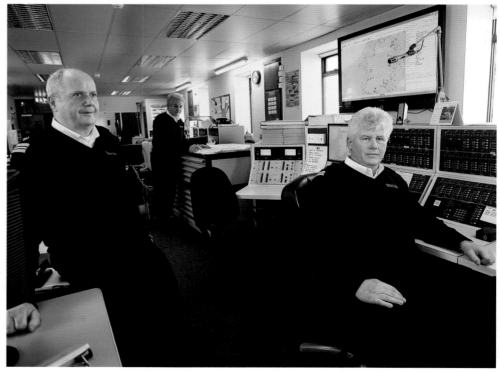

Above: In the summer of 2011, Dutch artist Andy ten Broek set up a curious 15m/50ft-long rijnhoorn – a sound installation based on the ancient Celtic horn, Swiss horn and the Tibetan horn – which could be heard up to 12km away. Andy ten Broek chose the location on the edge of the Atlantic deliberately. He was also attracted to the ancient landscape of Valentia, with its 385-million-year-old tetrapod prints, as he was in search of 'an ancient sound'. Listening to the tones was landowner Patrick Curran and his niece Emma Curran.

Right: Manning the only full-time Irish Coast Guard station in the southwest of Ireland are (l–r): Peter Drake, James Frances Lynch and Jim Guirey.

Opposite: A view from the slate quarry, overlooking Beginish Island and Cromwell Point Lighthouse.

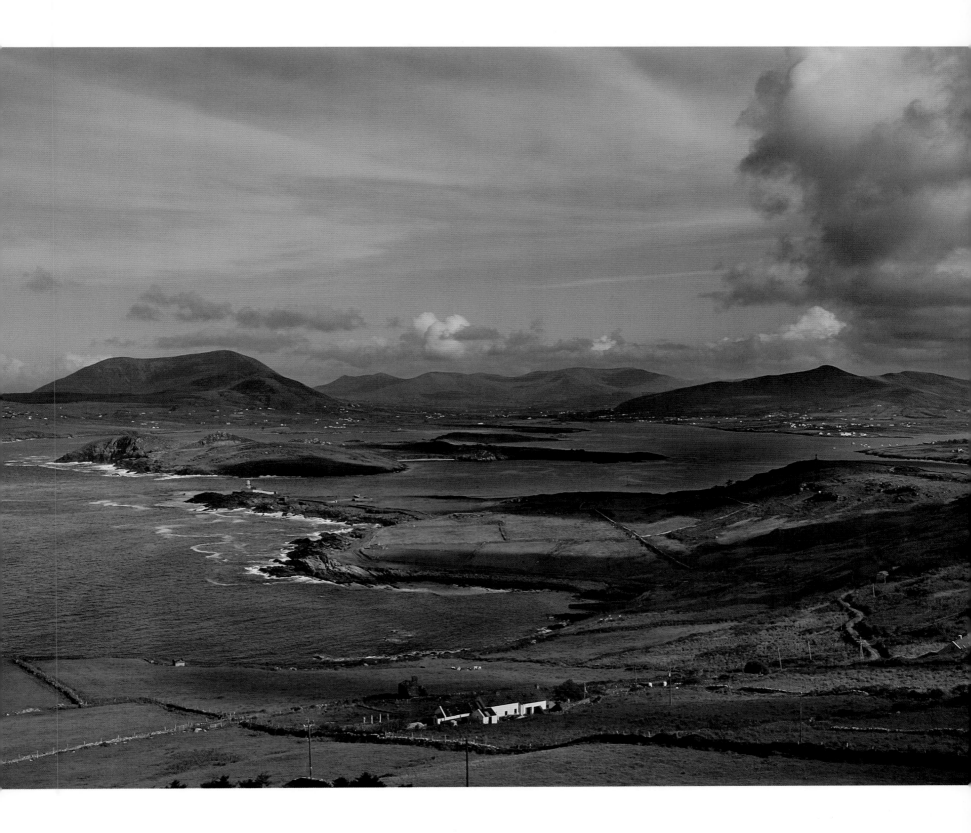

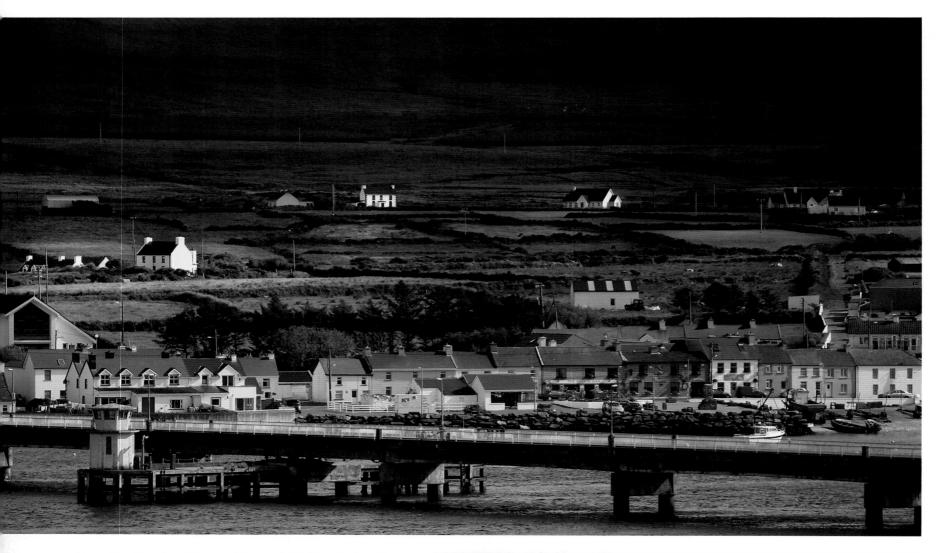

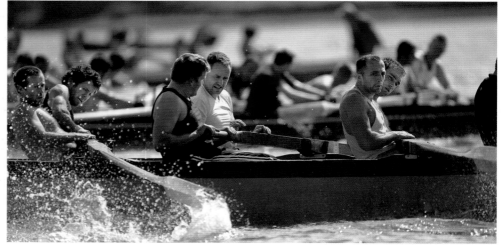

Above: The Maurice O'Connell Memorial Bridge, linking Valenta Island to the fishing village of Portmagee on the mainland.

Right: Callinafercy men in action in the Seine boat race in Cahersiveen. Seine boats were the traditional fishing boat of the Iveragh Peninsula. The hotly contested 30-minute race, which is held every regatta season in south Kerry, sees twelve strong men per boat – two per oar – take part from clubs including Valentia Island, Portmagee, Ballinskelligs, Caherdaniel, Over the Water, Cahersiveen, Callinafercy, Sneem, Cromane, Ardcost, Sive and Templenoe.

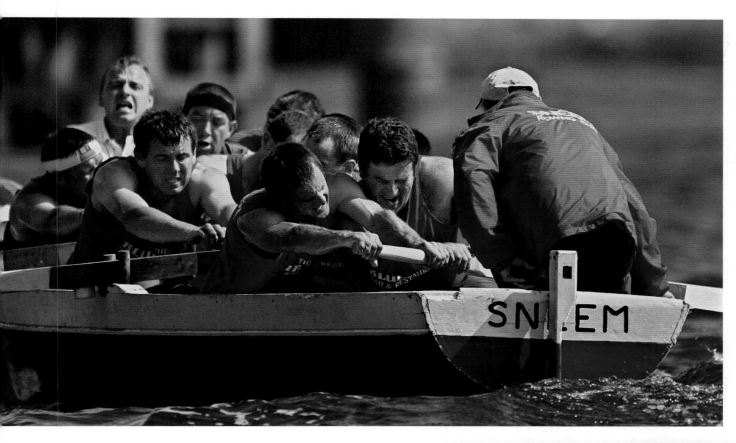

Above: 'Push for the line, lads': Sneem cox John O'Shea urges his team to the finishing line of the gruelling traditional Seine Boat race over 8km from Portmagee to Beginish.

Right: Valentia Island's Mick O'Connell unveils a plaque to mark the site of the first official transatlantic cable communication between Europe and America in 1858. Mick is one of the greatest Gaelic football players the country has ever seen, famed for his catch-and-kick style. Most comfortable in the midfield position, he played in nine All-Ireland football finals, winning four of them. He was named on the GAA's Football Team of the Century and, in 2000, named on the GAA's Football Team of the Millennium. Mick has an enormous knowledge of the history and folklore of the island. He and his wife, Rosaleen, gifted land for the building of Tigh an Oileáin, a residential home for six young people with special needs, which was opened in 2005.

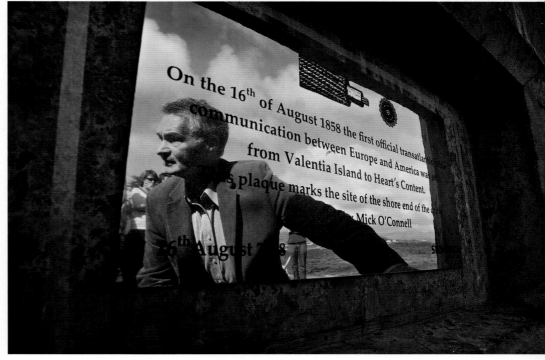

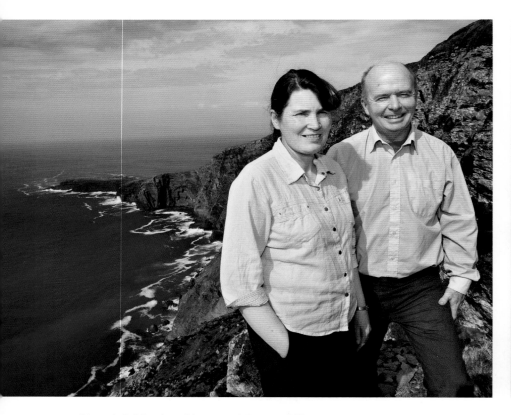

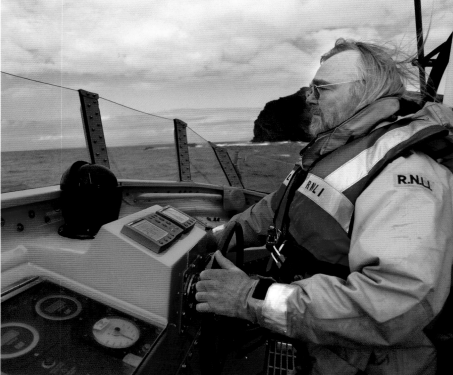

Above left: Islanders Muiris and Bernie O'Donoghue developed their farm on Goekaun Hill and Fogher cliffs into a wonderful walking and viewing site. Geokaun is the highest mountain on the island, at 180m (600ft), and from its summit, there are magnificent views of the Skelligs, Cahersiveen, the MacGillycuddy's Reeks and Dingle Peninsula.

Above right: Acting Coxwain Martin Moriarty, Valentia RNLI boat crew, surveys the coastline. An island man, Martin and his wife, Sandra, run Valentia Island and Sea Sports. Between them, they have a wealth of diving experience and they have recently opened an organic coffee shop at Knightstown Harbour. They are both involved with the annual King Scallop Festival, which takes place in June each year.

Right: Paul Duff, who runs the Lighthouse Cafe with his wife, Paula, on Valentia Island. They pride themselves on the organic island-grown vegetables used in all their recipes.

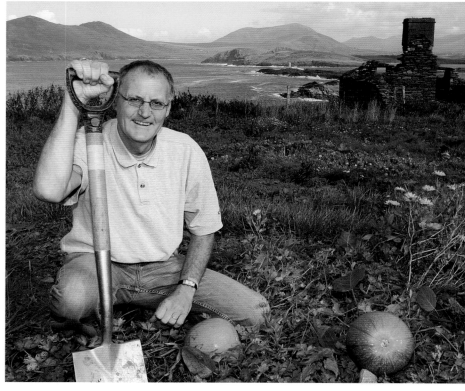

CAHERSIVEEN

I am Kerry like my mother before me,
And my mother's mother and her man.
Now I sit on an office stool remembering,
And the memory of them like a fan
Soothes the embers into flame.
I am Kerry and proud of my name.

From 'I am Kerry' by Sigerson Clifford (1913–1985)

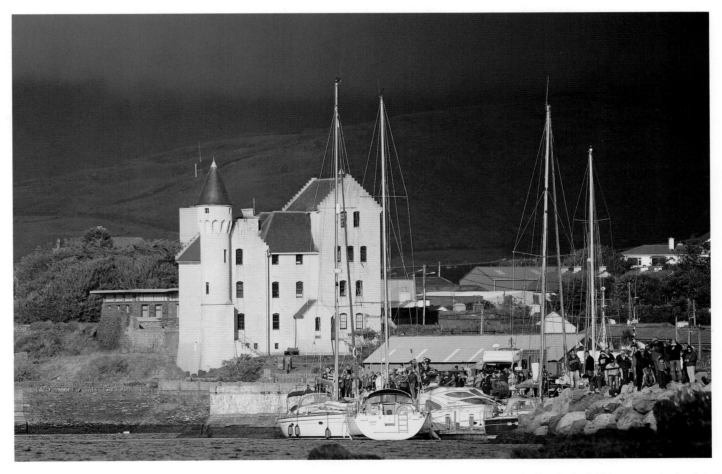

Cahersiveen is nestled at the foot of Bentee Mountain, overlooking Valentia Harbour. *Cathair Saidhbhín* means 'Little Sadhbh's stone ringfort'. It is the biggest town on the Iveragh Peninsula and has the only Catholic church in the country named after a lay person: Daniel O'Connell, the nineteenth-century Irish politician and campaigner for Catholic Emancipation and the Repeal of the 1801 Act of Union. An imposing out-of-commission Royal Irish Constabulary barracks is located close to the shore. Now a heritage centre, it was – according to modern myth – built from plans for a British barracks in India.

Right: Footballer and sportsman Maurice Fitzgerald of Cahersiveen finishes the swim in the annual Sive Triathlon Sprint Distance Triathlon – a 750m (half-mile) swim, 20km (12-mile) cycle and 5km (3-mile) run in aid of Sive Rowing Club.

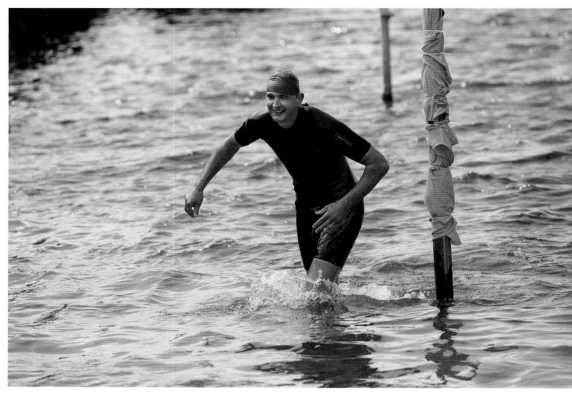

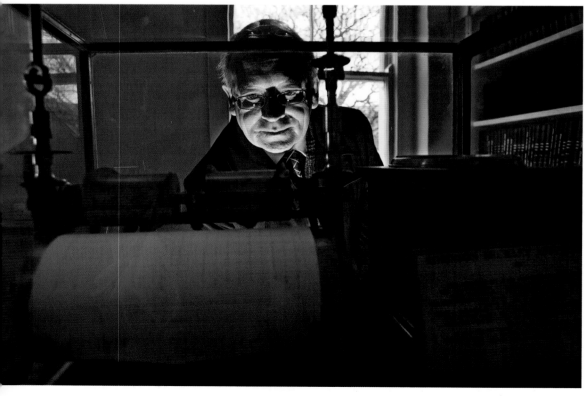

Left: Paud Mahoney, former Senior Meteorological Officer, takes great pride in the old weather instruments which can still be used to record weather today. He retired in 2006 from Met Éireann Valentia Observatory, which is based in Cahersiveen.

Right: Listening for the right note: local man Jimmy Moriarty takes part in the annual Cahersiveen busking competition at the August bank holiday weekend festival.

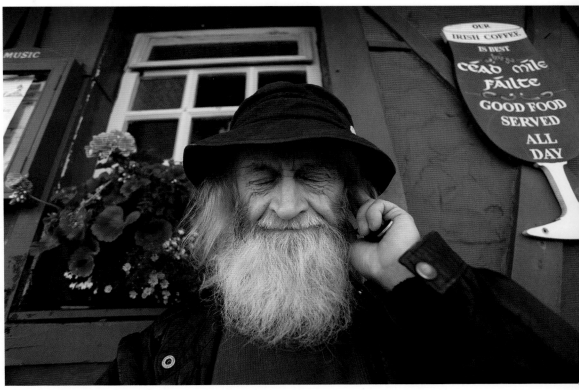

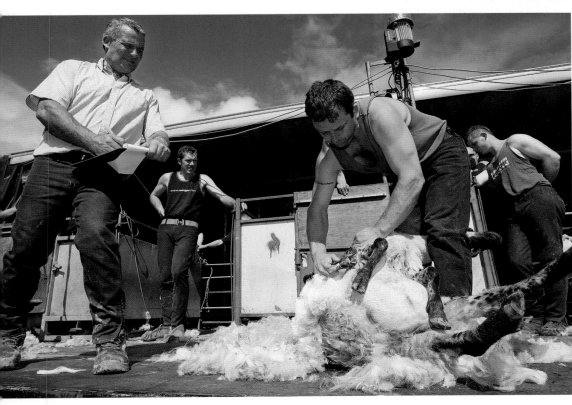

Left: Peter Hussey of Portmagee is judged by Patrick Moran, Waterville, as he competes in the sheep-shearing competition at the Cahersiveen Festival.

ROSSBEIGH

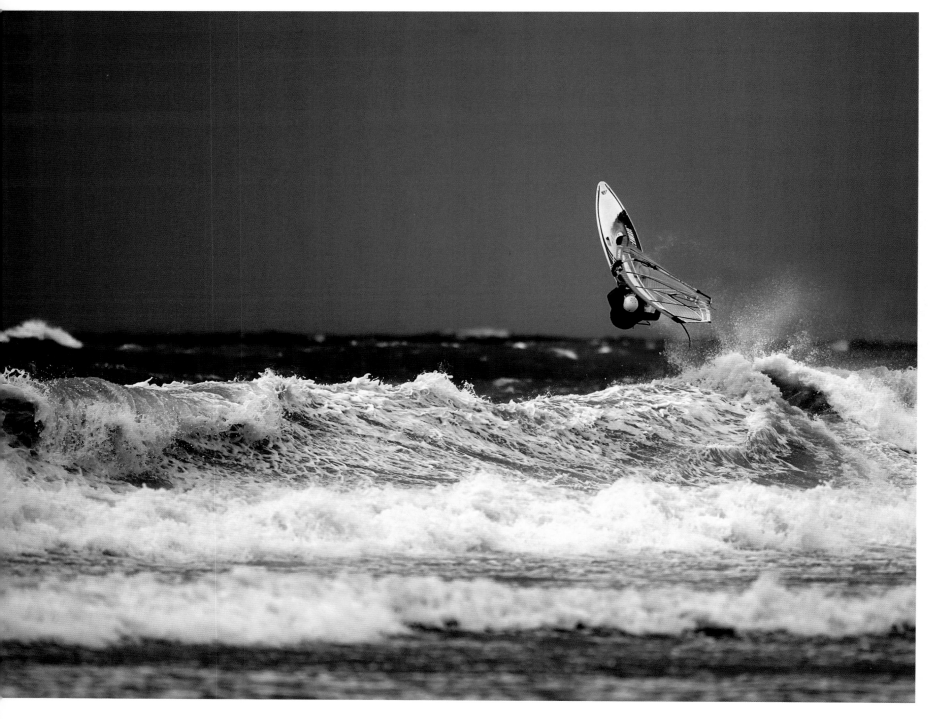

Ben Cronier of Cromane makes use of great windsurfing conditions at Rossbeigh Strand.

CROMANE

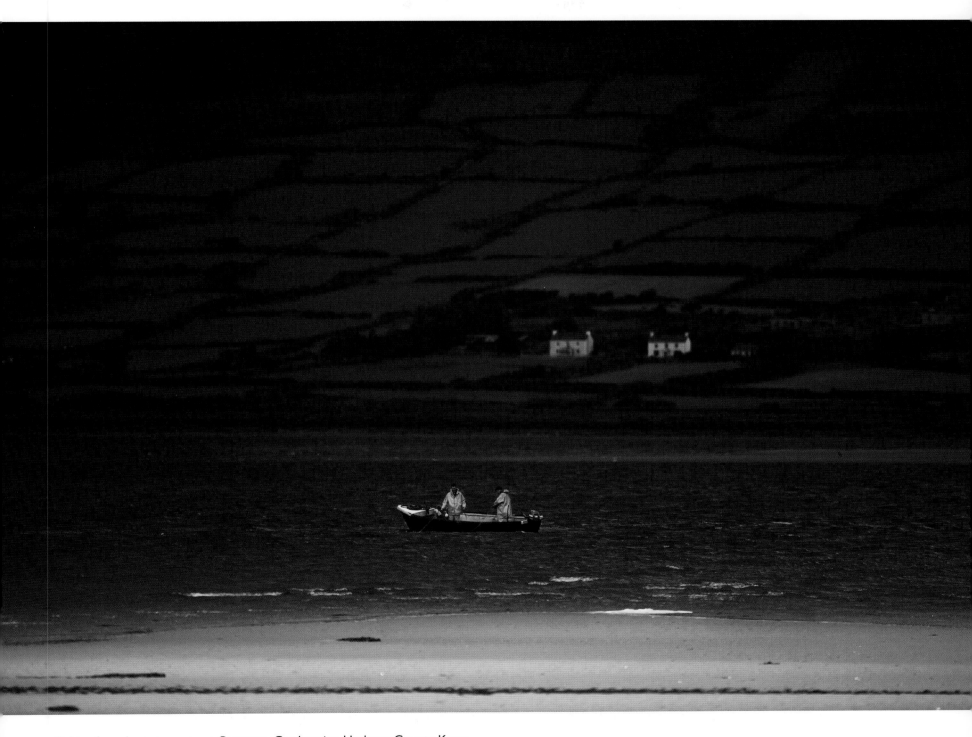

Fishing for salmon in punts at Cromane, Castlemaine Harbour, County Kerry.

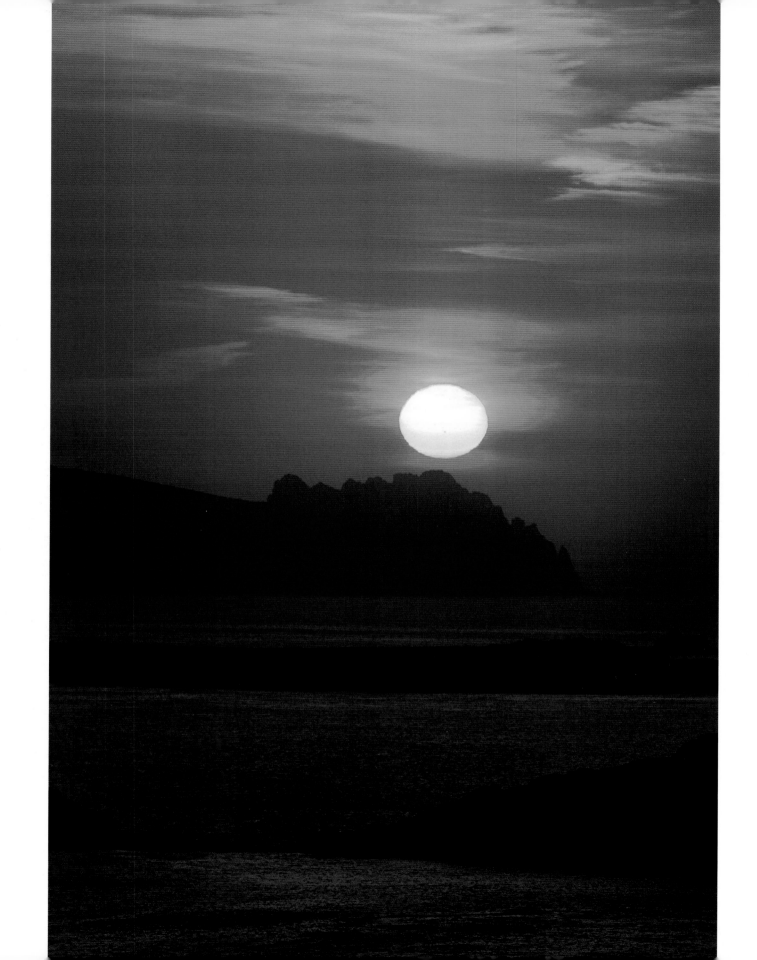

DINGLE PENINSULA

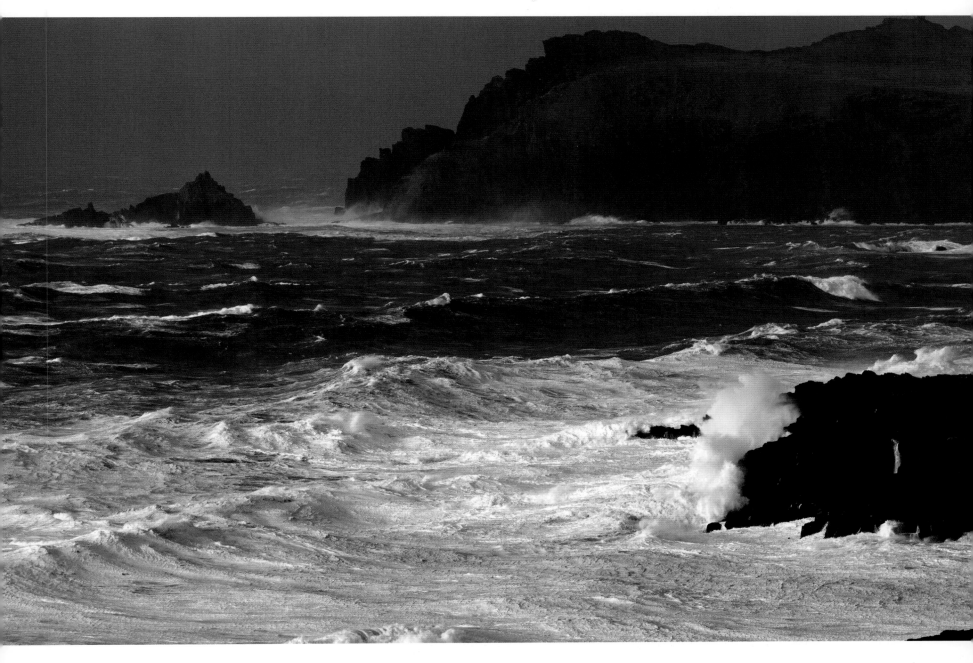

Above: Strong Atlantic swells and winds of 120km crashing in on Dún Chaoin on the Dingle Peninsula.

Opposite: The sun sets over Inis Tuaisceart, the most northerly of the Blasket Islands. The name means 'northern islander' but it is known locally as 'An Fear Marbh' or 'The Sleeping Giant'.

MOUNT BRANDON

A view from the top of Mount Brandon, Dingle Peninsula, overlooking Cappagh Strand. The name in Irish, *Cnoc Bréanainn*, meaning 'Brendan's hill', is associated with Saint Brendan the Navigator, patron saint of boatmen, mariners and sailors. He embarked on many voyages, sailing to Scotland, Wales and the Canary Islands and quite possibly reached America in the sixth century, although this cannot be proven.

Mount Brandon is 952m (3,123ft) in height and is the ninth highest peak in Ireland.

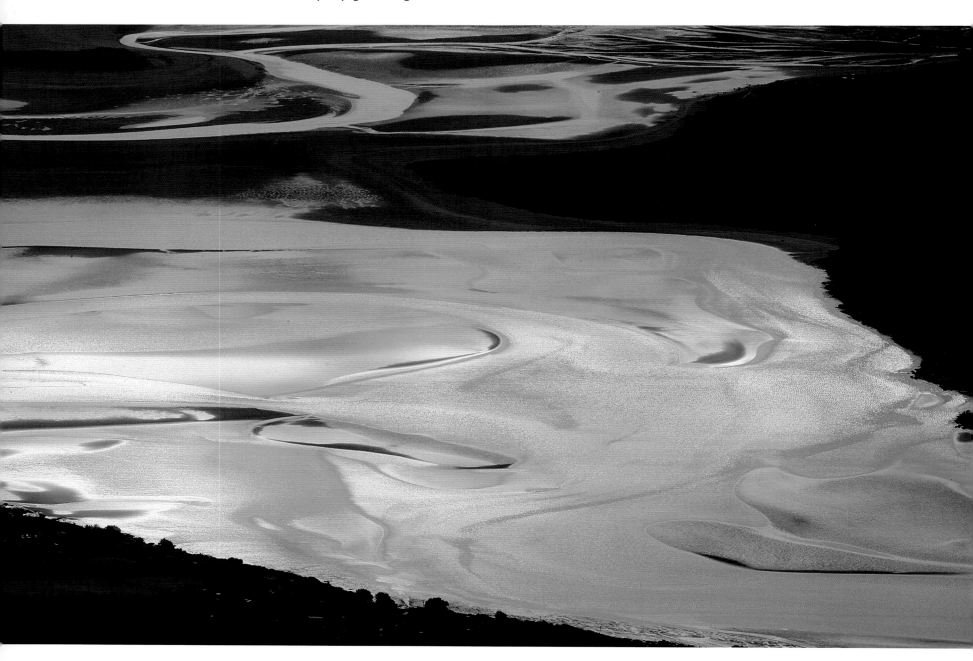

Right: Life begins at eighty: legendary broadcaster Mícheál Ó Muircheartaigh, who was born in Dún Síon in Dingle in 1930, celebrated his eightieth birthday by climbing Mount Brandon with his family.

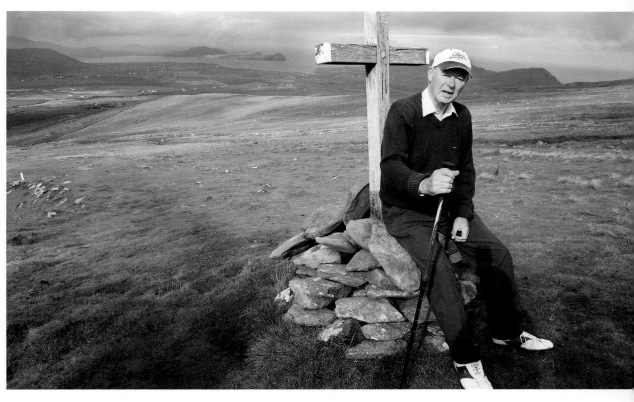

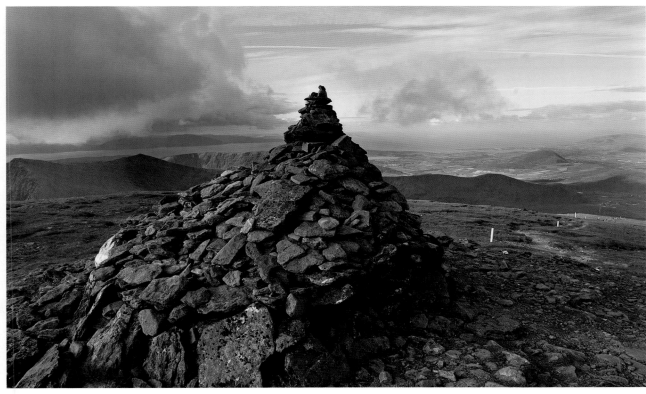

Left: Because of its association with St Brendan, Mount Brandon has an important pilgrim path, the popular *Cosán na Naomh* route, usually celebrated on the second Sunday in May.

POWER TO THE WIND

By Breda Joy

GROWING UP not far from Tralee Bay in the townland of Lismore, Mike Barry's very first memories of the sea are of 'shivering and freezing' on the beaches of Banna or Inch. But that cold had nothing on the sub-zero temperatures he was to experience in January 2004, when he became the first Irishman to ski to the South Pole as part of an international expedition which trekked and skied over 1,000km (700 miles) over 50 days. He was following in the footsteps of fellow Kerryman Tom Crean from Anascaul, who was within 240km (150 miles) of the Pole in 1912 when team leader Robert Scott ordered him to turn back.

Ironically, the Tralee father-of-three, who has challenged himself in some of the planet's most inhospitable seas in the Antarctic, got his first taste for adventuring in books. 'I started reading quite a lot on mountaineering and travels to Arctic and the Antarctic,' he says. 'Even if Tom Crean was not high profile then, I certainly became aware of him and his expeditions. There was very little written about him except for some by lines in Roland Huntford's books on Shackleton, Amundsen and Scott until Michael Smith published his book which raised his profile.'

The idea of going to the South Pole germinated for some years until, in 1997, he took part in the South Arís Expedition – a re-enactment of the voyage of the *James Caird* in a replica boat from Elephant Island to South Georgia and crossing the island. But, first, having climbed in various parts of the world and having made the first Irish ascent of Aconcagua, the highest peak in the western hemisphere, he was invited in 1993 to join the first Irish Everest Expedition and played a key role in supporting leader Dawson Stelfox who reached the summit on 27 May 1993. He was one of eight climbers on the expedition, which was one of the last traditional-style expeditions carried out without high-altitude porters. 'It was the beginning of the end of the traditional expedition to Everest,' he said. 'It was just at the turning point when the mass popularity of commercial expeditions was beginning. We were privileged to be in there at that time.'

Then, in 1997, on the seventy-fifth anniversary of the death of Sir Ernest Shackleton, he joined Frank Nugent, Paddy Barry, Jamie Young and Jarlath Cunnane on the South Arís Expedition which set about crossing 1,300km (800 miles) of the Southern Ocean to recreate the voyage from Elephant Island to South Georgia in the *James Caird*, the lifeboat from the ship *Endeavour*. 'Halfway across, we were hit by hurricane force winds, which blew for thirty-six hours and which capsized our boat three times in a twelve-hour period, and rolled us completely,' says Mike. 'It was a fairly wild experience for me. On one occasion, I had gotten into my sleeping bag in the coffin bunk. I dozed off. Next, we were upside down in gurgling water. My face was in water. I was a happy man when we popped around.'

'As a storm rages, you think this can't get any stronger, the waves can't get any bigger and the wind can't get any louder,' he says. 'You look out and the wind is screaming louder and the waves are getting bigger. It's the noise.' The forecast was for an even bigger storm in three days. The decision was taken to abandon the boat and, when the winds abated, get on board the support vessel, which took them to South Georgia where they retraced the footsteps of Shackleton and Crean across South Georgia over three days. In 2004, Mike Barry became the first Irish man to ski to the South Pole as part of an international expedition. The five-man expedition covered 1,200km (750 miles) in 52 days, dragging sledges weighted with 80kg of provisions. 'Possibly, the hardest part of the journey was the monotony of it because the

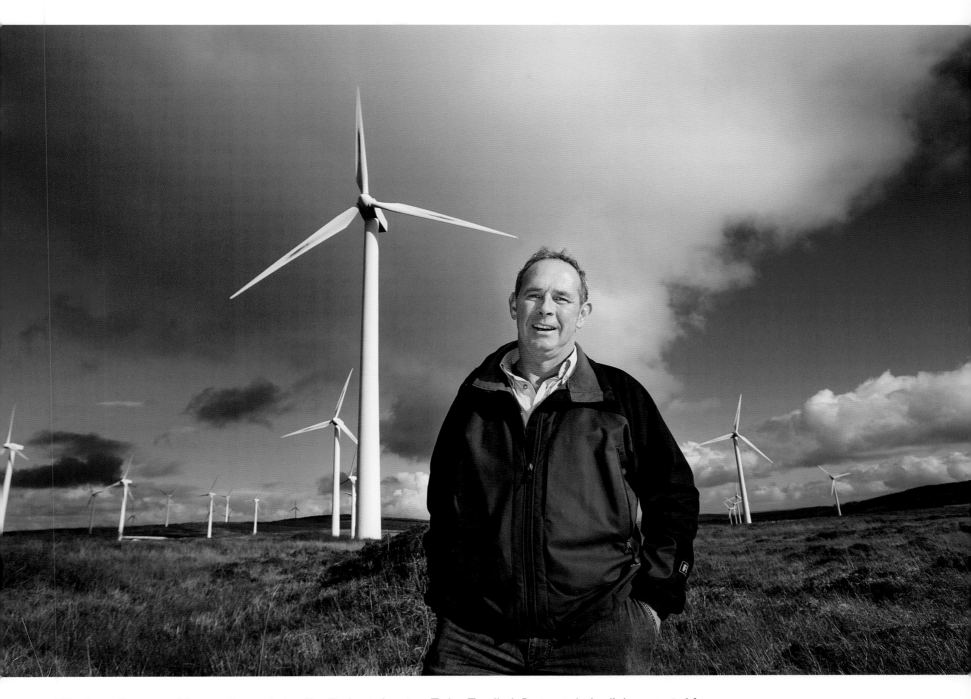

Mike Barry, Director of Saorgus Energy Ltd, at Tursillagh wind project, Tralee. Tursillagh Project is Ireland's largest wind farm.

environment doesn't change compared to the Arctic where the ice changes all the time,' Mike explains. 'We finished what was started in 1912 – the Irish journey to the South Pole. There was very little about Tom Crean then. It was nice to have a Kerryman finish what a Kerryman started with Shackleton.'

Having been at the mercy of the elements in some of the most inhospitable terrain in the world, Mike Barry, together with Killarney man Aidan Forde, turned his attention to the relatively new sector of renewable energy and set about harnessing the untamed Atlantic winds. The two men formed Saorgus Energy Ltd in 1993 and commissioned its first wind farm at Tursillagh, Tralee, in 2000.

'In Kerry, you can't but be aware of the energy in the natural environment, between the wind, the oceans and the rivers,' Mike says. 'We have some of the best prevailing winds in the world coming off the Atlantic with vast quantities of energy. If you look at the wind as being an invisible river, it's not the size of the Shannon, it's the size of the entire west coast of Ireland. It's an invisible river of energy flowing over the coast. To harvest even a fraction of

that will provide a vast amount of power. The difficulty is the wind is on the west and the power demand is on the east,' he explains. 'The infrastructure is not there at the moment.'

The sea and the outdoors are a shared family passion for Mike, his wife, Margo, and their children, Aron, Michelle, and Kay, who all enjoy kayaking, rock climbing and mountaineering. 'I love to go sea kayaking and sailing on the coastline around Kerry,' Mike says. 'There are some fabulous sea caverns, cliffs and inlets around our coast. From Kinsale to Dingle is one of the best sailing areas in the world.'

And he has discovered that you don't have to go literally to the end of the world to connect with the spectacular manifestations of nature. 'I was up on a wind farm one evening and the sun was setting. I said to my son, Aron, we might see the green flash. In special atmospheric conditions, you get a millisecond of a green flash that lights up the horizon. It's very rare and spectacular. Just when the sun goes below the horizon for a millisecond, you see it. And we did.'

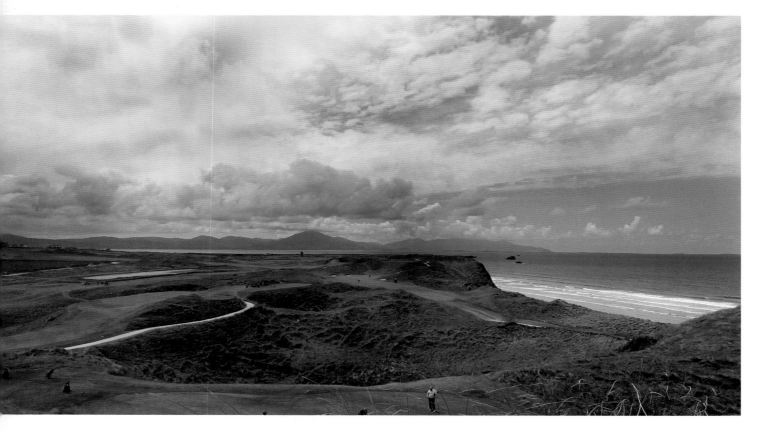

TRALEE

Tralee Golf Club, Barrow, County Kerry, is considered one of Ireland's most challenging Atlantic links courses. Its ruggedness is breathtaking. Instituted in 1896, Tralee Golf Club opened its present Arnold Palmer-designed course in 1984. Palmer later declared, 'I may have designed the first nine but surely God designed the back nine'.

CASTLEGREGORY

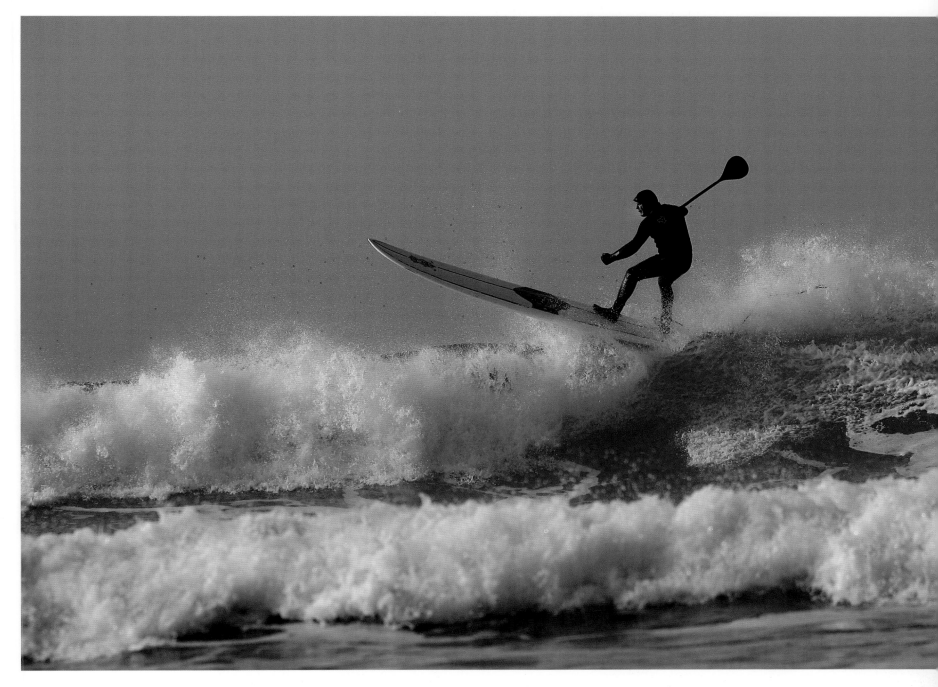

Jamie Knox of Castlegregory paddle surfs the waves at the Maharees. A former professional windsurfer, he runs his own watersports centre near Brandon Bay, close to Castlegregory, considered to be one of the best areas in the country for surfing, windsurfing and kitesurfing.

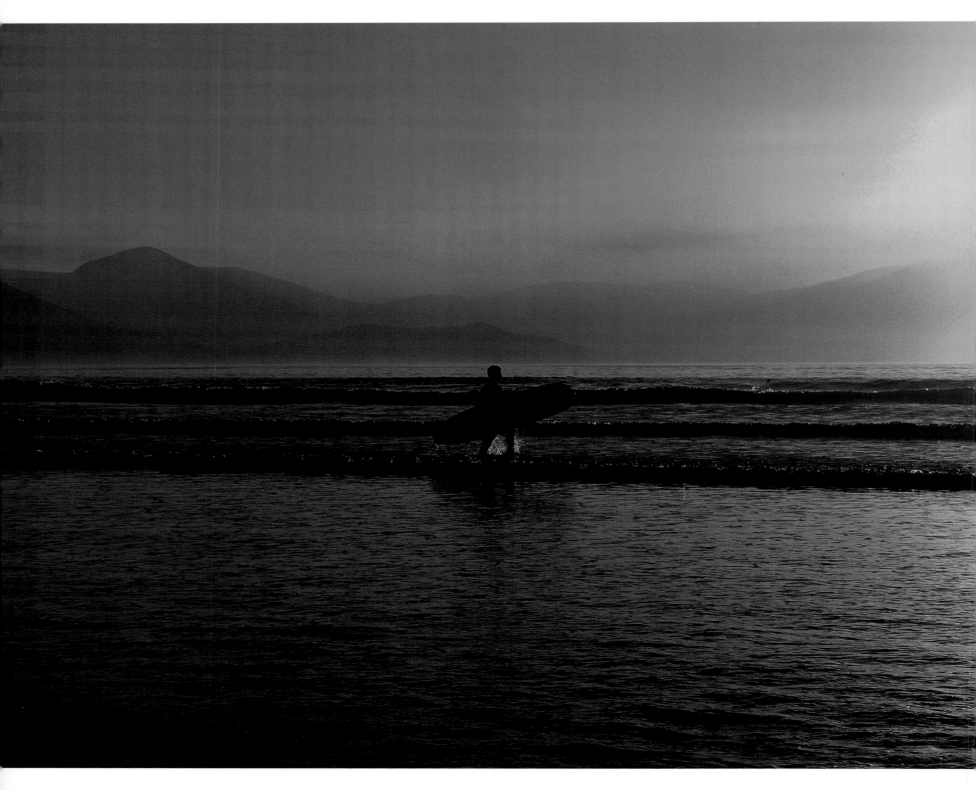

A cold February evening in the Maharees is nonetheless inviting for surfers.

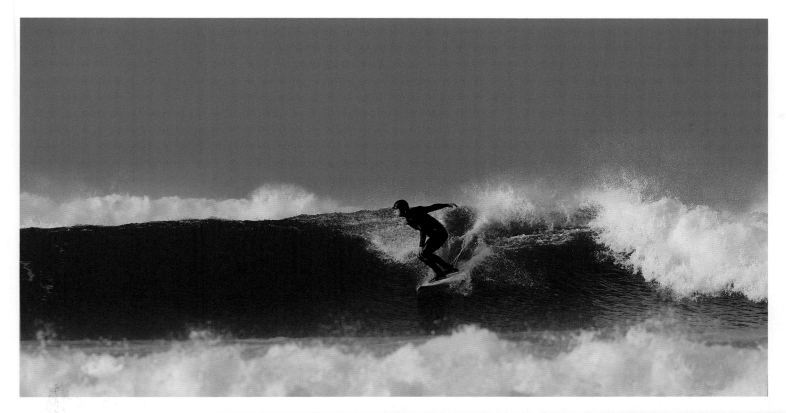

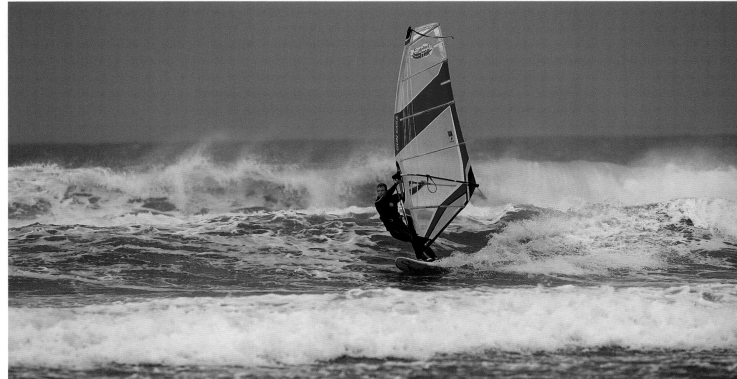

Above: Riding the Atlantic waves at Castlegregory.

Right: Windsurfing – the preserve of the brave.

FENIT

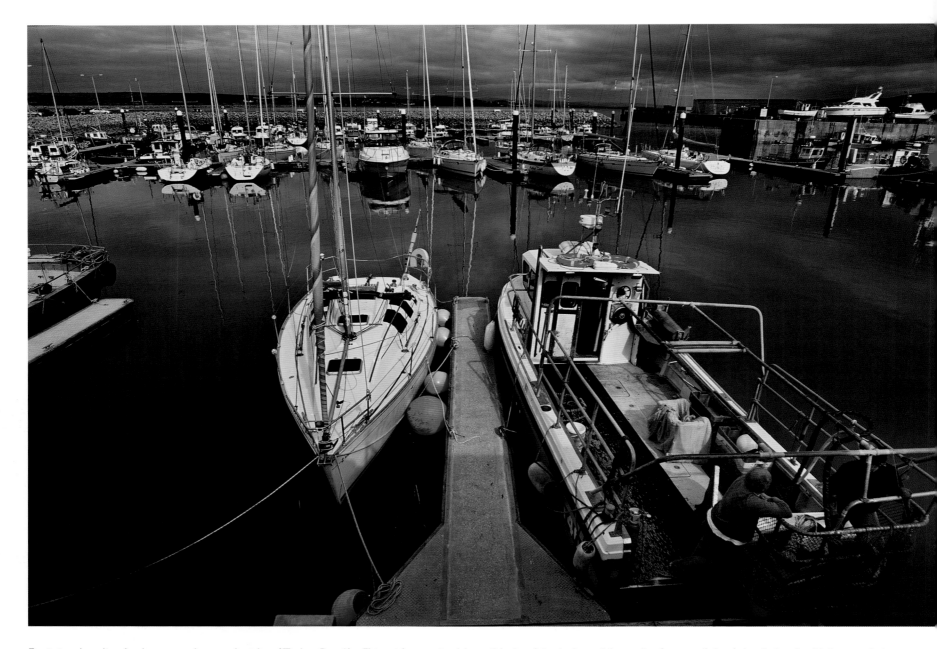

Fenit is a bustling harbour on the north side of Tralee Bay. 'An Fhianait', meaning 'the wild place', is sheltered from the forces of the Atlantic by the Maharees. It is a very popular harbour and marina with a variety of functions: fishing, sailing, leisure crafts as well as freight import and export.

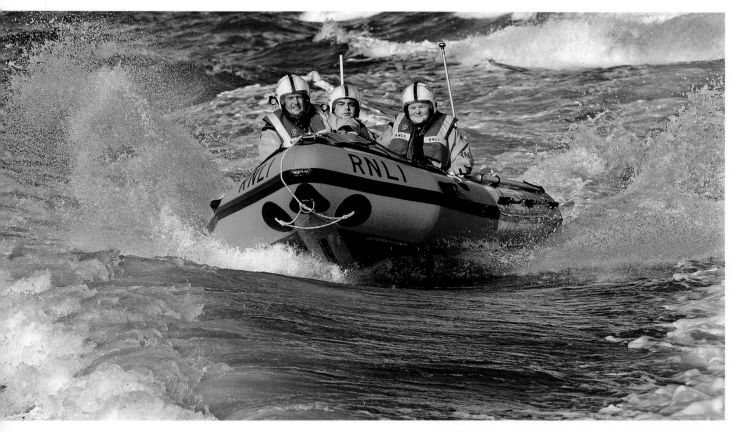

Above: (l–r): Lee Sugrue, Kevin Deady and Denise Lynch, volunteer crew members of Fenit RNLI Lifeboat, in an IB1 inshore lifeboat donated by Bangor RNLI volunteers and supporters, in memory of Bradley and Sonya Burns. Bradley was a helmsman and mechanic on the Bangor lifeboat and his wife, Sonya, was the lifeboat administration officer. The young couple died within ten months of each other in 2006, leaving two small children.

Right: Fishermen returning with their catch of oysters, which will be exported as well as supplying local renowned seafood restaurants in the Fenit and Spa area near Tralee.

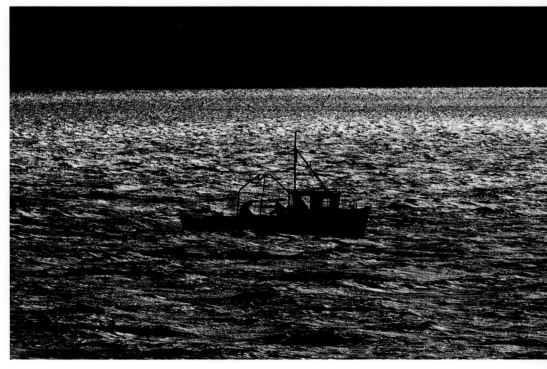

BANNA STRAND

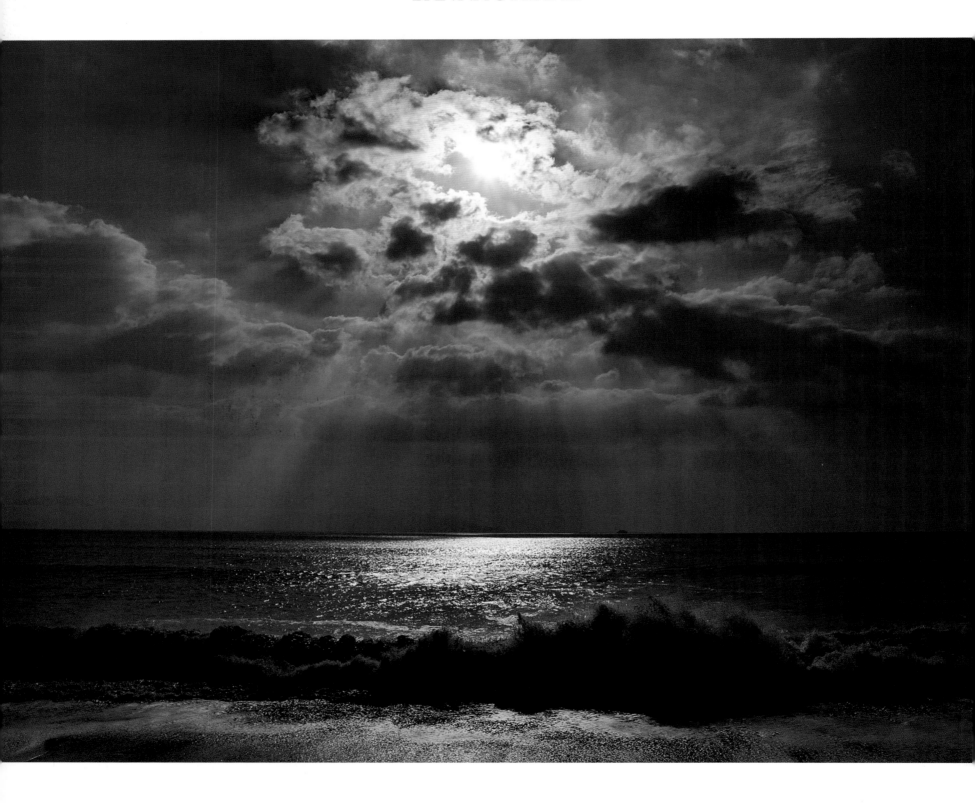

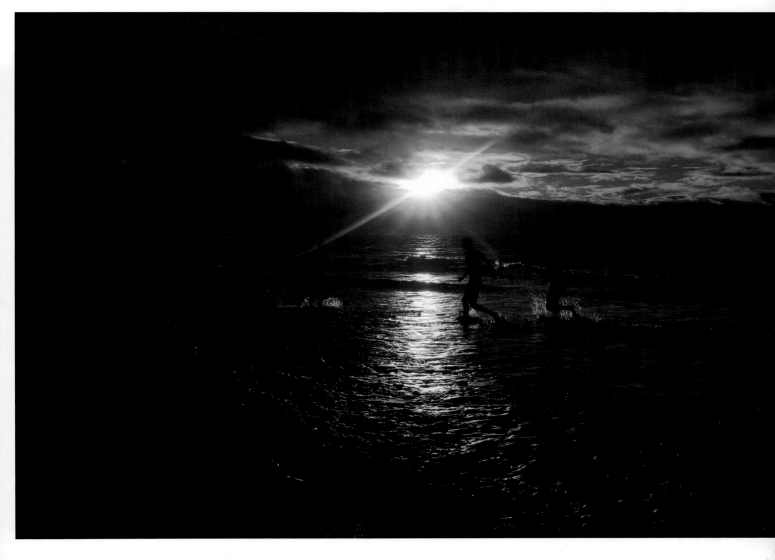

Above: Swimmers brave the Atlantic at Banna Strand in April, raising money for charity. Situated in Tralee Bay, Banna Strand is a popular beach for the Tralee and north Kerry population. An expansive Atlantic Ocean beach, it has 12km (7 miles) of rolling sand dunes and crystal-clear waters. It has a historical association with the Irish revolutionary patriot and diplomat Sir Roger Casement, who was captured on Good Friday morning, 21 April 1916, having landed from a German U-boat. Casement was involved in an attempt to land arms for Irish Republicans from the German vessel *Aud* two days before the Easter Rising at the GPO in Dublin. He was put ashore at Banna Strand, too weak to travel. He was discovered at McKenna's Fort, Ardfert, and arrested on charges of treason and espionage against the Crown. He was subsequently executed in Pentonville Prison, London, in August 1916. In 1965, Roger Casement's body was repatriated to Ireland and was awarded a state funeral and buried with full military honours in the republican plot at Glasnevin Cemetery, Dublin.

Left: Banna Strand on a hazy evening in April at sunset.

BALLYBUNION

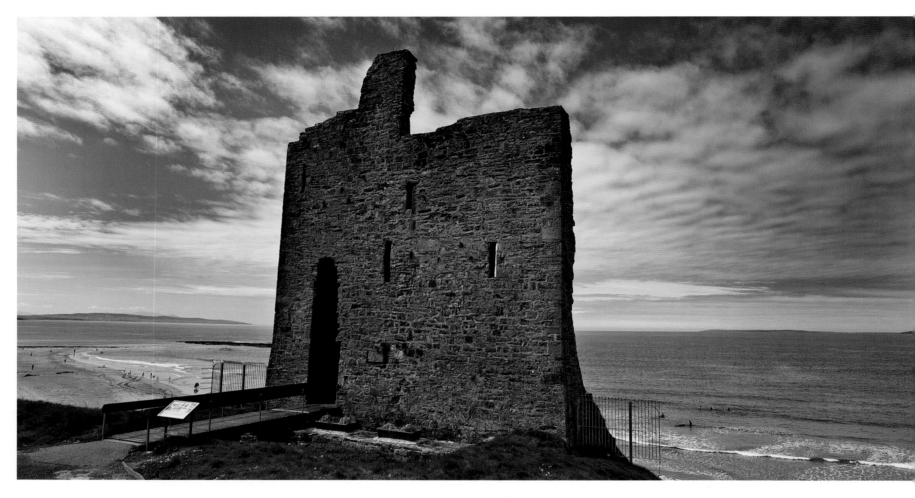

Above: Ballybunion Castle, a popular focal point and former Geraldine stronghold, was built in the fourteenth century and was the scene of many battles during the Desmond Wars. All that remains of the castle today is the East Wall.

Right: The Virgin Rock is located on Nuns' Strand, a magnificent strand with beautiful sea arches and cliff formations. The strand was formerly the preserve of the nuns who lived in the convent at the top of the cliff.

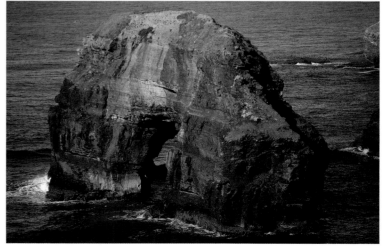

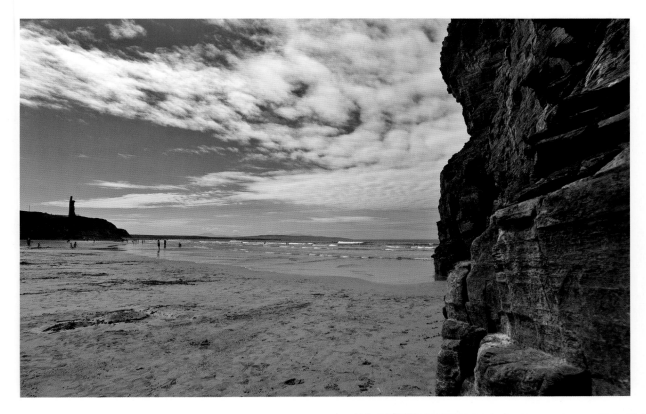

Left: Ballybunion is one of the great seaside resorts in Ireland. The seaweed baths, which have been run by the Collins family for almost 100 years, use seaweed hand-picked daily from the 'Blackrocks' and sea water pumped straight from the Atlantic Ocean.

During the summer months, cooked periwinkles are sold in paper bags, with a pin to extract the small sea snails. Ballybunion has two world-class golf links and a walk along its cliff face, with its unusual rock formations and sea stacks, is a paradise for geologists.

TARBERT

Tarbert Lighthouse, situated on the Shannon Estuary in north Kerry, came into operation on 31 March 1834. Built on a tidal rock off the north side of Tarbert Island, its stairs and wall are made of limestone while its floor and lantern are made of blocking granite.

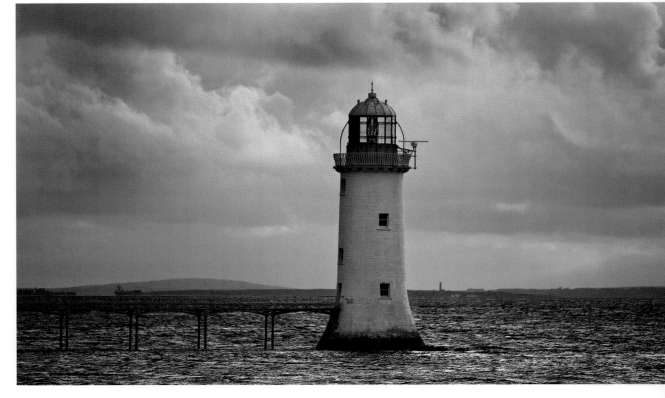

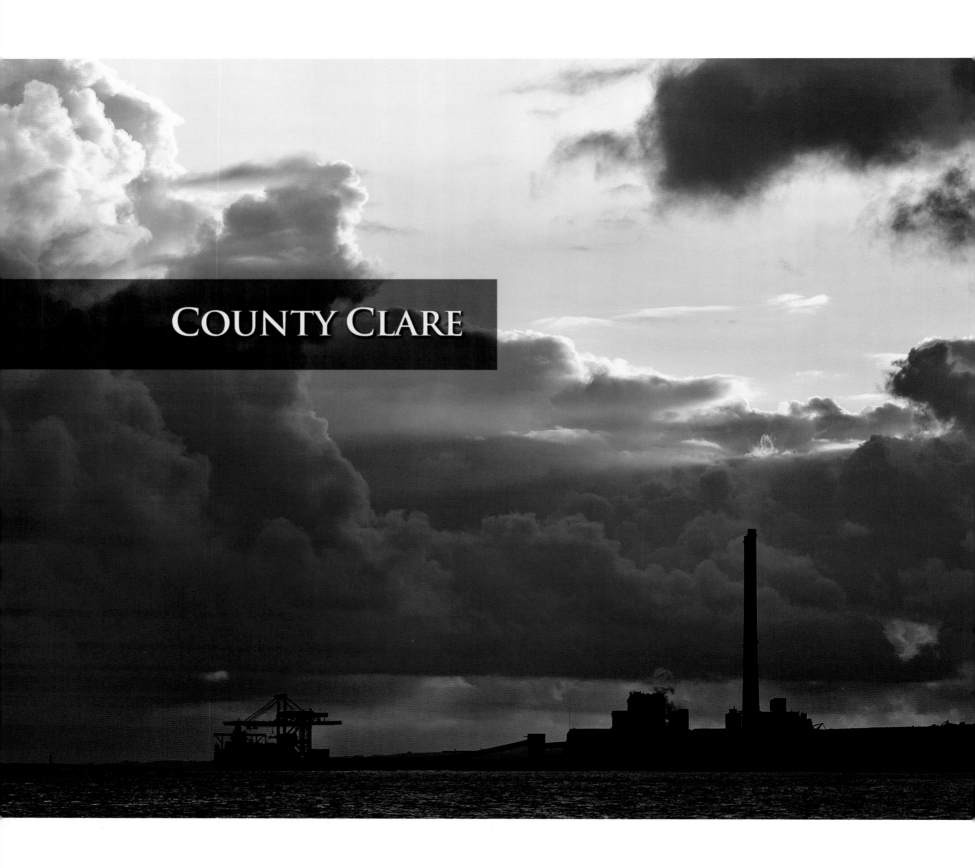

COUNTY CLARE

SCATTERY ISLAND

This isolated and ancient island is located at the mouth of the River Shannon, approximately 1.6km (1 mile) from Kilrush in southwest Clare. It is home to a sixth-century monastic settlement founded by a local saint, Senan. It had seven churches, all now in ruins, and a round tower, one of the tallest in Ireland, which, unusually, has a door on the ground floor. St Senan's monastery was strict and conditions for the monks were austere. Women were not allowed on the island. However, Senan's sister's last wish was to be buried there, so her remains were taken at low tide, when it was not considered an island.

Near the round tower there is a holy well, named after St Senan, 'Tobar Sinean'. He is reputed to have performed miracles there. The local saint is said to have died on the island in 544, and is buried in St Senan's Bed beside Temple Senan, a twelfth-century Romanesque church. Scattery monastery was raided by Vikings in the ninth and tenth centuries. Irish King Brian Boru also attacked it. It was practically demolished in Tudor times when all monastic settlements in Ireland were suppressed. Scattery Island was used by the ill-fated Spanish Armada as a safe haven from Atlantic storms in the sixteenth century.

The last inhabitants left the island in 1978. Now abandoned, the lighthouse, old cottages, monastic ruins and graves of the islanders are all that remains of this unusual and turbulent island. It is still an important island of pilgrimage, and noted birdwatching paradise.

Opposite: Evening at Moneypoint electricity generating station. The station is located near Kilrush, County Clare, on the Shannon Estuary. It is the largest power station in Ireland, with three generating units, each capable of producing 305MW. It was commissioned between 1985 and June 1987 and uses coal as its principal fuel source.

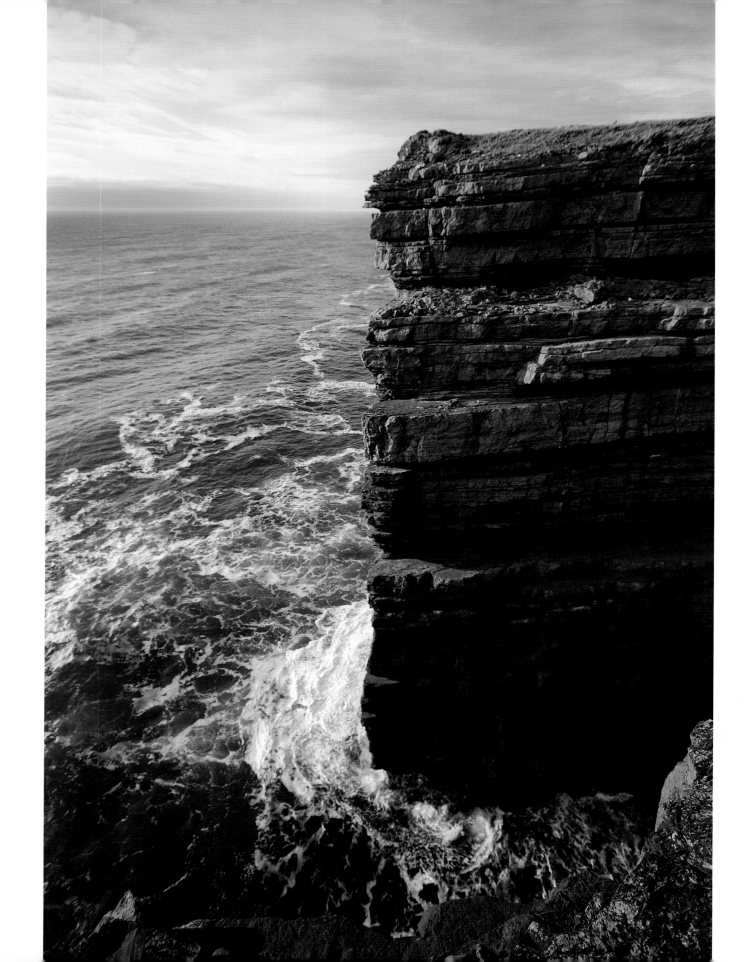

DIARMUID AND GRÁINNE'S ROCK, LOOP HEAD

Opposite: Diarmuid and Gráinne's Rock is located at Loop Head, over 30m (100ft) high and detached from the main headland by a vertical narrow channel called 'Lovers' Leap'. This exhilarating cliff is often climbed and abseiled by elite and experienced climbers.

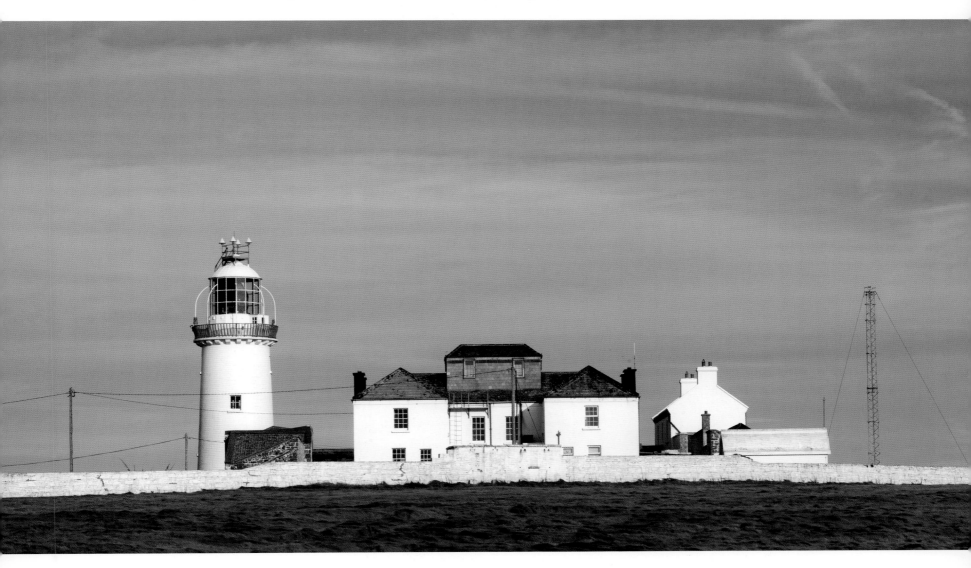

LOOP HEAD LIGHTHOUSE

Loop Head lighthouse station, Kilbaha, west County Clare, is a major landmark on the northern shore of the Shannon river. This stronghold has watched over the Atlantic's seafarers for more than three centuries. The light was manually operated until 1971, and officially fully automated twenty years later. It was opened to the public in the summer of 2011.

KILKEE

Kilkee is regarded as one of the safest bathing places in Ireland, being protected from the full force of the Atlantic by a reef known as the Duggerna Rock. The pollock and diamond holes on the west end of town are three natural rock-enclosed pools. They retain seawater when the tide recedes, forming natural swimming pools. Kilkee was rated by the late oceanographer Jacques Cousteau as the best diving location in Europe and among the top five in the world. The diving boards allow for dives of up to 13m (45ft) into the open sea. The Diamond Cafe overlooks the pollock holes, well worth a call after a swim or a walk along the cliff face.

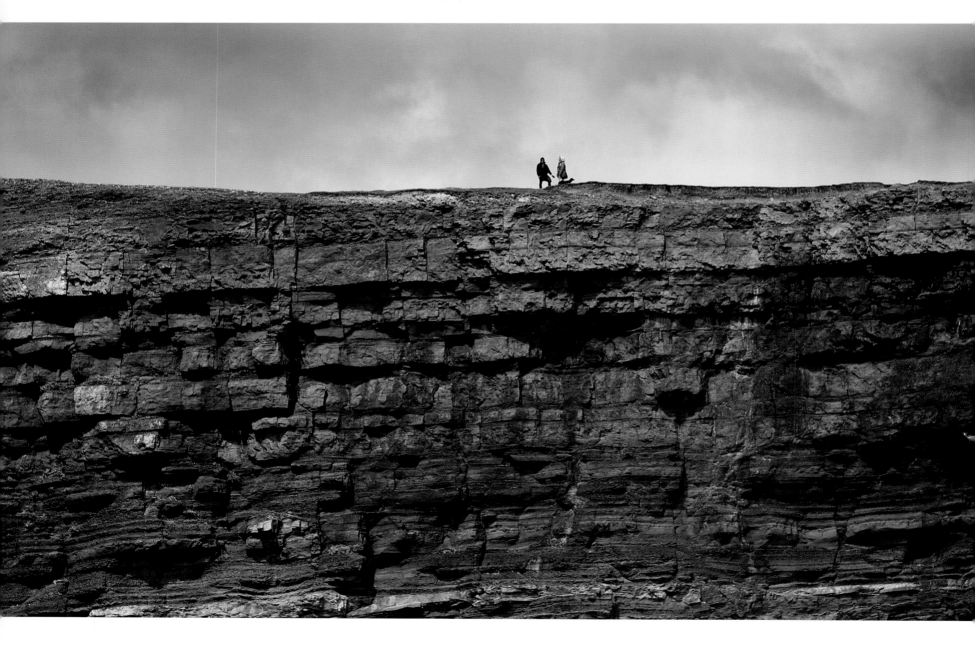

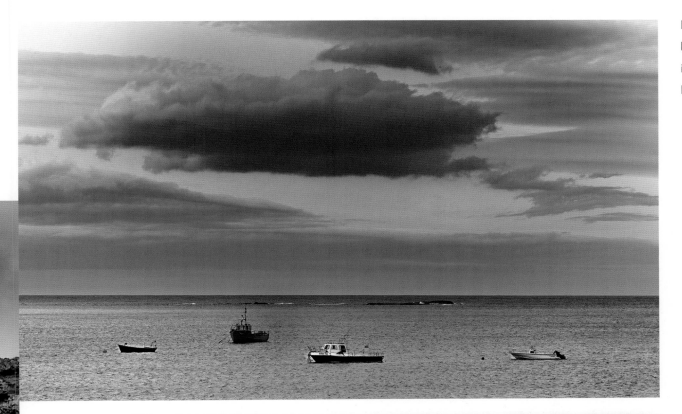

Not surprisingly, Kilkee Beach is a blue-flag beach. Just off the town centre, it affords beautiful views with the cliffs keeping it sheltered from the elements.

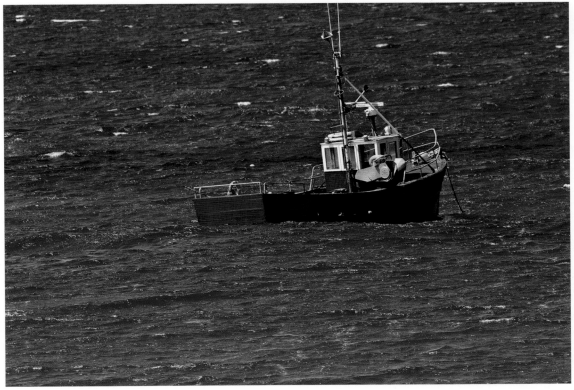

In the nineteenth century, fishing was important to Kilkee, a tradition maintained today.

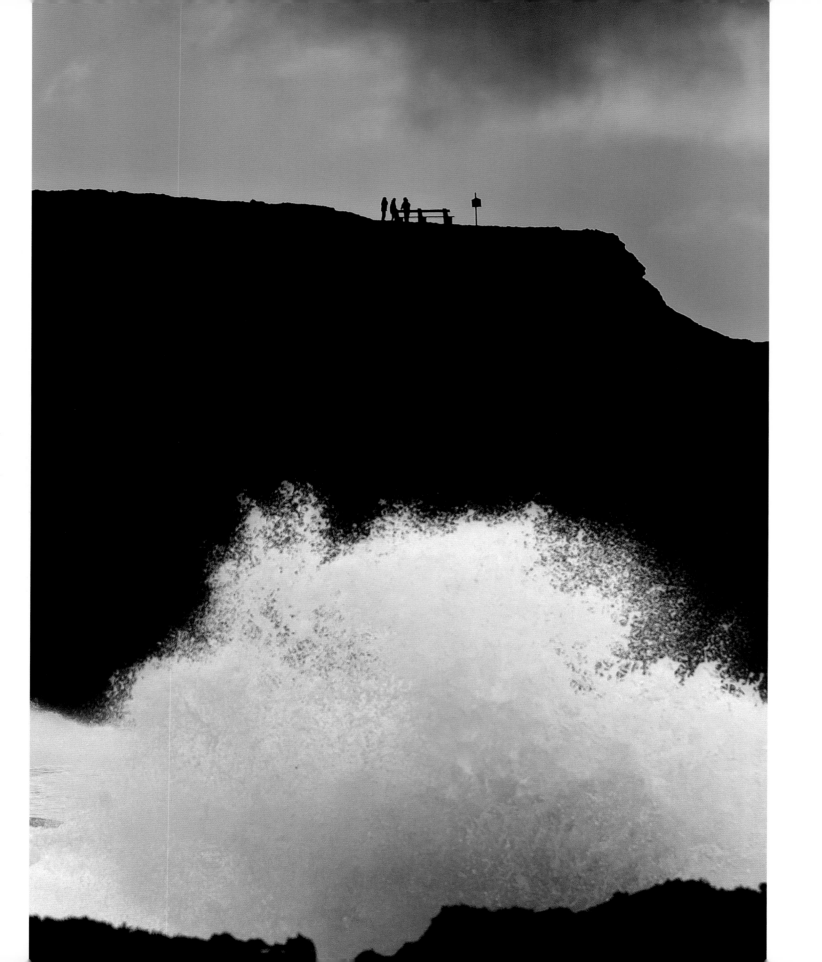

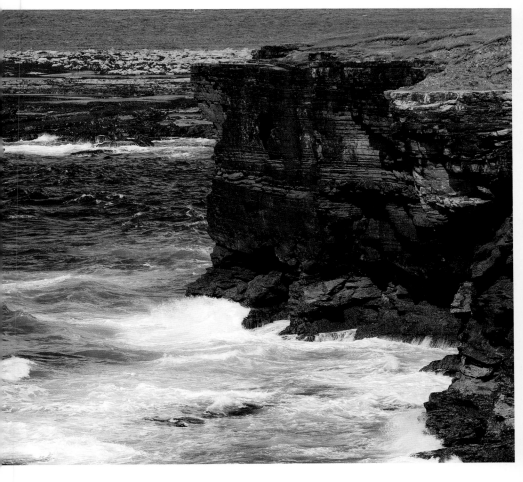

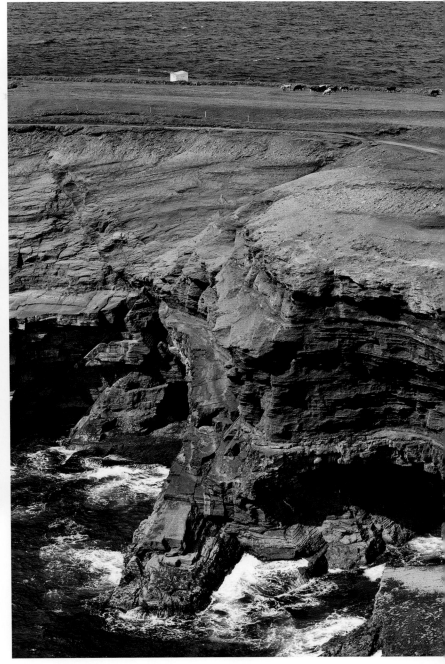

Above and right: Kilkee's cliffs are famous with the diving fraternity worldwide, with sheer cliffs, deep ravines, rock formations, underwater landscapes, sunken reefs and dive drop of over 40m. Landmark dive sites include Biraghy Mór and Biraghy Beag, Chimney Bay, Bishop's Island, Diamond rocks, George's Head, Middle Rock, Muragha Reef, and 'The Skinny Dog', named for the Greyhound Bar in Kilkee.

Opposite: As a bleak August evening falls on Kilkee, rain is about to return. The famous Kilkee waves are 10m high along the cliff face.

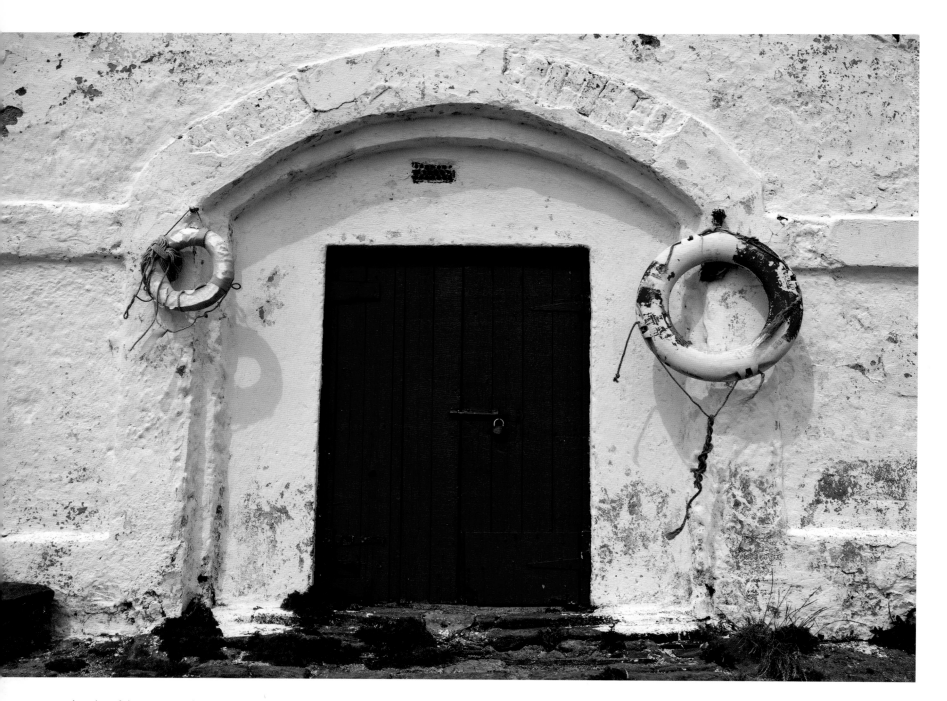

A colourful remnant of the nineteenth-century fishing village of Kilkee.

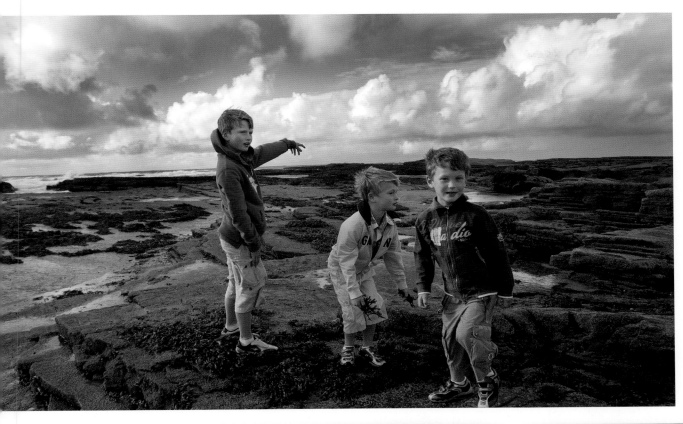

Left: Playing in the pollock holes on Kilkee are Ben (ten), Robert (eight) and Alex Sullivan (six) from Ballybeg, Ennis, in County Clare. The boys attend Clare Castle National School. Ben is a member of Ennis Rugby club, Robert is in the Beaver Scouts and Alex hurls with Clare Castle GAA Club.

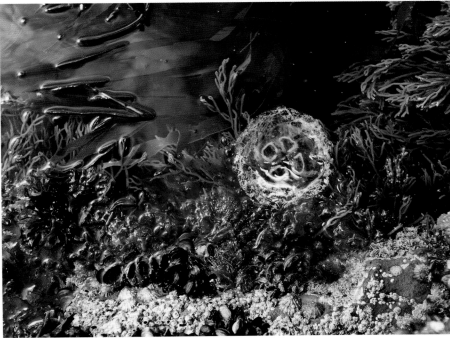

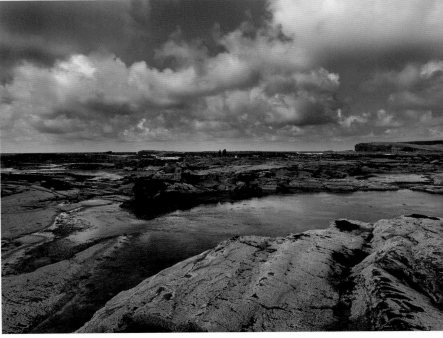

Above: The pollock holes, on the west end of Kilkee, are natural rock-enclosed pools, with water that is changed with every tide.

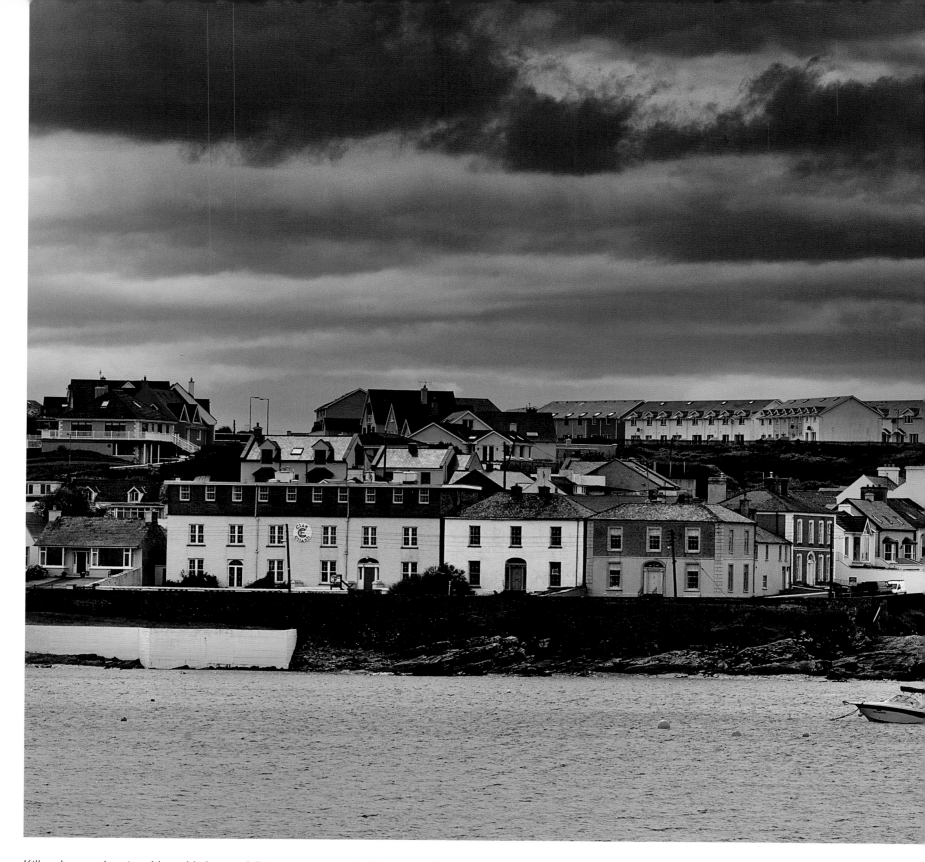

Kilkee has not lost its old world charm while its renown as a holiday resort has grown.

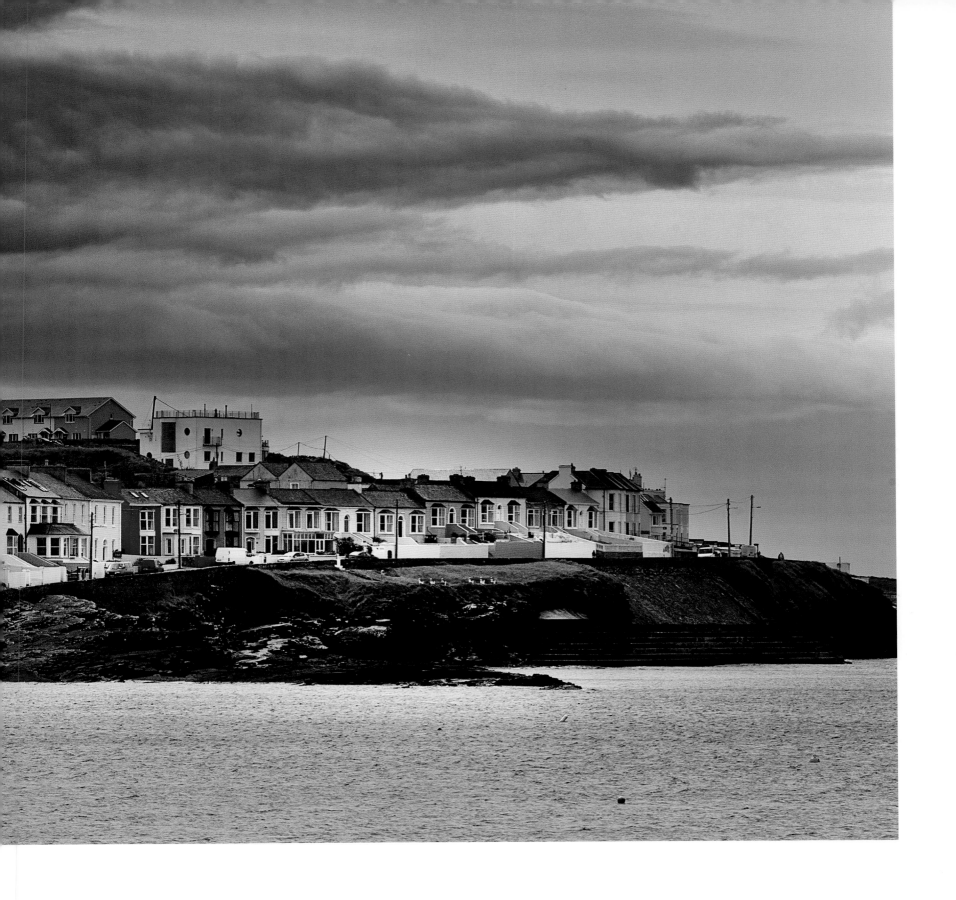

TALTY'S SEA VEGETABLES

By Maria Moynihan

FROM TRADITIONAL carrageen moss and dillisk to über-trendy wakame smoothies, Irish seaweed is big business. And having harvested it for four generations, the Taltys of west Clare have their sights set far from Spanish Point. Gerard Talty – in best L'Oréal 'because you're worth it' mode – makes a persuasive pitch on the properties of his seaweed bath mixes, just one of a portfolio of products in his family's Spanish Point Sea Vegetables range; a commercial twist on a tradition stretching four generations along the shoreline at Caherush, between the Cliffs of Moher and Kilkee in west Clare. With listings in almost 300 health food and independent stores nationwide for their edible seaweeds – ranging from traditional carrageen moss and dillisk to the audibly more exotic wakame and sugar kelp – there is also a growing market for their recently launched Atlantean seaweed soil conditioners and animal feeds.

Following the nuclear disaster in Japan, the Asian market is ravenously interested in the iodine-rich superfood from the west of Ireland ('each Japanese family roughly eats about two kilos a week of seaweed,' says Gerard) while there have also been enquiries from international high-end stores like Dean & DeLuca in New York.

It is a long way from Gerard's grandfather's time, when he would load his pony and trap and set off at four o'clock in the morning on the 25-mile trip to Ennis, where seaweed was sold as fertiliser to fill the barren limestone fissures and cracks of the Burren. Then there were the old cures, whether it was carrageen for coughs and chest colds in cattle (and even TB for their owners) or dillisk for worms. 'Whether that's the high salt or the iodine content that the worms didn't like, they got out of there anyway,' laughs Gerard. His own father, Michael, also supplemented his farming income by harvesting seaweed for Irish Marine Products, used in the manufacture of animal feed and for the export market. 'I suppose it was similar to somebody from an inland area doing a bit of turf as the supplement,' says Gerard. 'Every family in our area did it. There was no one who could afford not to pick it. At that time it was £2 a stone and a family would pick 15 stone in a day, so five days of that – £150 – was a nice little supplement in 1980.' The advent of chemical substitutes turned the tide on the practice in the 1980s, but four years ago, Gerard spotted an advertisement looking for seaweed harvesters for a start-up venture.

'At the time, there was probably nobody interested and very few answered the ad. It was still "good times",' says Gerard. 'I was working, but I answered the ad because I said I want to know more about this. I love the sea and I walk the shores and I always felt it was a total disgrace that we had thousands of tonnes of fertiliser rotting on our shores every day that was free of charge.'

While that project fell through, it brought Gerard in contact with Dr Prannie Rhatigan, who had investigated the nutritional benefits of seaweed and published a cookery book, *Irish Seaweed Kitchen,* with recipes ranging from soups and salads to cakes and even ice cream. Aware of the market for edible and agricultural seaweeds – from the traditional west Clare man looking for his dillisk fix, to the trendy vegetarian, vegan or raw foodie who downs wakame smoothies like shots – Spanish Point Sea Vegetables was launched, with a slot in the rejuvenated Limerick Milk Market, followed by stockists nationwide. And sticking to tradition, it has re-emerged very much as a family business, with Gerard's father, Michael, his wife Eileen and son Evan all involved.

At the mercy of the tides, the Taltys get five to ten days a month to harvest. Like their on-land counterparts, sea vegetables are seasonal: wakame and nori thrive in winter waters, sugar kelp in spring, and dillisk, carrageen and kombu in late summer/early autumn. Sustainably nipped, they are spread out to dry for six hours on Atlantic-washed flagstones before being rinsed and packed for the market.

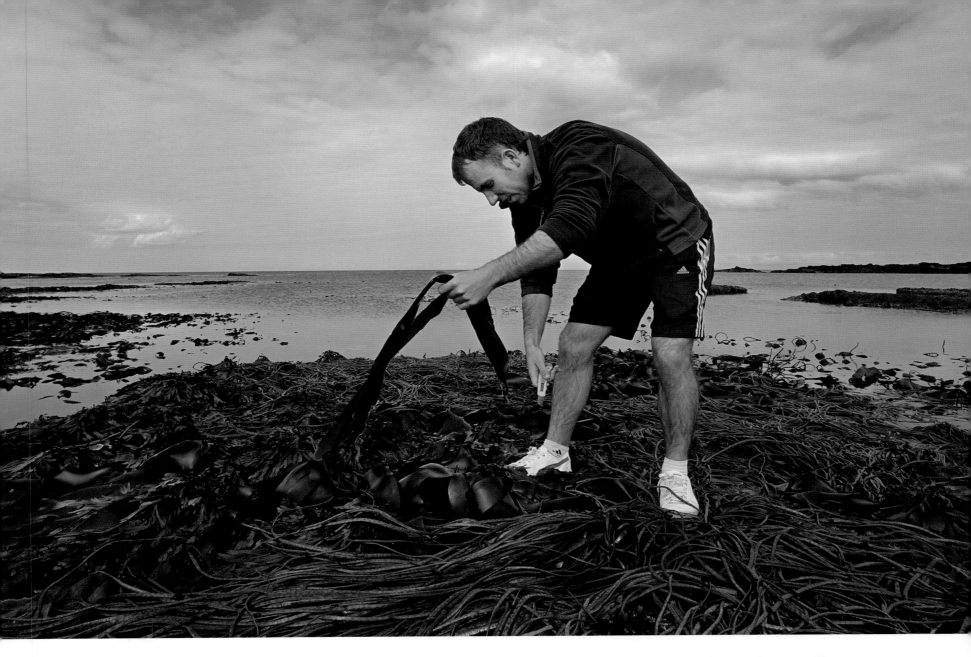

Evan Talty, collecting and cutting dillisk and sea spaghetti from the shoreline at Caherush, Quilty, near Ennis. Evan is probably better known in Clare as a fine Gaelic football player with Kilmurry Ibrickane. The club won the Munster Senior Club Championships in 2004 and 2009, and reached the All-Ireland Senior Club Football final in 2010.

'Every type of seaweed can be got in a square mile,' says Gerard. 'We harvest on our own land, we have no travel expenses, no drying expenses, so we can pass it on to the customer at a reasonable price.' The Taltys are keen to act on the interest in Spanish Point Sea Vegetables overseas, but want to secure an export partner first. In the meantime, the next generation is already on board. 'If you boil carrageen, strain it and add sugar-free lemon barley or lime, it will set like a jelly and the kids can take a spoon of it whenever they want,' says Gerard. 'My granddaughter is six and she'll go for carrageen any day.'

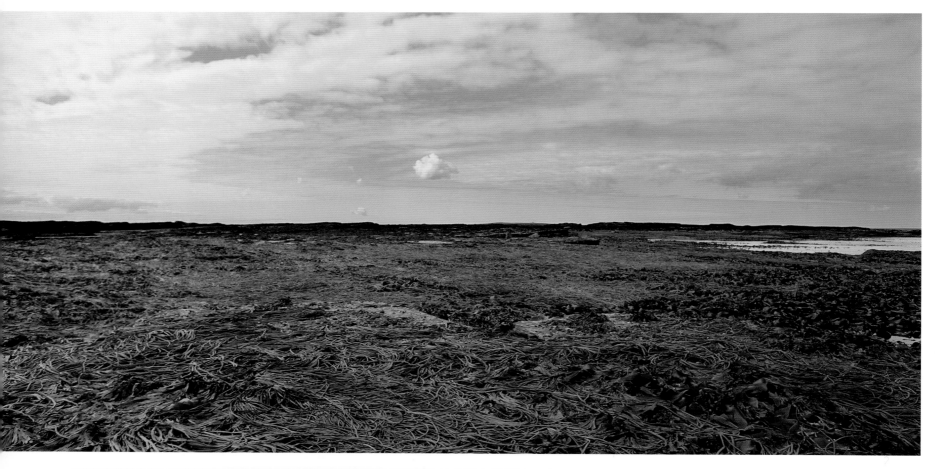

Above: Sea spaghetti *(Himanthalia elongata)* is a brown seaweed that can be eaten like normal spaghetti – just boil for ten to fifteen minutes and add to pasta or chop it up within a salad.

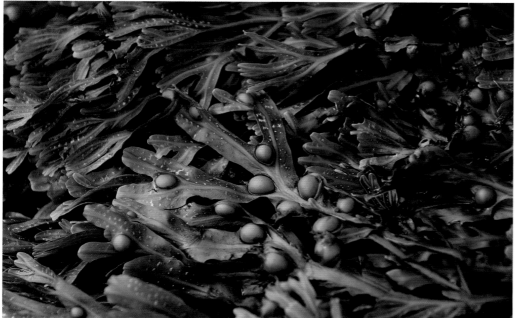

Left: A close-up of bladderwrack *(Fucus vesiculosus)*. It is a form of kelp that has been used medicinally for centuries. Bladderwrack is used for thyroid disorders, for boosting the immune system and increasing energy. Some people also apply bladderwrack to the skin for skin diseases, burns, ageing skin and insect bites.

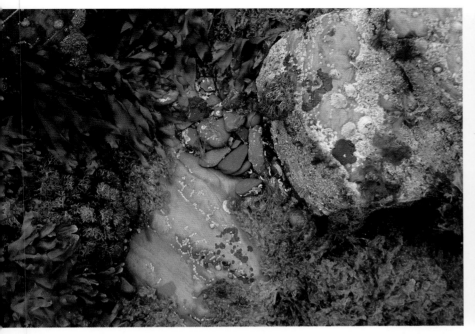

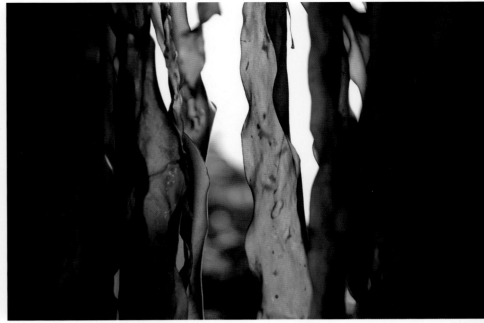

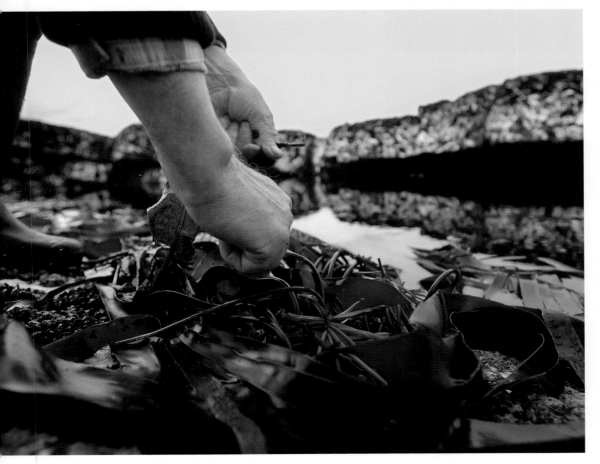

Above left: Common sea vegetables area in abundance on the shoreline: sea lettuce or *Ulva lactuca* (bottom right), dillisk (top left) and carrageen, or *Chondrus crispus* (centre left). All these beautiful species are rich in iron, iodine, minerals and protein.

Above right: Drying out dillisk. The earliest records of dillisk *(Palmaria palmata)* being used was by St Columba's monks 1,400 years ago. It is a cold-water alga, reddish brown in colour, and is a great snack food, full of important nutrients and minerals.

Left: Harvesting is carried out between the shorelines of the Burren in north Clare to Loop Head in west Clare.

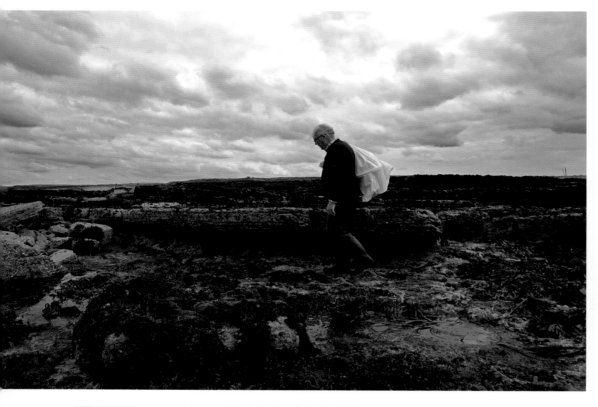

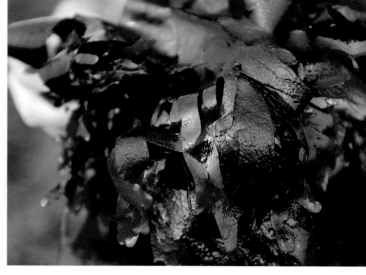

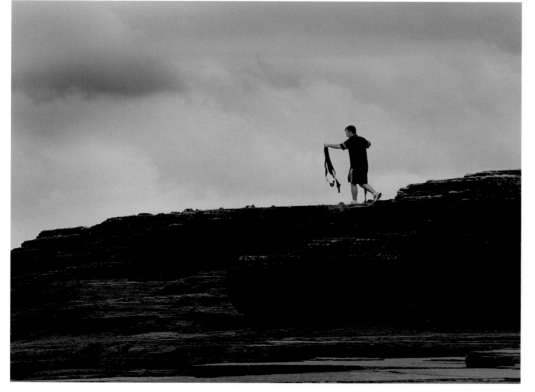

Above left: Homeward bound: Michael Talty loves working the land and the seashore. His knowledge of sea vegetables for use as old remedies is encyclopaedic. Carrageen is still his favourite. It is harvested by hand, air- and sun-dried in a traditional, sustainable way.

Above right: In English, dulse or dillisk, in Irish, *dilleasc* or *creathnach.*

Left: Evan Talty lays out the seaweed on the sea cliffs, the first process of harvesting.

SPANISH POINT

Spanish Point takes its name from the doomed Spanish Armada which sailed from Spain in 1588. The 130-strong fleet was sent by Philip II to invade England during the reign of Queen Elizabeth I. The Armada was led by the Duke of Medina Sidonia. Following its defeat at the Battle of Gravelines, the Armada turned for home. Ferocious North Atlantic storms, with driving winds and mountainous waves, led the ships to the treacherous and rocky coastline of Ireland's Atlantic seaboard. Up to two dozen ships of the Armada were wrecked. Many of them were destroyed near Spanish Point. Of the sailors who survived the storms and made it to dry land, many were executed by Sir Turlough O'Brien of Liscannor and Boethius Clancy, MP, landowner and High Sheriff of the day. Five thousand perished in Ireland as a result. Today one of the shipwrecks can still be seen on the reefs off Mutton Island, 3km from the shore.

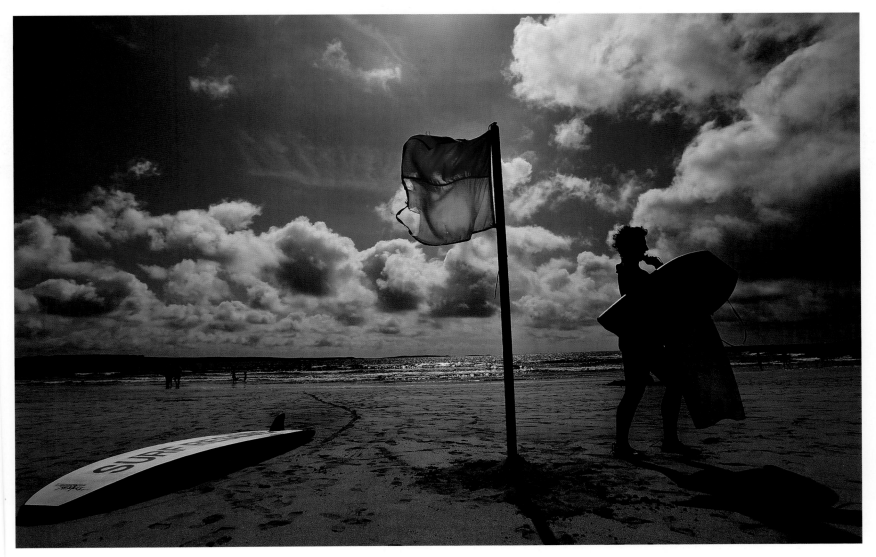

A surfer emerges from the sea at Spanish Point.

Right: Paddle surfers enjoying a rare calm summer's day at Spanish Point.

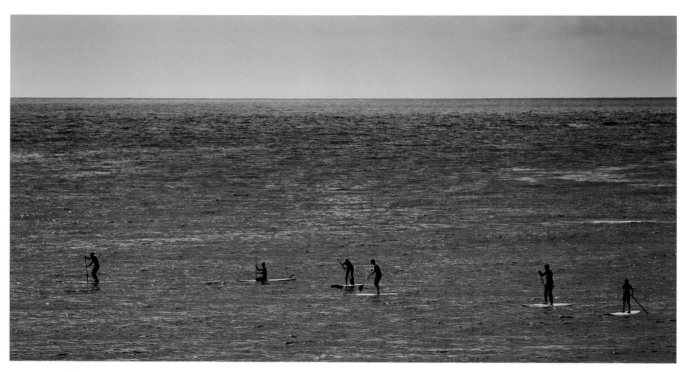

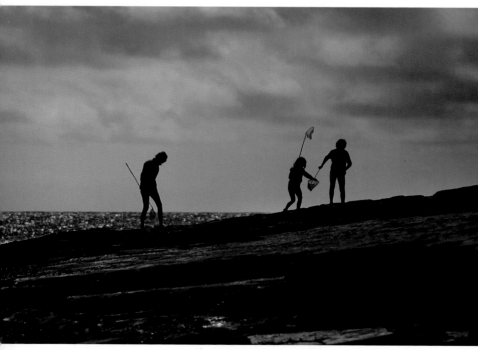

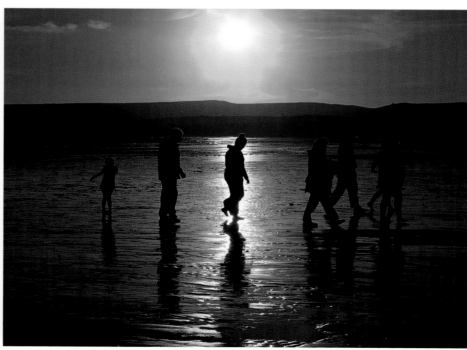

Above left: Children still love to explore and fish, and examine every rock and crevice along the rock face at Spanish Point.

Above right: Walkers enjoy a golden sunset along Lahinch Beach.

LAHINCH

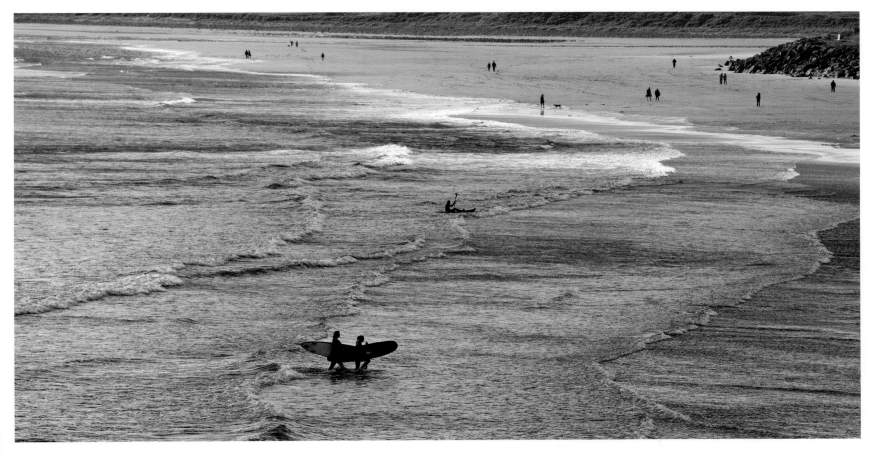

Above: Lahinch is a traditional family beach destination. It sits perfectly on the Atlantic Ocean, between Spanish Point and the town of Ennistymon. It came to prominence in the nineteenth century with the historical West Clare Railway, which linked Kilrush, Kilkee, Miltown Malbay and Ennis, and made Lahinch easily accessible to visitors who came to enjoy the long sandy beach with its beautiful promenade.

Right: Last swim of the day on a fine summer's evening.

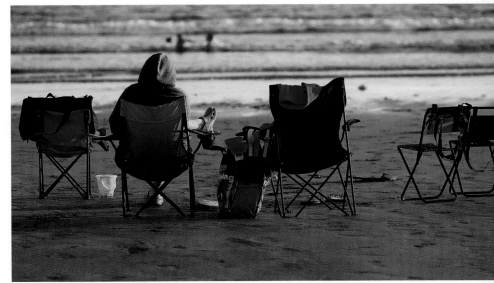

THE IRISH COAST GUARD

By Lorna Siggins

A HAG OR 'cailleach' was chasing Cuchulainn across Loop Head, County Clare, when he leaped onto a rock several metres offshore. She attempted to follow him, fell into the sea, and her body was washed up on the headland, which was named after her. Were she to repeat her unfortunate experience now, the 'cailleach' might well have survived and found herself at the end of a winch suspended from Shannon's Irish Coast Guard air-sea helicopter. Airman Jim O'Neill might even have told her a few jokes to calm her, having already spotted her in the briny with his heat-seeking infrared camera before leaving the aircraft by cable and karabiner with his bag of paramedical gear. For just as Hag's Head is a distinctive part of the southern Clare shoreline, so the Shannon rescue helicopter has become an institution – taken for granted now in the skies above the west coast. There's a constant patter on the high-frequency radio, with talk about results of football matches mingling with communications between Shannon air-traffic control and the helicopter, call sign Golf Charlie Echo. Should that call sign change to Rescue 115, it is a signal that the training run has become a rescue 'tasking'.

'Bring some money and your mobile phone,' Captain Cathal Oakes had advised this writer, before becoming airborne with co-pilot Micheal Moriarty, winch operator Ciarán McHugh and winchman Jim O'Neill. 'Just in case we have to drop you down somewhere en route.' It didn't arise; but when Captain Oakes donned a pair of plastic glasses, almost completely covered in tape, it was a reminder that even a routine training flight is accomplished under pressure. The glasses simulate night-time conditions. There will be several more exercises by crew members, each having to update his skills constantly, before we land. Moriarty's career path reflects the broad experience of the crews who sign up to search and rescue. A Kerryman, born and reared in the Gap of Dunloe and now settled down with his partner Fiona and two children Mikey and Ellen, he has been flying since 1995.

'It has brought me from California where my initial training took place,

to Panama where I flew from tuna boats looking for fish, to the Middle East, to the Kinsale gas field, and to the southern part of the North Sea,' he says. Naturally, he has taken particular pride in rescues undertaken in the MacGillycuddy's Reeks and Kerry area. 'Each rescue has its own challenge,' he says. Ironically, the most successful missions are often those no one hears about. Only a fraction of the thousands of rescue flights Shannon recorded over the past two and a bit decades have made headlines.

It wasn't always like this, as those who campaigned over decades for adequate aerial support for the Royal National Lifeboat Institution (RNLI) clearly remember. Back in 1958, the crash of *Hugo de Groot*, a KLM flight, off Galway, with the loss of 99 lives, prompted such demands. 'Many people will wonder why air-sea rescue operations should have to be coordinated from Scotland and southern England when the accident took place within the air-traffic control area of Shannon Airport. Had there been a helicopter in the Republic – not necessarily at Shannon – it could have searched the crash scene by mid-afternoon at latest,' *The Irish Times* reported on 15 August 1958. There were to be more such calls, particularly from the fishing industry, over subsequent decades. For although pioneering Air Corps pilots undertook many rescues from Baldonnel from as early as 1963, capability was severely restricted by geographical location and helicopter flying range. Much of the coastline was dependent on the goodwill of Britain, principally through the RAF.

It took the death of Donegal skipper John Oglesby on the deck of his boat *Neptune*, off the north Mayo coastline, in 1988 to change all that. Oglesby, whose son was among the crew, had his leg severed by a trawl warp. The nearest lifeboat station at the time was Arranmore, County Donegal. By RAF calculations, the vessel would have reached port before the closest available helicopter could have reached it. Oglesby bled to death within sight of land. Joan McGinley was distraught and angry at the manner in which Oglesby, a

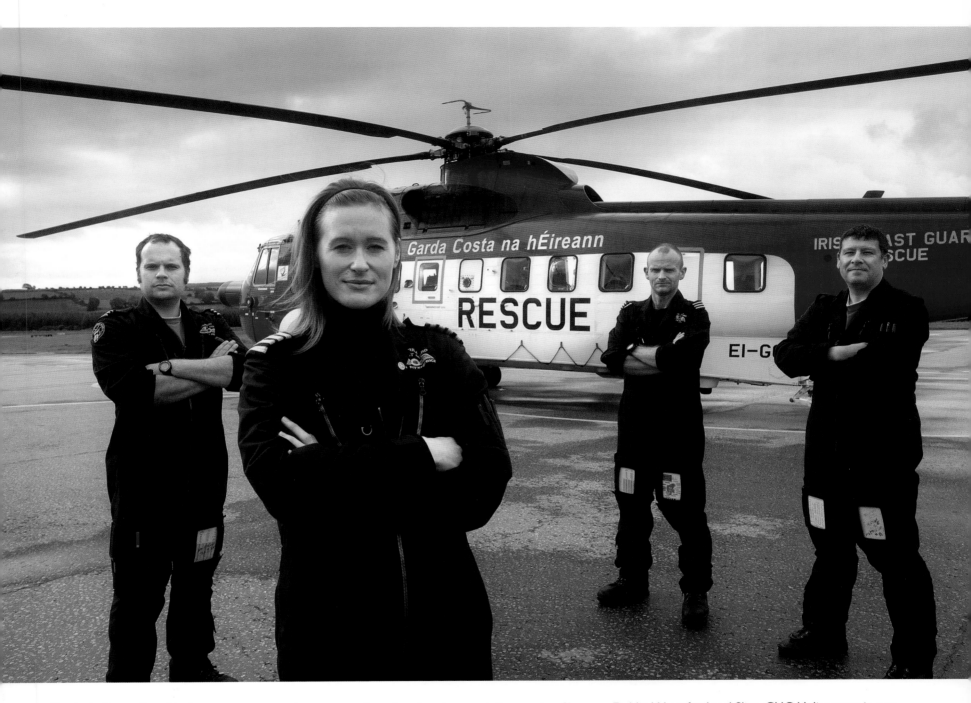

The Irish Coast Guard helicopter rescue service operates from four bases around the country: Shannon, Dublin, Waterford and Sligo. CHC Helicopters is one of the largest helicopter services company in the world, and they have provided search-and-rescue (SAR) helicopter services on behalf of the Irish Coast Guard since 2001, with a fleet of six Sikorsky S-61N helicopters. SAR crew are (l–r) Benny Meehan (winch operator), Dara Fitzpatrick (chief pilot, Waterford base), Jim O'Neill (winchman), and Andy Rees (pilot).

close friend of her partner, had died. After a public meeting in Killybegs not long after the accident, McGinley established the west coast search-and-rescue campaign, run with a group of people including Aran Island GP Dr Marion Broderick, Joey Murrin of the Killybegs Fishermen's Organisation, Bryan Casburn of the Galway and Aran Fishermen's Co-op, former Naval Service commanders Eamonn Doyle and Paddy Kavanagh, former Air Corps pilot Commandant Fergus O'Connor and solicitor Peter Murphy.

Its single-issue focus yielded swift results. An interdepartmental review group, chaired by former Garda Commissioner Eamon Doherty, recommended that the Air Corps place a Dauphin helicopter on permanent 24-hour standby at Shannon as an interim measure – and so the first dedicated west coast air-sea base was in operation by September 1989. A final report recommended that a medium-range helicopter service be provided to the State on contract from Shannon, with an operating radius of 200 nautical miles, and that the Air Corps Dauphin at Shannon be relocated to Finner military base in County Donegal.

The Irish Coast Guard also owes its origins to that report, and to McGinley's campaign. The first Coast Guard director, Captain Liam Kirwan, effected a radical transformation of capability, assisted by the RNLI, which

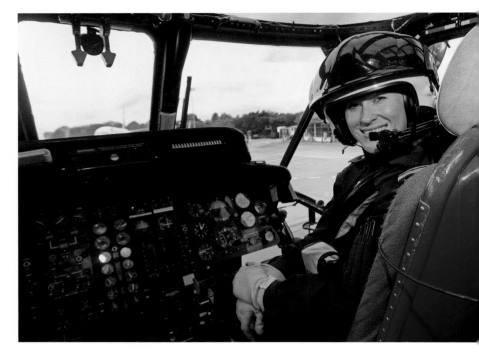

moved rapidly to open a new lifeboat station in Ballyglass, County Mayo, as part of a further expansion. Now run by Chris Reynolds, the Irish Coast Guard service can provide coastal, offshore, mountain and inland rescue. Aircraft cross the Border when requested and can assist Britain when required. Shannon became a commercial rescue base within two years, with Irish Helicopters initially replacing the Air Corps. Air-sea rescue bases at Sligo (replacing Finner camp), Dublin and Waterford were to follow, with the contract for all four now held by CHC Helicopters. A somewhat controversial government contract which approved the purchase of new and second-hand S-92 helicopters was to be phased in during 2012.

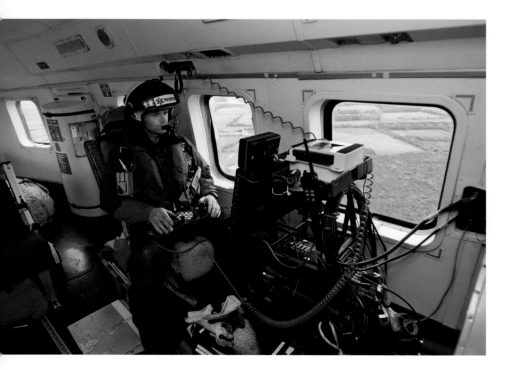

Above: Captain Dara Fitzpatrick is one of only a few female civilian rescue pilots in the world. A Dubliner, she has over twenty years flying experience.

Left: Winchman Jim O'Neill uses highly specialised camera equipment on board the Irish Coast Guard helicopters, which are fitted with forward-looking infrared radar (FLIR) to detect the heat signature of a person, especially useful if a person is stranded in the water.

Captain Dave Courtney, a former search-and-rescue pilot, recalls in his autobiography *Nine Lives* how operating procedures blended the best of experience from the RAF, Royal Navy, Air Corps, British Coastguard and commercial companies serving the North Sea oil industry. Challenges, such as the near ditching of the Shannon helicopter shortly before Christmas 1993, helped to refine those procedures. The S-61 had been called out to assist an Irish-registered Spanish fishing vessel, *Dunboy*, with thirteen crew on board, which had lost engine power some 65km (40 miles) west of Slyne Head in winds of up to 150km/h (90 mph). Winchman John McDermott had just landed on the vessel's deck in a heaving sea when the boat listed 70 degrees, the cable broke and about 35m (120ft) wrapped itself around the aircraft's blades. A Mayday call was issued, but the helicopter, flown by Captain Nick Gribble and co-pilot Carmel Kirby managed to recover and fly to Galway, leaving McDermott to be picked up by the RAF hours later.

There was a tragic outcome to a rescue incident involving another rescue agency – the Air Corps – almost six years later in July 1999. Captains Dave O'Flaherty and Michael Baker, Sergeant Paddy Mooney and Corporal Niall Byrne were returning from the first night of the rescue mission in the early hours of 2 July 1999, when their helicopter collided with a sand dune

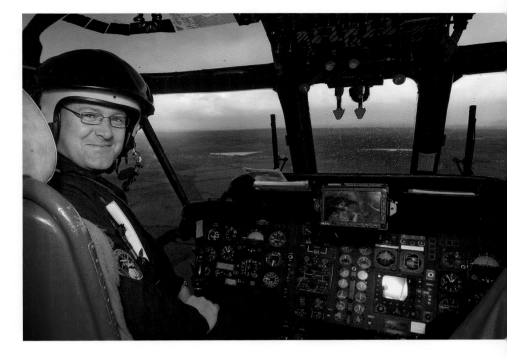

in thick fog. The official investigation highlighted 'serious deficiencies' in the support given to the four crew. The four had learned only on 1 July – the day the search-and-rescue base at Waterford Airport was converted to 24-hour cover – that there was no provision for after-hours air-traffic control. An agreement had not been concluded by the Department of Defence and the airport management.

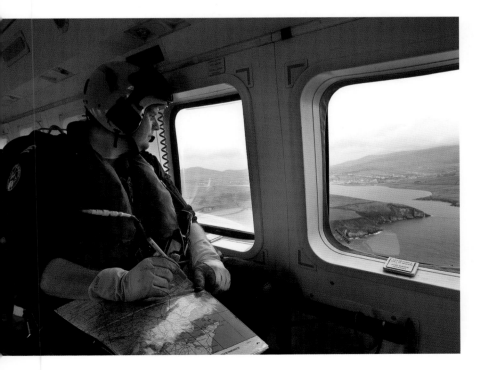

Above: Pilot Michael Moriarty at the helm of a Sikorsky S-61, based at Shannon.

Right: Winch operator Benny Meehan checks conditions and map positions for the winchman of this crew, Jim O'Neill.

The report by the investigation unit specifically noted that considerable pressure was brought to bear on the late Captain O'Flaherty, as detachment commander, to accept the rescue mission in search of a small boat with four adults and a child. In June 2008, Minister for Defence Willie O'Dea awarded posthumous Distinguished Service Medals to the crew of Dauphin 248.

Not only has flying become safer, but the decision to approve paramedic training for use by winch crew on missions has also helped to save lives. 'We used to scoop and run to the nearest hospital,' O'Neill explains. 'Now we can give certain types of treatment en route.' Even before the training for that, though, the Shannon S-61 marked its first emergency birth. On 17 March 1996, Sorcha Ní Fhlatharta first saw light of day in the helicopter cabin, when her mother, Mairéad, delivered her with the assistance of two nurses and the helicopter crew en route from Inis Oírr to University Hospital Galway. 'The crew were great and it was a sort of a distraction,' the mother said some years afterwards. 'I really didn't have time to think about the pain.'

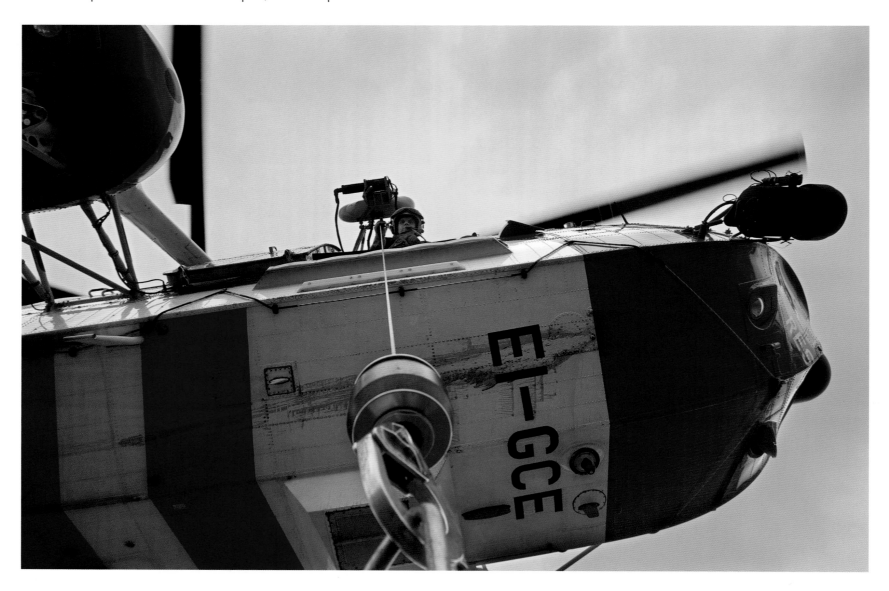

Winch operator Benny Meehan, operating the winch.

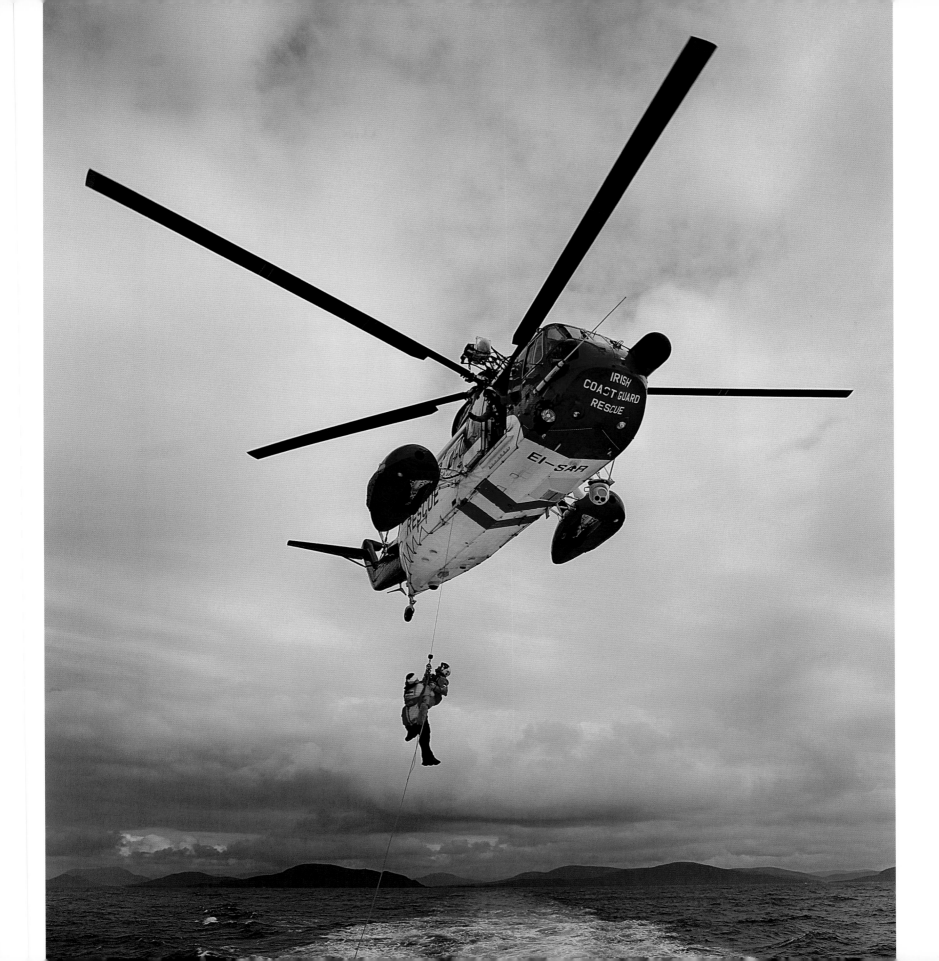

Previous page: Irish Coast Guard crews from Shannon and Waterford take part in a test-run emergency plan to Skellig Michael in conjunction with other rescue and emergency services.

Right: Winchman Mike Sandover is successfully winched back to the helicopter during a training exercise in Ailladie in the Burren.

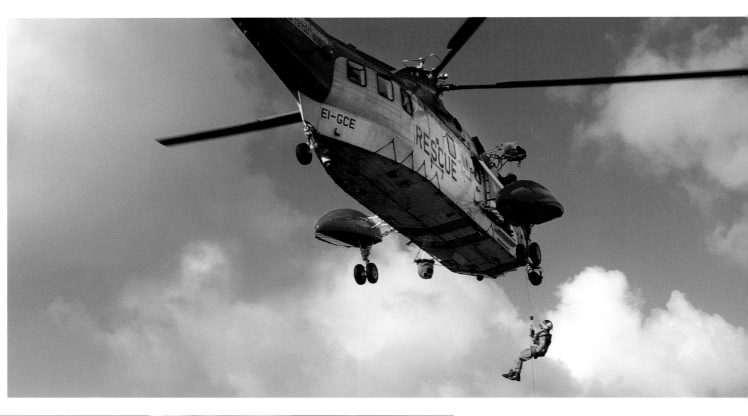

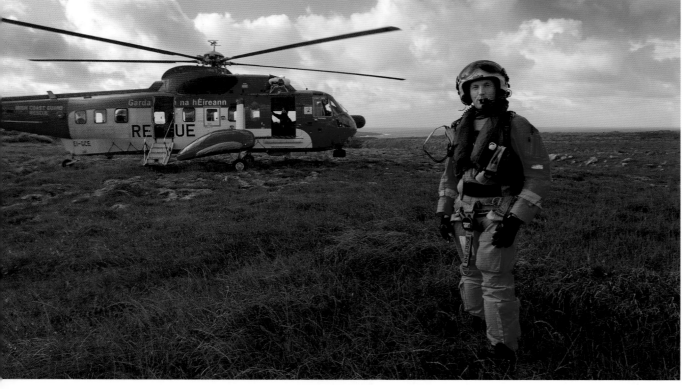

Left: Mike Sandover, from Killarney, is also a member of Kerry Mountain Rescue Team, and is an accomplished mountaineer. Prior to joining the Irish Coast Guard, Mike worked as a paramedic with the HSE ambulance service.

CLIFFS OF MOHER

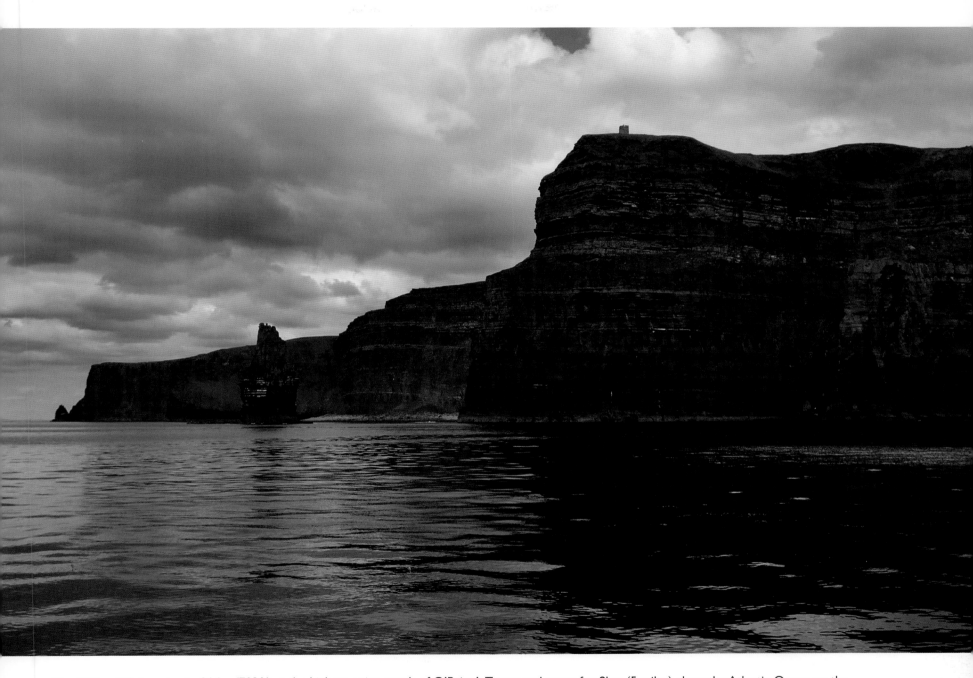

The Cliffs of Moher rise to 214m (702ft) at the highest point, north of O'Brien's Tower, and range for 8km (5 miles) along the Atlantic Ocean on the west coast of County Clare. From here, on a clear day, it is possible to see the Aran Islands in Galway Bay, as well as the Twelve Pins and the Maumturk Mountains in Connemara and Loop Head to the south. The cliffs are listed in the top 28 of the global online campaign for the New Seven Wonders of Nature.

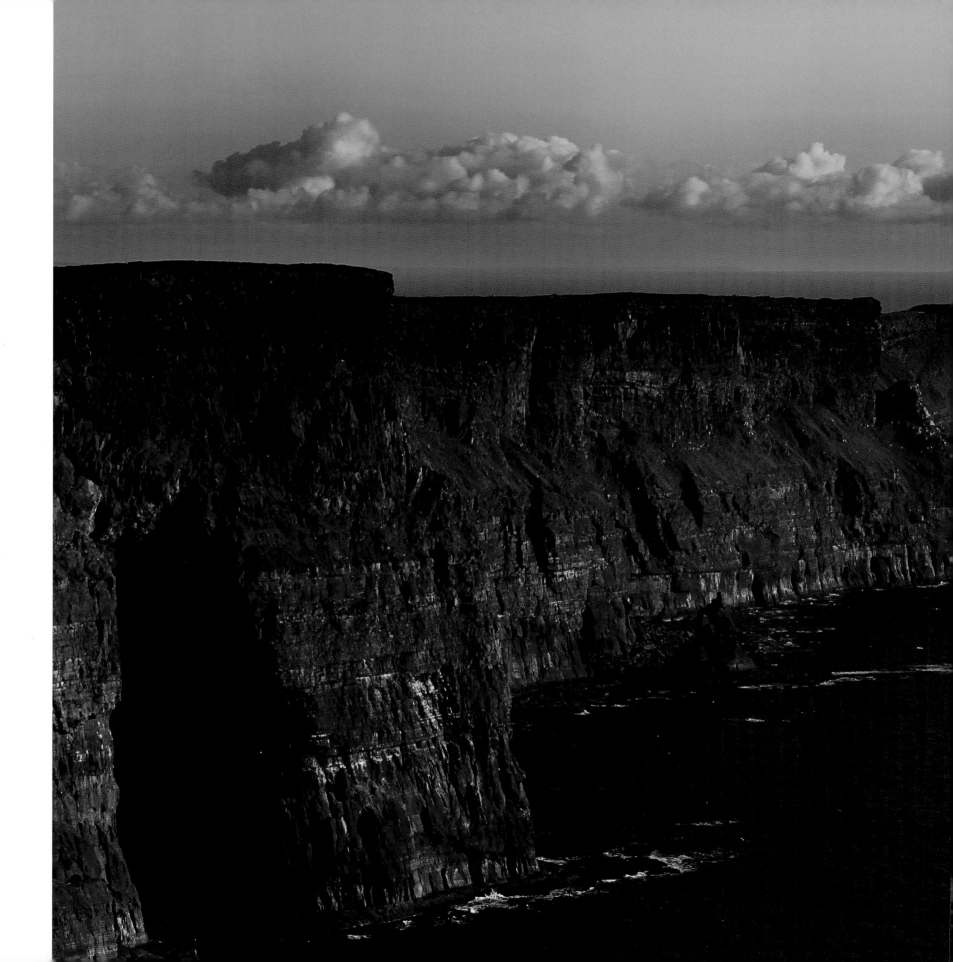

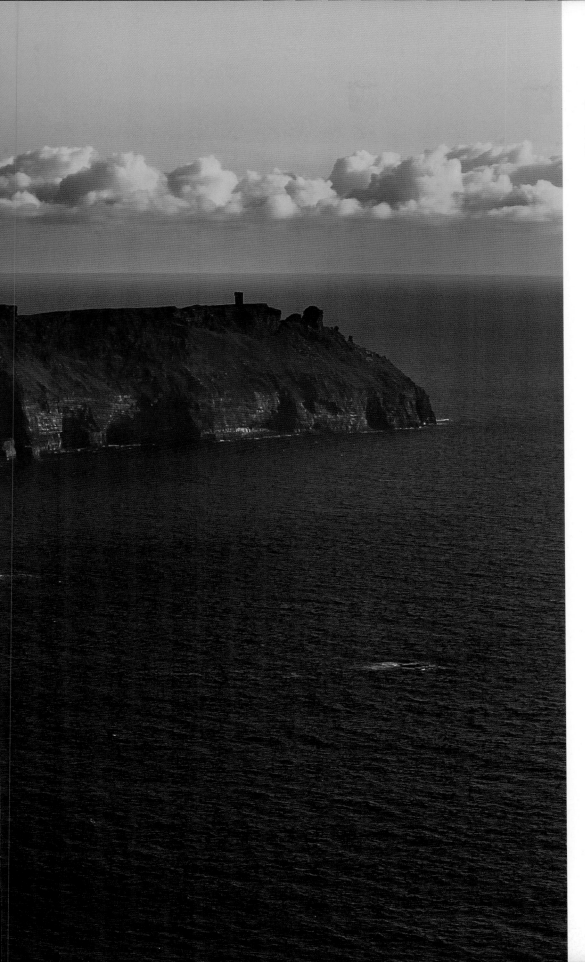

Sheer beauty: the Cliffs of Moher on a summer's night, looking southwards, with the Hag's Head in the distance.

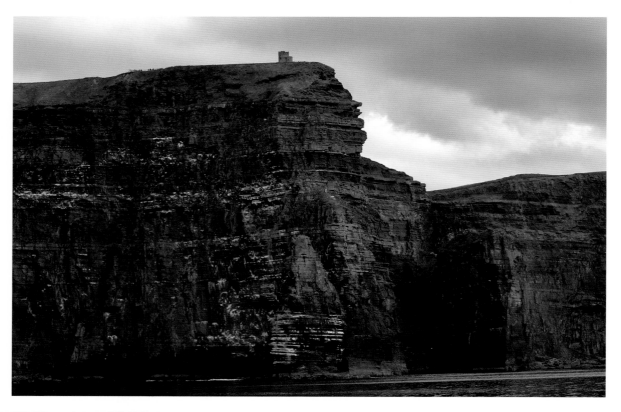

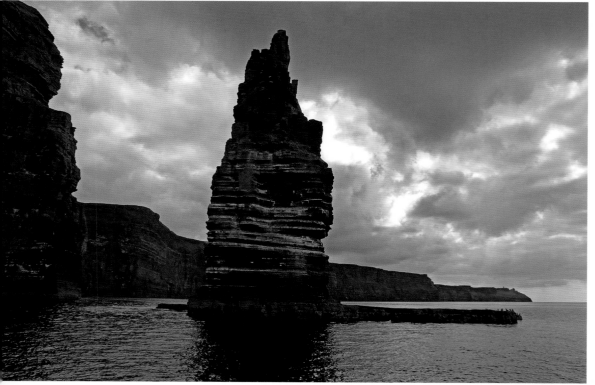

Above: At the centre point of the 8km/5-mile stretch of cliffs is O'Brien's Tower, built by Cornelius O'Brien in 1935. He was a descendant of the Irish hero Brian Boru. Cornelius was a man of vision and believed that tourism would be a sustainable business for the area. He built the tower as an observatory to entice tourists to visit the cliffs. They came in their hundreds and, today, visitor numbers are counted in millions.

Left: The large offshore sea stack known as Branaunmore. The Cliffs of Moher were formed about 320 million years ago during the Carboniferous period, mainly Namurian Shale and Sandstone. The Napoleonic signal tower at Hag's Head was built built in 1803, close to the site of a long-vanished first-century BC ruined fort, hence the name: *'Mothar'* in Irish meaning 'ruin'.

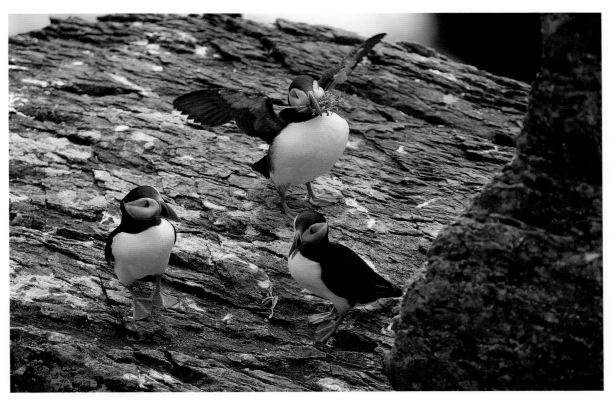

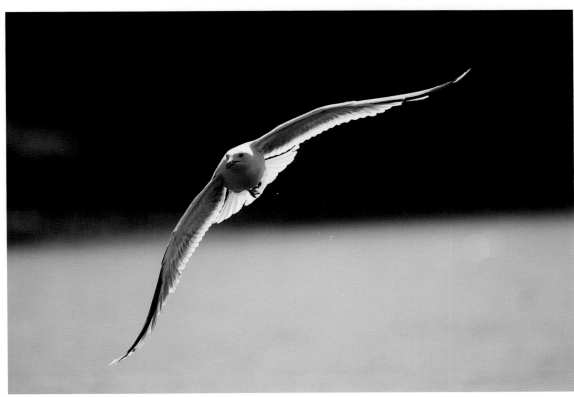

The Cliffs of Moher are home to a huge number of nesting seabirds, including Atlantic puffin, razorbill and a range of gulls. They are a designated Special Area for Birds (SPA) under the EU Birds Directive, 1989.

MURROOGHTOOHY, THE BURREN

The Burren in County Clare is a botanical wonder, where Mediterranean and alpine plants rare to Ireland grow side by side, in deep limestone crevices. The Burren – the name is derived from the Irish word *'boíreann'* which means 'rocky place' – is internationally renowned for its abundance of flora, fauna, history and archaeology. What makes it unique is the lack of soil cover and the extent of exposed limestone. Further inland there are examples of Ireland's ancient civilisation, from round towers, dolmens, high crosses, tombs and holy wells. The Burren is a designated Area of Conservation. Mammals that thrive in the Burren environment include pygmy shrew, field mouse, bank vole, rabbit, Irish hare, pine marten and lesser horseshoe bat. Birds include peregrine falcon, ravens, kestrels and meadow pipit. The Burren is also renowned for the variety of its orchids, such as the dense flowered orchid, early-purple orchid, bee orchid and lesser butterfly orchid.

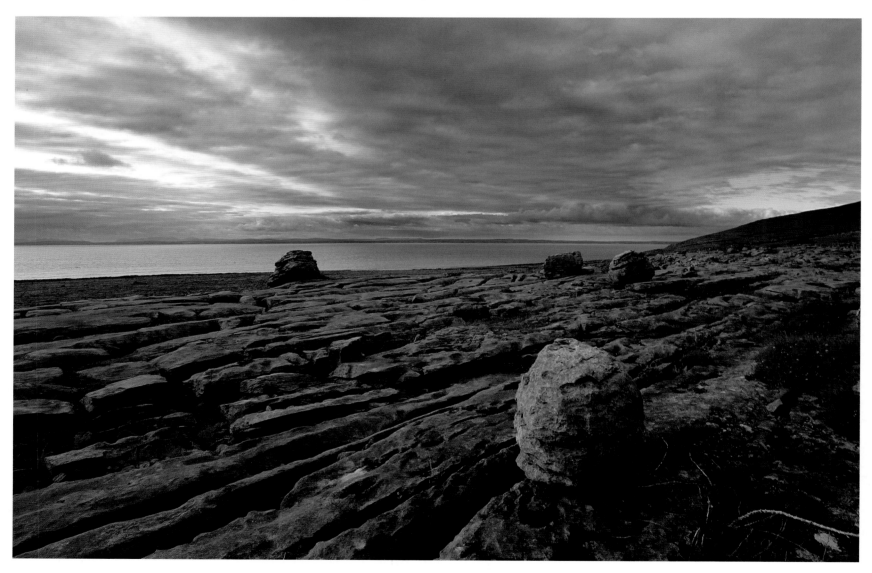

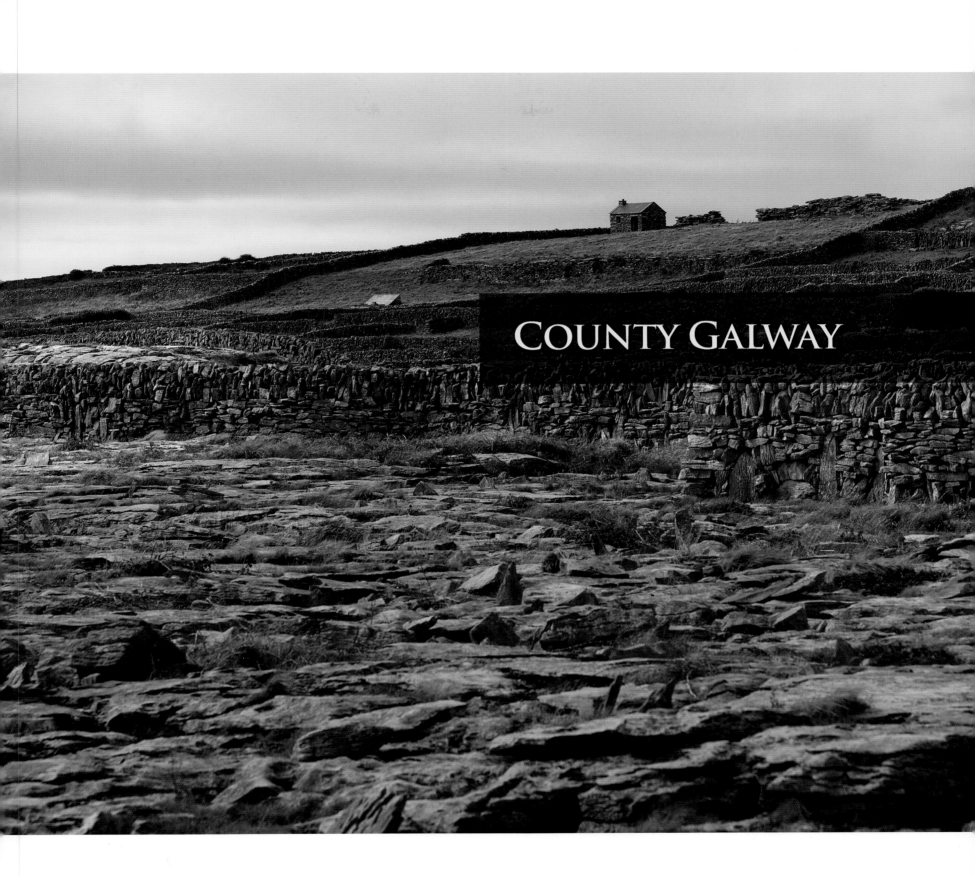

COUNTY GALWAY

INIS OÍRR

Inis Oírr, the smallest of the three Aran Islands, is located close to the mouth of Galway Bay, the other two islands being Aráinn and Inis Meáin. Irish is the main language spoken on the islands. Inis Oírr's population of just over 250 rises in the summer months. The island has been inhabited for 5,000 years. Its landscape is similar to that of the Burren, with the grikes and clints typical of limestone areas. Fishing and tourism are important to the area. There are beautiful walks, bike hire, traditional pony and trap rides, water-based activities and Irish language courses. Accommodation and eating out are well catered. The island is served by a ferry from Rossaveal Harbour in Connemara and Doolin Pier in County Clare.

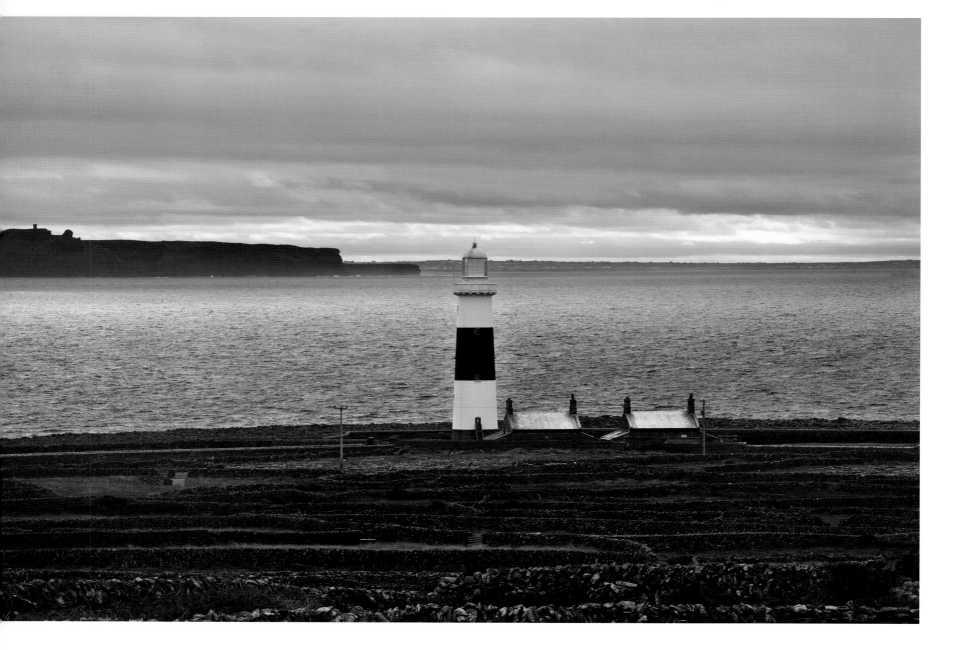

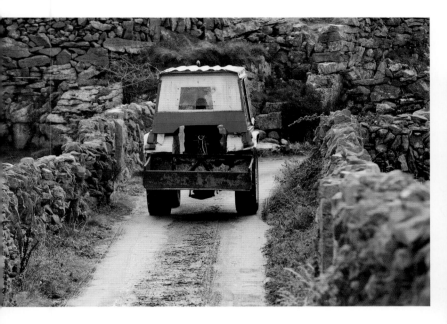

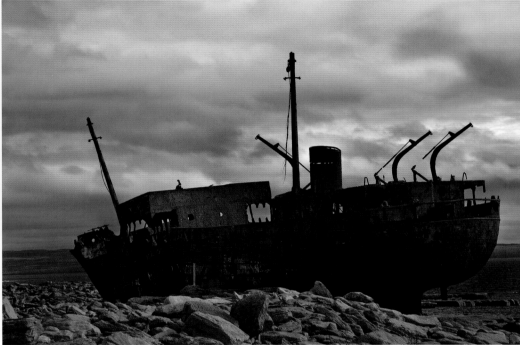

Above: The sturdy tractor is the favoured mode of transport on the island for farmers.

Top right: The wreck of the *Plassey* is one of the most visited shipwrecks in Ireland, thanks largely to the much-loved comedy *Father Ted* which featured the ship and Inis Oírr in the opening credits. The *Plassey*, a cargo ship, was wrecked off Inis Oírr in the 1960s. The islanders rescued the entire crew from the stricken vessel and acquired a special mention in the National Maritime Museum in Dún Laoghaire, County Dublin.

Bottom right: Inis Oírr is said to having the longest growing season in Ireland. Average temperatures rarely go below 6 °C.

Opposite: Inis Oírr Lighthouse, Fardurris Point, overlooking the Cliffs of Moher, is an impressive sea light on the southernmost edge of the three Aran Islands, guiding boatmen into the southern entrance to Galway Bay. The tower was built with local crystalline limestone, identical to that of the Burren.

P. 127: Inis Oírr is a haven for flora and fauna, steeped in folklore and culture, and home to 300 inhabitants.

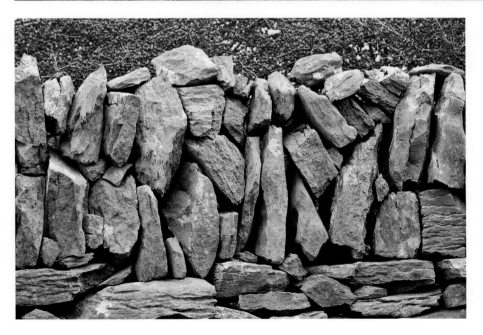

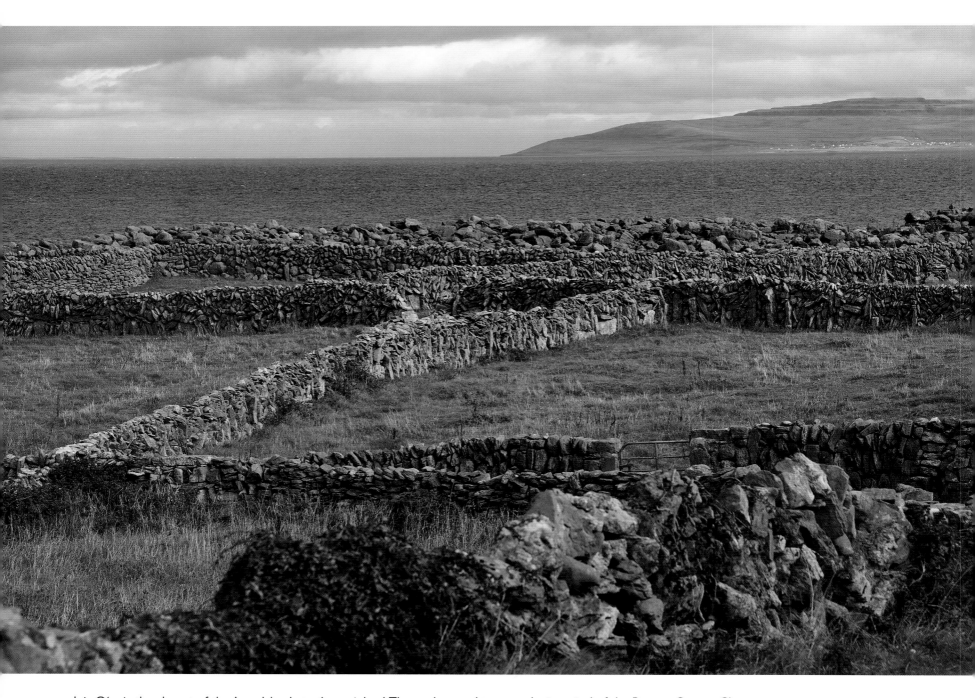

Inis Oírr is the closest of the Aran Islands to the mainland. The geology and topography is typical of the Burren, County Clare.

PÁRAIC PÓIL, MAN OF ARAN

By Lorna Siggins

PÁRAIC PÓIL BAKES the best brown bread and fries the finest fresh mackerel between the Burren and Boston. That's not the fresh air talking, mind, although we had absorbed a fair bit of it on the sea passage over to the Aran island of Inis Óirr. Having served us up copious grub just minutes after our unfamiliar faces appeared at his window, he pours us out large mugs of thick, black, freshly brewed tea from his pot.

And he asks a few questions, diplomatically, as we eat hungrily, while one of his sons engages in a friendly wrestle with a pal on the living-room floor. After days of rain, the weather forecast is vaguely promising. Póil hopes he might get some of the last of a season's very late cut of hay. Normally, it would have been done by June – if at all, for the mild climate on Árainn supports almost year-round grass growth, and cattle don't have to be wintered indoors. Where hay is required, it is often imported from the midlands. Póil glances out the window and offers us second helpings. Sustenance is very important, he explains, with the wisdom of a man who has a meadow to cut. He puts down his mug, steps up to clear the dishes, and we pile into his blue Ford tractor. More accurately, his young daughters, Bébhinn and Saoirse, clamber into the cab with their dad, and their young friend Eileen. We take 'standing room only' in the bucket at the back.

We're with his sons, Micheál and Réamoinn, their friend Fiachra, and the scythe. 'Ah, the *speal*' the boys exclaim excitedly. Eyeing the sharp reaping blade with a little less enthusiasm, we've just grabbed a tight grip of the vehicle when we are elevated, suspended, and find ourselves moving briskly down the hill.

There will be a short stop en route to the land at the Rian, Póil had explained beforehand. His friend, Gerry, will be coming along. Gerry, a Tyrone man, says he came to Inis Óirr for peace, and found passion. After passion passed, he says, he found peace. When he and his wife separated, he was determined not to quit the island totally for fear of losing contact with his two children. Póil, a soulmate in every sense, offered him the use of a one-roomed cottage which he had built on his land.

We're 'ag dul suas arís' at a 75-degree angle, and I am trying to calculate whether the Ford's front wheels and engine will counteract the weight of us all at the rear. It is only when we reach the Rian that I notice that we had a dog for company also. 'A lady in Connemara advertised him on the local radio,' Póil says. 'He's called Roger. A man of the same name died recently on the island, and I felt we needed another Roger for the summer at least.'

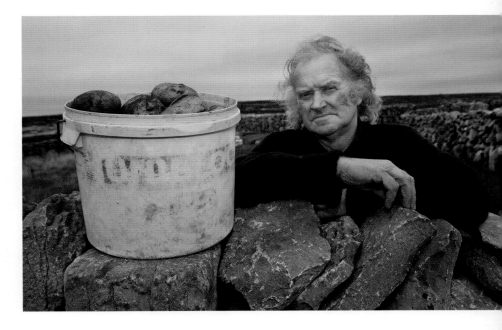

We alight, climb over the gate into the first in a series of eight fields, which Gerry proudly declares to be the best pasture on the island. Looking over the narrow lane, I can see why. 'I used a crowbar and a lump hammer, and it took me seven to eight years,' Póil says simply. Anyone who knows the Árainn landscape knows what that entails – unearthing boulder after boulder, and tackling virtual menhirs of limestone to create cultivable land out of rough and unforgiving ground. One has to look only at the walls for further evidence of this. High limestone windbreaks they are, and Póil explains how turning the slabs upright to create what he calls a 'claidh shingle' makes for better shelter. He built neat steps into each wall, and filled the crevices carefully with scores of small stones.

'I covered the land with sand, the sand with topsoil, planted grass seed, and waited,' he says. 'It was a lot of work, but it is very satisfying. And we had no JCB and no rock breakers then.' He took eighty baskets of seaweed from the shore to cultivate potatoes, he says. 'Eighty baskets,' he repeats. Thinking about it later, a passage from Tim Robinson's *Stones of Aran* springs to mind. Recounting how the islanders created land by covering rock with sand and seaweed over generations, and how seaweed ash or 'kelp' was a lucrative cash crop for several centuries, Robinson noticed that the shorelines of Inis Oírr's south coast bore names testifying to the hardship. Weed gathering at

low tide was never easy. 'Aran's back was bent to the rule of the moon, for lifetime after lifetime,' Robinson wrote.

Póil takes his scythe and starts working the grass, looking out on the island's lighthouse and an indigo sea extending to the Cliffs of Moher in north Clare. We pad across, knee-deep in meadow, as he explains how he found stones and shells in one of the fields, which suggests there had been inhabitants thousands of years before. 'I planted trees and put a wall around them, to mark the spot,' he says. 'As Roger sniffs and scratches and roots for rats along the wall, his master sharpens the *speal* on all sides. He moves then in a series of ever increasing circles, switching between Irish and English to find the right words which might explain what he is about. With two neat strokes for each cut, there is only the sound of the wind and lowing cattle in the distance, and the soft swish of the blade in the grass.

This is good clean pasture, he explains, with few thistles, and an abundance

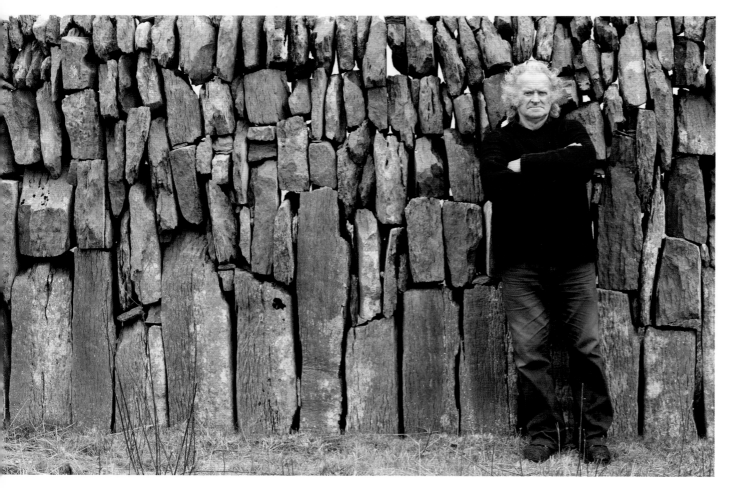

Left: Páraic Póil loves the artistry of drystone wall building; each stone and rock is chosen and placed with great care and attention.

Previous page: Páraic grows his own potatoes, cabbage and an assortment of vegetables despite the challenges presented by the natural conditions.

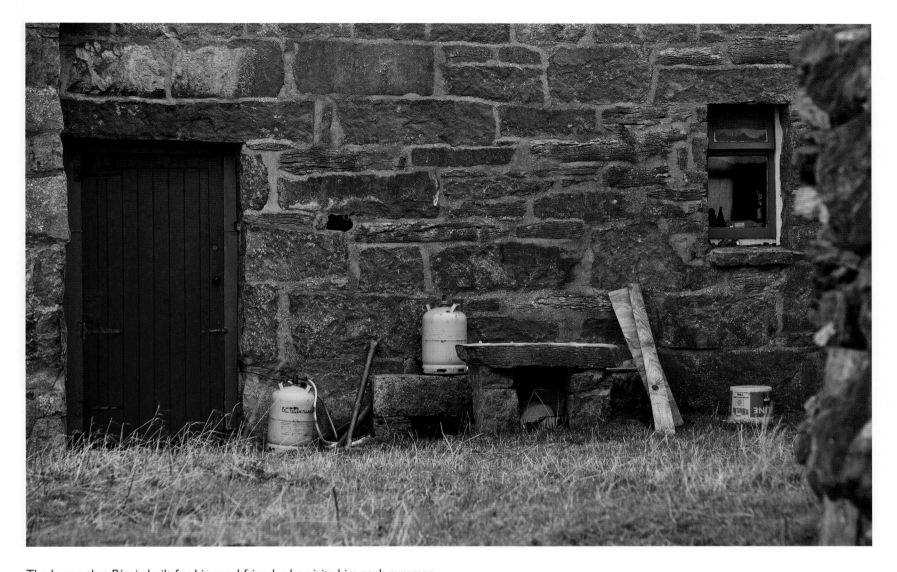

The house that Páraic built for his good friend, who visits him each summer.

of bluebells, several types of dandelion, cow parsley, dog daisies, sea pinks and Bloody crane's bill. Póil sharpens the blade again, before showing me how to employ the *speal*. 'Because it is late in the season and the weather has been so bad, the wind and the rain have flattened the grass and it makes it harder to cut,' he says kindly, and then discreetly observes my feeble efforts.

In his grandfather's time, the *speal* was made of wood, with a straight handle, and one had to bend down low and strain one's back. 'It is much easier now with the curved steel handle,' he says. 'Really?' I wonder, feeling every stroke pull on the shoulders. 'Move with the wind,' he advises, and this seems to work. I've tried a scythe before, and know how disarmingly easy it looks. 'If you were here in this field on your own, you wouldn't be long struggling,' he laughs, and quotes the proverb '*namhaid í an cheird gan í a fhoghlaim*', or 'a trade is the enemy until it is learned'.

Póil learned young, as one of nine children, born to Micheál and May Póil, who also farmed on Inis Oírr. 'There were ten of us,' he says, 'but one brother died before I was born.' He left school after primary, learning life skills with his hands – building, farming, rearing a family with his wife, Anita, and opening an organic restaurant half a mile from the harbour, named An Mhaighdhean Mara.

He grows most of the vegetables for the restaurant. For a time, the couple offered seaweed baths in their home. 'You feel so terrific after it, and visitors loved it,' he says. 'Then the price of fuel went up, and it meant we would have had to charge 20 euro. We didn't think that people would want to pay that.'

Gerry and several of the children are watching us from the cottage roof. Póil turns the cut grass over with his blade to create swarths, which he will leave to dry and season for twenty-four hours before turning and shaking again. 'Three more good days, and we can make haycocks, and we'll have it saved,' he says. 'That's where the children will help.'

He loves using the scythe, relishes manual work and the silence that it brings. The pause to sharpen the blade again, the spit of the hands, is interrupted by a skylark. 'There wouldn't be too many saving hay like this, when it isn't needed, but there's plenty of scythers around as a *speal* is always handy for nettles,' he says. He remembers snow and frost only once on Inis Oírr, when he was a small boy. The mild climate makes for healthier, cleaner animals, and finer meat, he believes. 'I used to kill my cattle until the regulations came in that stopped us doing that,' he says. 'Now I send them to Galway, and the meat comes back. I'd kill four or five a year for the restaurant and for customers on Inis Meáin and Inis Mór. You should come back and taste one of my steaks.'

It has been a rough enough summer for farming, and a rougher season for an island ferry dependent on tourism, where there is a constant challenge to provide fresh drinking water due to relatively low rainfall. Inis Oírr is served daily by ferry from Ros-a-Mhíl, County Galway, and by air from Indreabhán, but the shortest sea link is with Doolin in north Clare. 'Many days this summer the boats didn't leave Doolin at all,' Póil says. He was fortunate in that he hosted a team of sculptors engaged on a two-week-long symposium, Umha Aois, with Áras Éanna, the island's arts centre. The sculptors experimented with Bronze Age casting techniques. A replica of a Bronze Age horn housed in the National Museum of Ireland was cast during the second week.

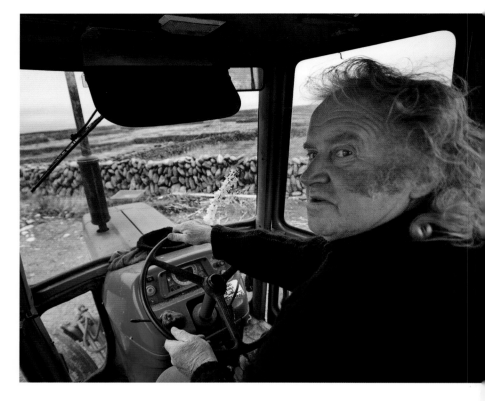

The mode of transport for many islanders is the trusted tractor.

It will take a full day to cut this field, and we have a ferry to catch. There's something missing, and we're not sure at first what it is at all. Ah, no horseflies! No midge bites! Maybe there's some value to the fresh weather after all. 'You can see Kerry on a clear day,' Gerry says, as he shows us the house that Póil built – complete with heating, running water and a sofa that doubles up as a bed. 'And on a really quiet night,' he whispers, 'you can even hear the dogs barking in Boston …'

KINVARRA

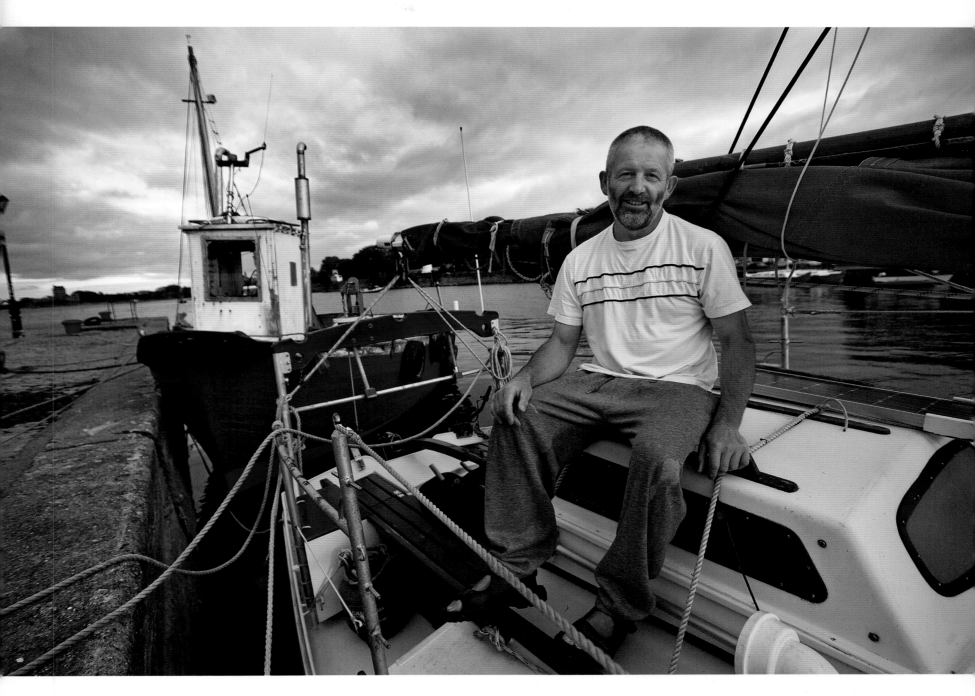

Paul Corbett lives on his boat at Kinvarra Pier, County Galway. Kinvarra in English, from the Irish *Cinn Mhara* meaning 'head of the sea', is a beautiful sea port village located in south County Galway.

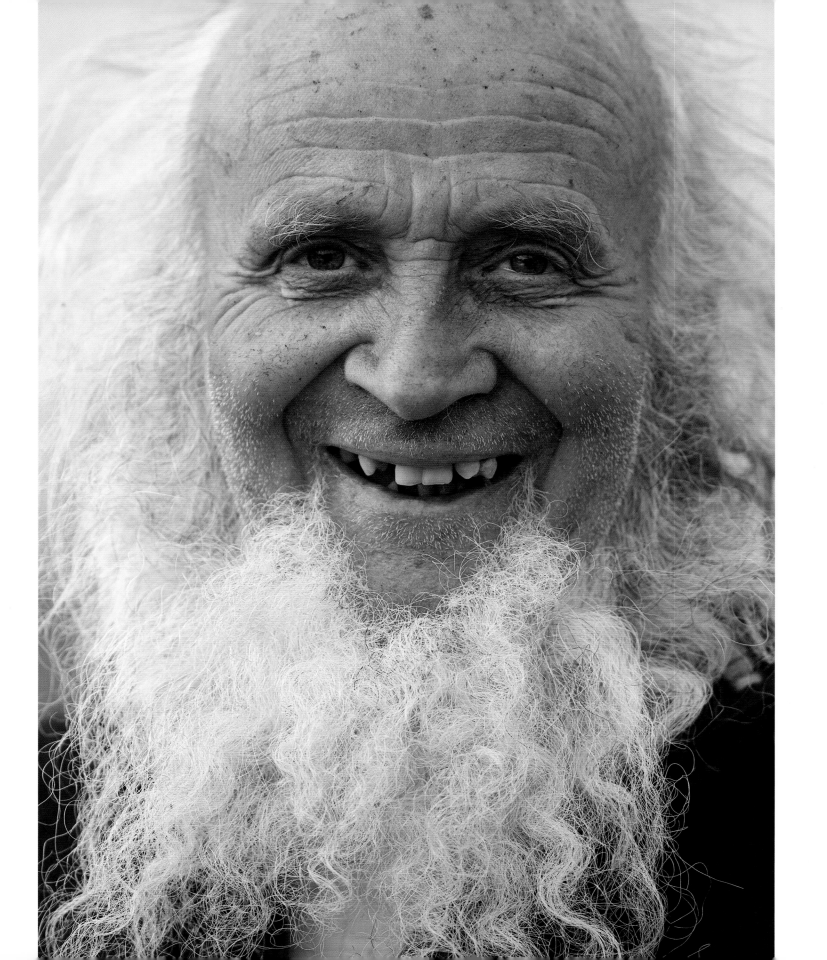

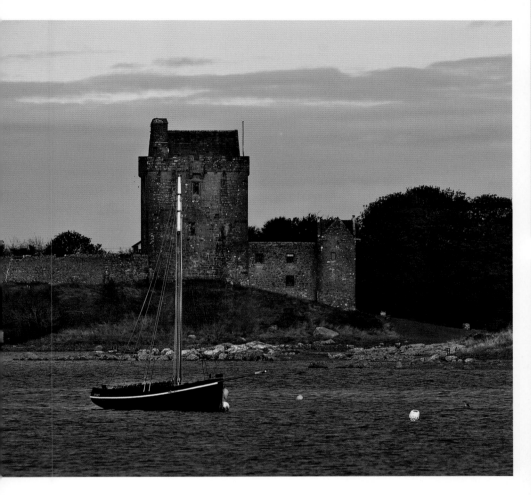

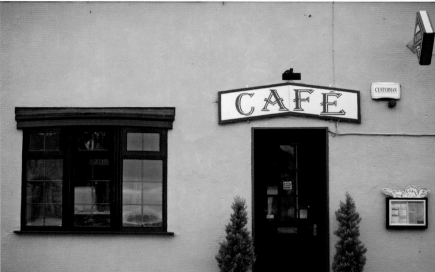

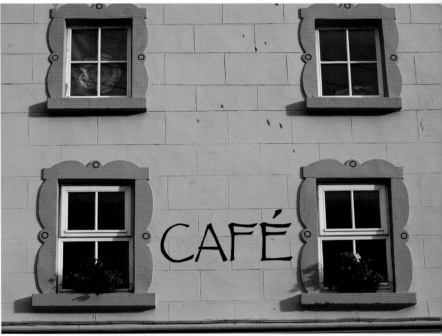

Above: Dungaire Castle is a sixteenth-century tower house built by the Hynes clan in 1520, a celebrated stronghold of nobility located to the east of Kinvarra on the shores of Galway Bay. Nightly entertainment during the summer months celebrates the works of the Irish literary greats William Butler Yeats, George Bernard Shaw and John Millington Synge.

Right: Brightly painted shop fronts in Kinvarra.

Opposite: Rainer Krause, a traditional fisherman from Dungora, Kinvarra, came to Ireland from Germany in 1964. He farms oysters and mussels and fishes for mackerel and pollock.

SALTHILL

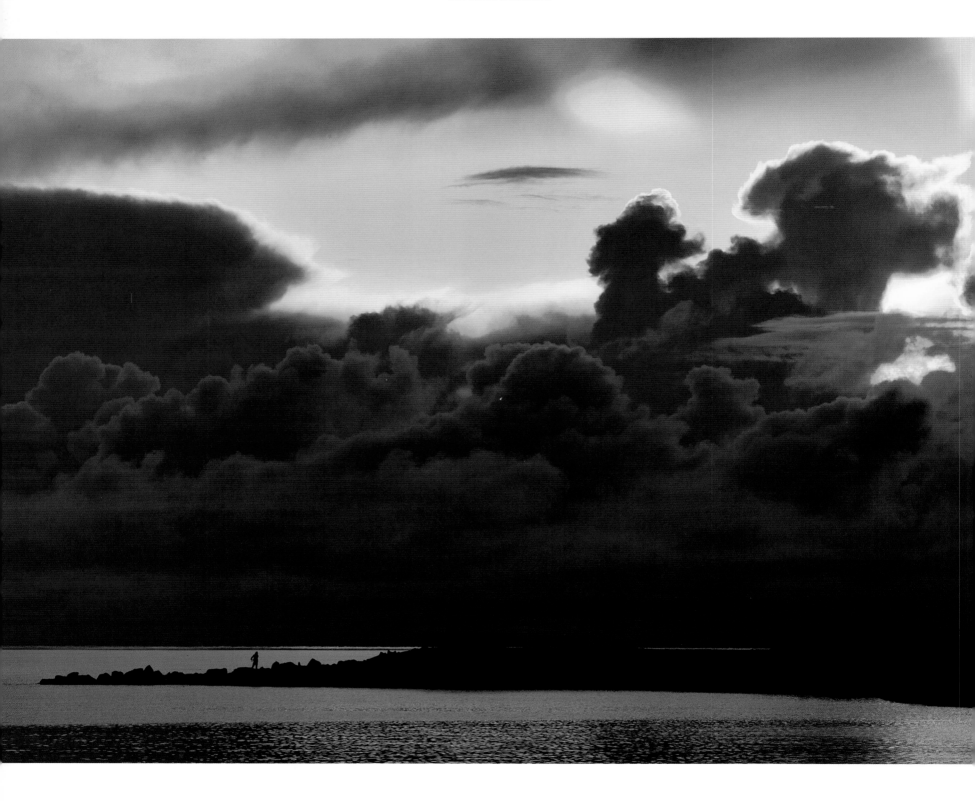

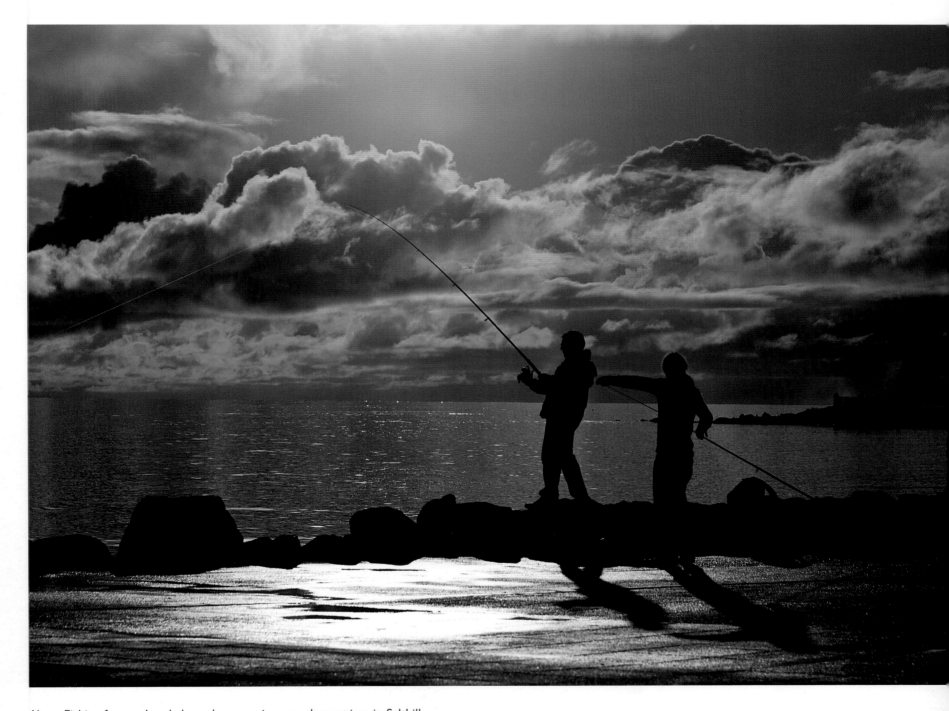

Above: Fishing for mackerel along the prom is a popular pastime in Salthill.

Opposite: Salthill – *Bóthar na Trá* – is Galway city's most popular seaside village, with its 2km promenade walk, known to Galwegians as 'The Prom'. It has a host of seaside indoor and outdoor activities: located along the bay are Blackrock Diving and Viewing Tower, Leisureland swimming pool and fun park, Atlantaquaria (an aquarium), Seapoint Leisure Centre, casinos, Palmer's Rock scuba diving, a boat and jet ski slipway, and any number of hotels and cafes.

ROSSAVEAL

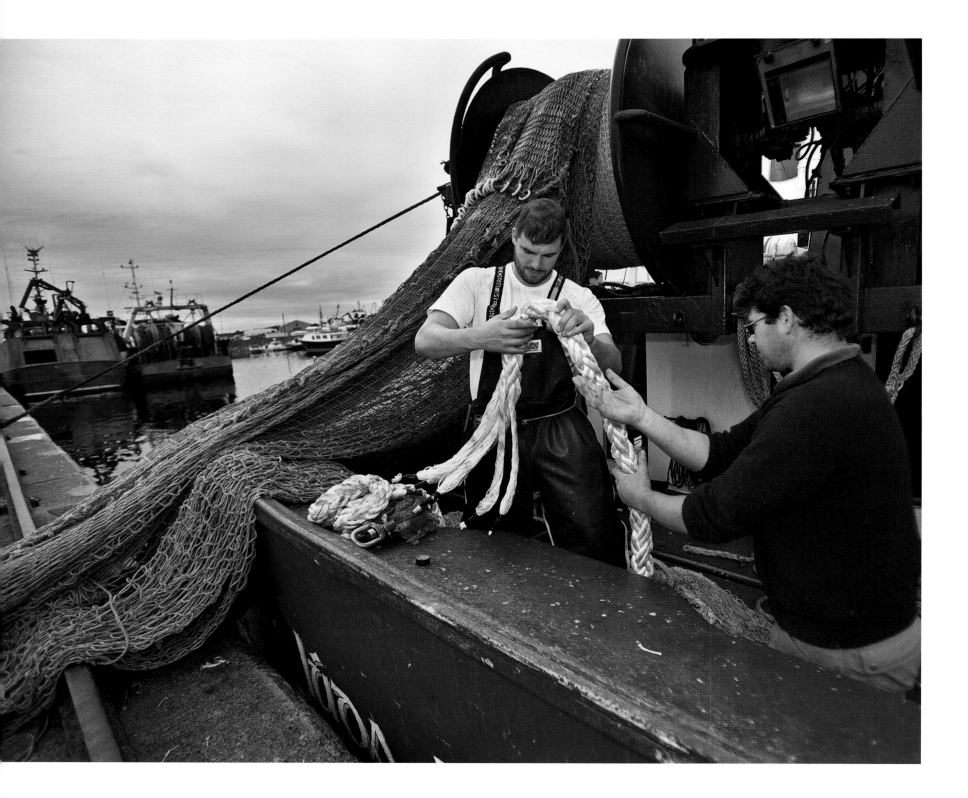

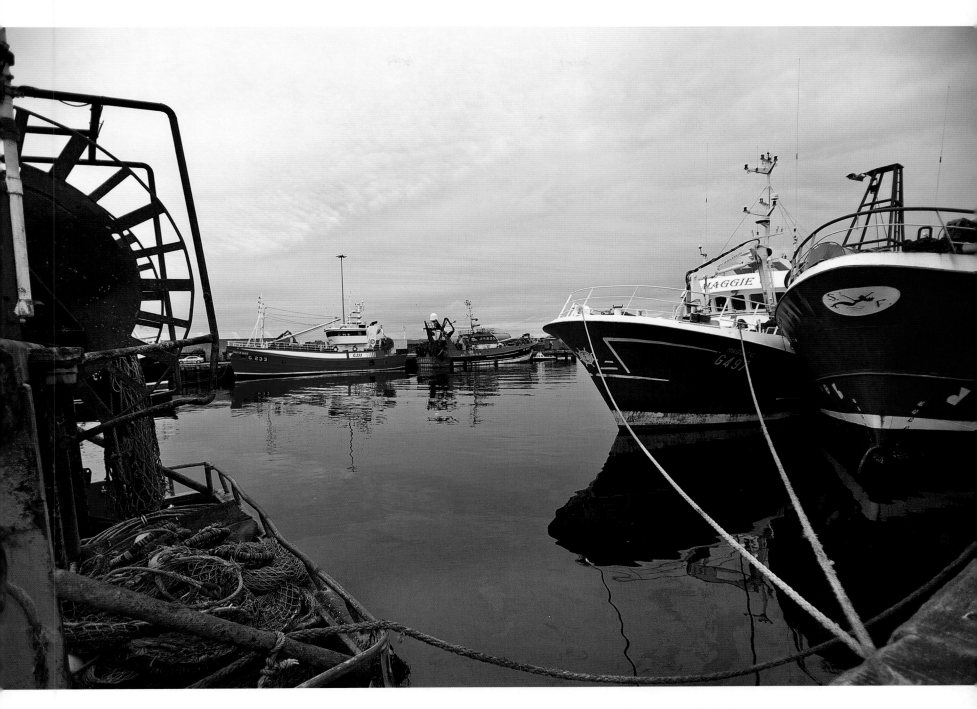

Above: Rossaveal is a fishing village in Connemara near Carraroe. The village is situated in the heart of the Connemara Gaeltacht. The name *Ros an Mhíl* translates from the Irish as 'peninsula of the whale/sea monster'. Two ferry companies operate a regular service from Rossaveal to Kilronan, the main village on Inis Mór.

Opposite: Fishermen Macdara Breathnach (left) and Oscar Ó Cualáin, Carna, tend to their fishing ropes at Rossaveal Harbour.

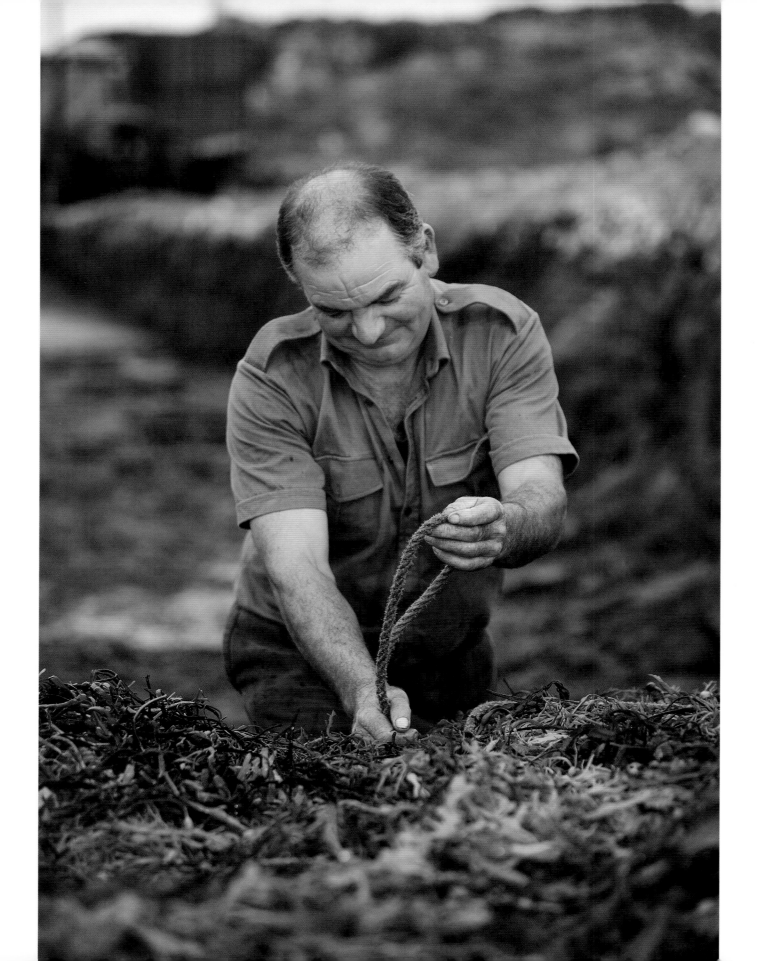

JOHNAÍ DUBH, THE SEAWEED MAN

By Lorna Siggins

THEY CALL HIM 'Johnaí Dubh', and his nut-brown complexion reflects a life spent through all weathers and all seasons on the south Connemara shoreline. When we caught up with him on an early morning low tide in Carna, County Galway, he had already put in almost half a day's toil – on his own, and entirely by hand.

With his back to the sea and bent over double, Johnny Clochartaigh was sliding his knife over rocks as deftly as a barber trimming heads. 'I'm working on a *climín*,' he explained, ie a bale of seaweed. Effortlessly, he gathered the *feamainn bhuí – Ascophyllum nodosum* by its official Latin name – to make several bales for the factory. Watching his technique, it seemed as if this might take forever. In fact, he estimates that one *climín* takes an average ninety minutes to prepare.

Clochartaigh, in his early fifties, was born and bred in Mweenish, one of seven brothers in a family of eleven. He is the only professional seaweed harvester among them, in what was a dwindling profession on the Connemara coast – until the recession hit the construction industry in 2008. 'My grandfather did it, and my father did it, and my eldest, now twenty-one, was with me till he was eighteen. But you would never get rich on this, and it is such hard work that it is not something that the young people want to do.' 'I don't blame them either,' he said, as he continued working with his knife, transforming those first few clumps into a substantial mound. 'My son trained in film, and now he is with *Ros na Rún* for TG4, the Irish language television channel. The girls are finishing education and looking for work. Sean might help out when he is on a break, and Katie, the youngest, always liked to come shrimp fishing with me. But there are other, easier ways to make a living.'

Clochartaigh passed me a knife to show me how it's done, pulling the blade towards him with one neat stroke. Does he not use gloves? 'Never. You get a better grip of the weed with your fingers, but then you have to make sure you don't take the tops off your fingers too.' Catching a clump, the first

slice I made was a little too deep. 'You've got to make sure you don't take the holdfast,' he explained. 'That way, the *feamainn bhuí* grows back in the salt water and sunlight. It takes about five years for it to return to full harvestable length, then. Any earlier, and it isn't ripe enough for the factory.'

Apart from the knife, his only equipment is a good pitchfork, previously used by his father, along with ropes, wellington boots, and his currach tied to the pier. 'I start with the low tide, and I don't stop till the sea is behind me,' he laughed. In that six-hour cycle, he will have made several *climíní*, which will be bound up and towed by his boat into shore. A lorry comes from the factory in nearby Cill Chiaráin twice a week to collect his harvest. He would not become rich on the reward.

The 'factory' is Arramara Teo, a state-sponsored body and one of the longest surviving manufacturing operations west of the Shannon. In 2007, it marked its sixtieth anniversary supplying the agriculture, horticulture, aquaculture and alginate industries.

This 7,800km/4,900-mile-long coastline has 501 different species of seaweed, some 19 of which have commercial use worldwide and 16 of which are being exploited for substances such as alginates, which are used as gelling agents for ice-cream, binding agents for tablets, wound dressing and dental impressions, and in textile and electrode production. James Bond once had to risk his life for the formula. Various types of the weed – which the Japanese call 'sea vegetable' because of its many valuable nutritional properties – are also used in fertiliser, as top dressing for soils, in biochemistry and biomedicine, for cosmetics, thalassotherapy, and as a tasty food snack.

Clochartaigh has not been to Japan – he hasn't left Carna, and preferred to send his wife and kids on holidays when they were all younger. 'I like to stay here,' he explained. He doesn't drink or smoke. He can start work as early as 4 a.m. to catch the tide, yet he will still run 10km (6 miles) and more every night with his dog. He likes to keep a few cattle, uses seaweed to fertilise potatoes in spring, and knows that there is nothing like carrageen moss for a chest infection. Yet the full significance of the resource around him seems almost ephemeral, as he moves alone, along a largely deserted shore. Sometimes the only sounds are of the sea, a heron or two in the distance, scavenging rock pipits and the incessant chattering of almost invisible brown crabs all around him. 'Arramara drives as far as Belmullet, north Mayo, for harvest. There was always plenty of crop, but, during the boom years, not enough people to cut it.'

In countries like Norway, harvesting is done mechanically by boat in inshore areas, but the nature of the Irish west coast terrain is such that it is best done by hand. There has been a demand for what is perceived to be a wild, organic product among exports markets for raw material in the US, Asia, France, Germany and Italy.

Even Japan buys in *feamainn bhuí* which has been dried and bagged and graded by Arramara. It is used there as an animal feed supplement. Back in 2000 a report on the sector estimated that seaweed was then worth almost €9 million to the Irish economy, but forecast that there could be potential multiples of this figure earned with further research and development. The big challenge then for companies like Arramara was not only finding and maintaining skilled harvesters, but also working to add value, and maintaining access to the shoreline.

In Johnny Clochartaigh's case, his family has worked Mweenish for generations, but there are other areas of the Connemara coast where he might not be so welcome. *'Spiteanna feamainne'* is the local term for long-held seaweed rights, established at a much more difficult economic time, when the pickings from the shore sustained small farms and vegetable plots. Thus, even where the weed has not been recently cultivated, there are families who would defend their fiefdoms to the last.

And how would Clochartaigh feel if some of the new Irish from Galway – comprising over 17 per cent of the population in the last census – were

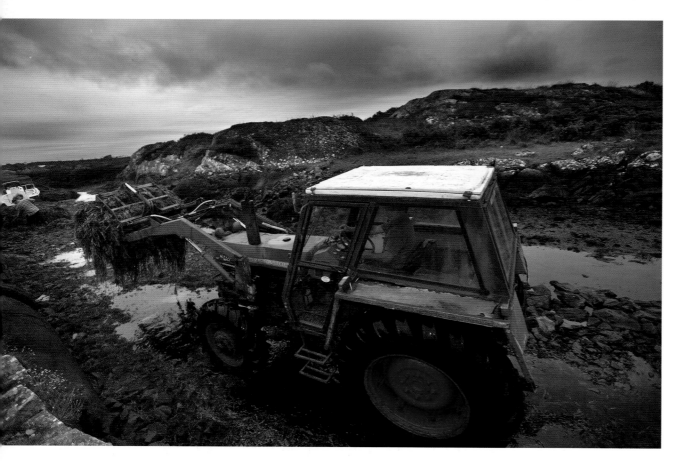

Left: The seaweed is harvested at low tide, when it is most exposed.

Previous page: Johnny ties the bundles of seaweed with his own special knot to hold them together before transporting them to Arramara Teoranta.

to join him on his patch of shoreline? 'I'd be delighted,' he said, without hesitation. 'There's way more than enough here for everyone.' We came across some upturned broken bottles, and other debris. 'You have to be so careful, but it is a lot easier now that people are no longer dumping rubbish off the pier,' he observed. 'Sure, it is all so regulated now that we are wearing life jackets when we are just towing in the *climíní*.' With that, he recalled how in 1989 he almost lost his life in his currach when collecting pots. 'I do the shrimp fishing for two months in the summer – there's a truck comes all the way from Spain to buy from me, imagine. This day, I was out just off Mweenish, when the currach went over and I had no life jacket. I was lucky to get out of it. I still remember climbing up on the boat.'

That coastal area, known as the Inner Passage, is replete with submerged rocks and shoals – a mirror image of the Twelve Pins mountain range which Clochartaigh can view to the north on a clear day. Just fifteen years after that, in September 2004, the *St Oliver* fishing vessel was lost with all four crew on its way from Carna to Rossaveal. 'It went up on the very same rocks,' he said.

Clochartaigh took his pitchfork, shook up the cut weed, and laid out his ropes at right angles. He forked in the *feamainn bhuí* to make a neat, rectangular bale, and showed me how to tie it up with slip knots. 'I'll be back this evening now at full tide to tow it in with the currach,' he said. Full tide, low tide – that's the pattern of his working day. 'The factory always needs the weed to be fresh, clean and not too soft, which is why I am hoping it won't rain before the truck comes. When I was working with my father, we had to fork it twice, as it was taken away on a donkey and cart.' He placed the tied rope under a sturdy rock. The shore looked fairly tranquil now at low tide. However, several years ago, a seaweed harvester preparing a *climín* further south was lost when he was washed into the sea.

'You're always watching that you don't slip,' Clochartaigh said simply. 'And then there are the days when the wind gets up before you have the *climín* tied, and it scatters the weed and breaks your heart. Best day is a good, dry, frosty day in winter. Then, I wouldn't want to be anywhere else.'

Bladderwrack *(Fucus vesiculosus)* is rich in iodine, calcium, magnesium, potassium, sodium, sulphur, silicon and iron, as well as being high in some B-complex vitamins. Not surprisingly, it is often used for medicinal purposes.

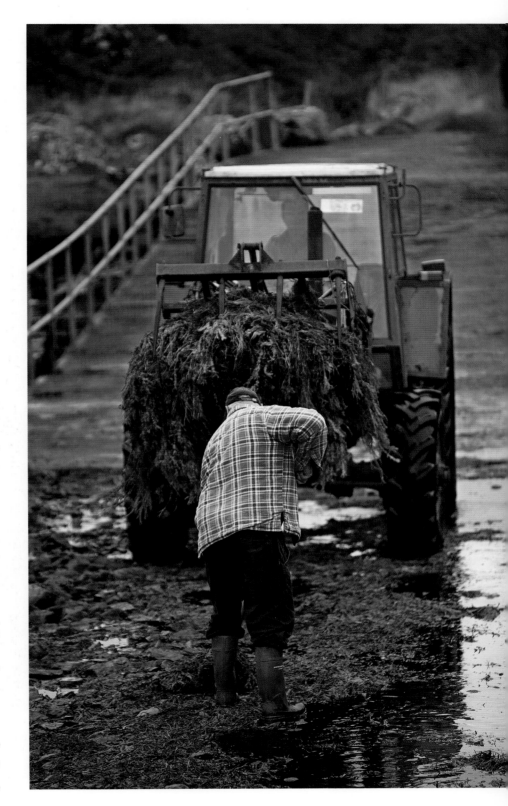

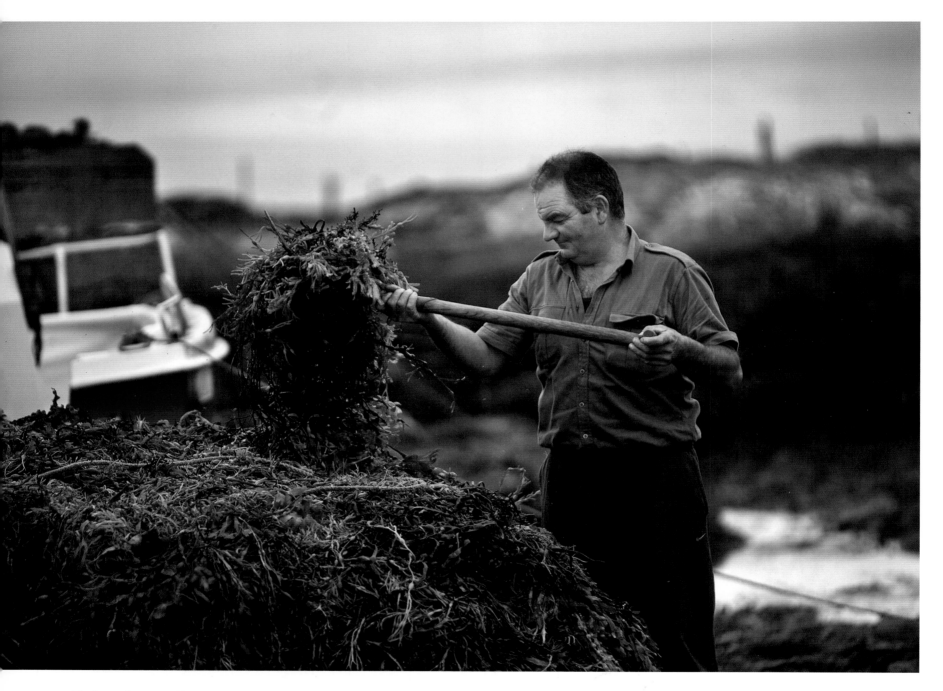

Traditional seaweed harvester Johnaí Dubh Clochartaigh sorts the *climín,* or bundle of seaweed. It is then transported 11km (7 miles) by tractor to nearby Arramara Teoranta, seaweed processors in Cill Chiaráin (Kilkieran), Connemara.

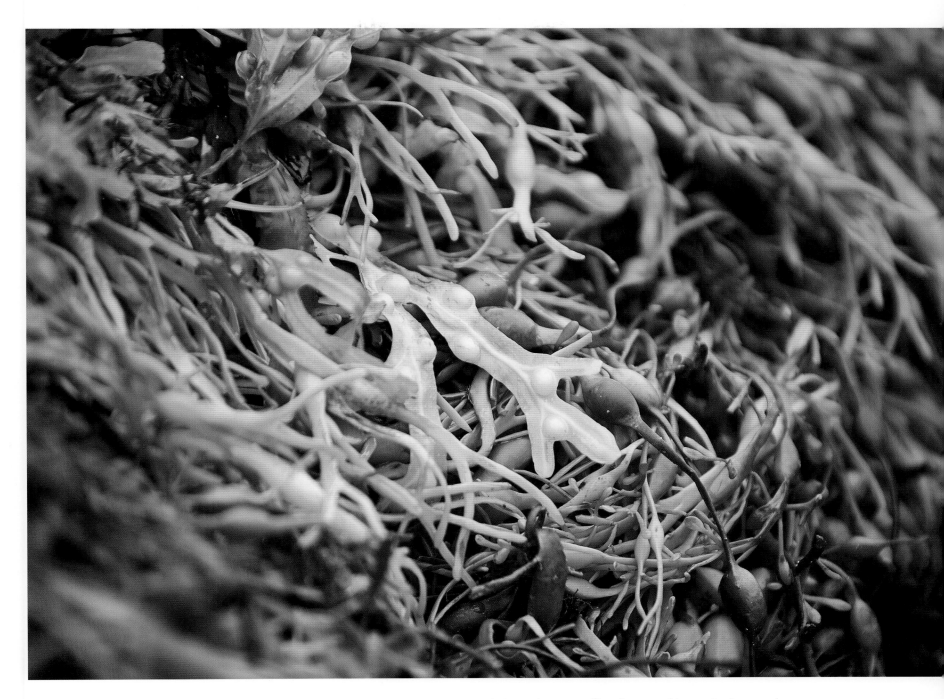

Bladderwrack, or *feamainn bhuí,* is the most common seaweed found along the shore. At least 4 tonnes of 'wet' seaweed is required to produce 1 tonne of seaweed meal.

ROUNDSTONE

The picturesque fishing village of Roundstone is in the heart of Connemara, County Galway. Its name in Irish is *'Cloch na Rón'* which means 'seal's rock'. Down through the years, famous artists such as Paul Henry and Jack B. Yeats have used this haven as a canvas to create some of their most celebrated works of art. Roundstone is also home to silversmiths, potters, sculptors, musicians and bodhrán makers.

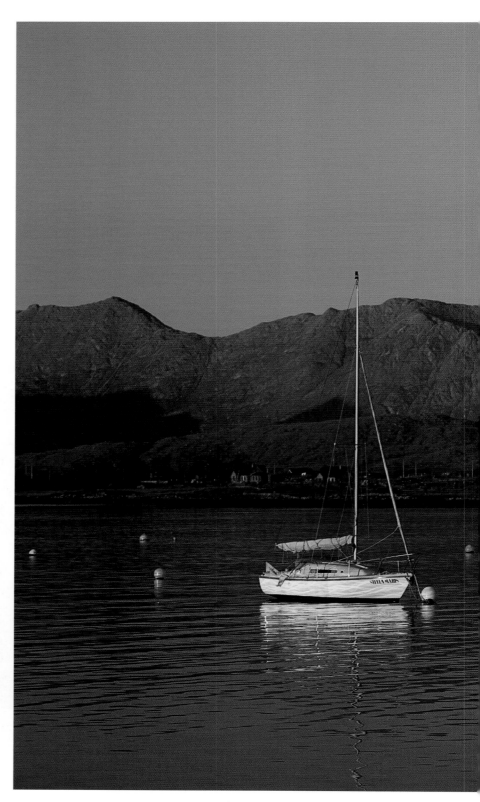

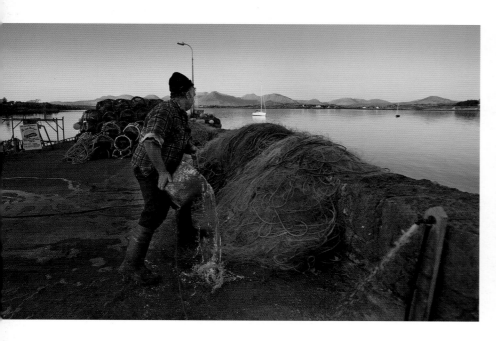

Above: Local fishermen quietly arrive back in the pier, landing their catch and preparing their boats and nets for the following day at sea.

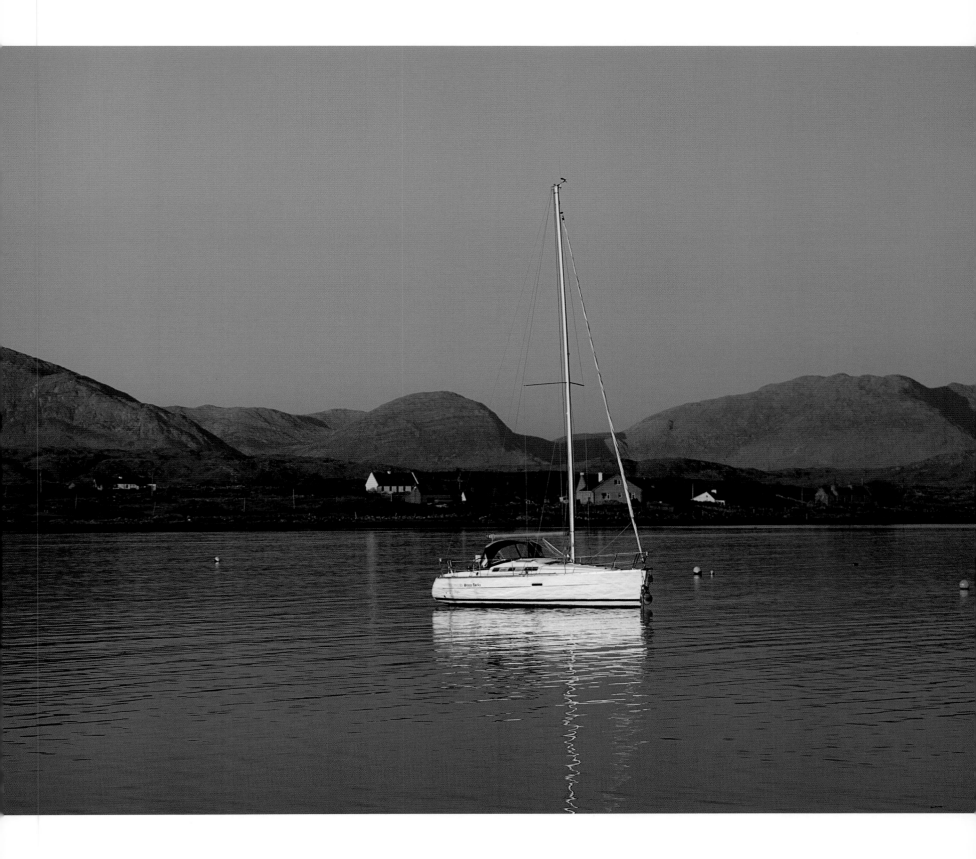

THE BODHRÁN MAKER

By Maria Moynihan

'WHEN I LOOK at the sea, I always ask myself, 'how can anybody not believe in God?' murmurs Malachy Kearns. 'Everything about the sea is divine. It has never been mastered by mankind. There's no war damage to the sea. It is beyond majestic. If you take the sound of the sea, it's kind of a therapy. The smell is healing. And if you add in the sound of the seabirds calling, it is another level of beauty. Every morning, I look out at the sea and I say, "Good morning, Ireland! Good morning, God!" There's usually a heron down on the same spot on the shore, has been and will be. You can see eternity straight away.'

For a big man, Malachy Kearns has an unexpectedly poetic, almost hypnotic, turn of phrase.

If you wanted to cobble a clumsily convenient metaphor together, you could compare his speech patterns to the soothsayer rhythms that resonate from one of his bodhráns. Played with subtle skill, this tough goatskin drum should send its sound 'straight to your gut, where the life centre is'.

Yet when Dublin-born Malachy quit his job with a Dutch engineering company to make bodhráns in the grounds of an ancient Franciscan monastery 'at the end of the last tarmac lane in Western Europe' in Roundstone, Connemara, over thirty years ago, his concerned sister wondered if he would consider 'discreet, psychiatric treatment'.

'There was a bit of madness in setting up here years ago,' Malachy acknowledges. 'The phones were still on the "windy up" system, so you had to book a call, maybe wait three hours to get it through and then you'd ring somebody in New York and the person who answered the call would say, "he's just popped out, can you call back in 10 minutes?"'

But the lure of the sea, which first brought him to Connemara, proved too powerful to resist. Malachy says he used to drink too much, work too hard. But trad music had caught him at 'soul level' at sessions in his aunt's bar, Rafter's, in Sligo. A neighbour in Dublin, harp maker Joe Porter, taught him

the rudiments of bodhrán-making; a skill he fine-tuned with Listowel master Davy Gunn. He decided to take a bash at it 'for a year or two'. 'There's a great gift in that I drifted into bodhrán making and moving west, not with a great plan,' says Malachy. 'I don't ever see bewilderment or confusion or pressure as being the end now. It can lead to a great, great place.'

Sticking to traditional techniques – goatskins are soaked in lime sulphide for seven to ten days before stretching – Malachy's bodhráns have found favour with musicians like Christy Moore, who plays with his knuckles and thumb, sent pulses racing in Riverdance and even appeared in the famous céilí scene in *Titanic* after director James Cameron visited the workshop twice, driving sales at home and abroad.

'When I see a finished bodhrán, I'm always thinking of where it is going and in my head I see it having a whole lively life, hopping, whether it is in New York or Kerry or Birmingham,' says Malachy. 'I can see the subtle veining in the skin. I see it as a life. We put our heart and soul into it really.'

Success, however, did not come without casualties. The pressure led to the break-up of Malachy's marriage to his wife of over twenty years, Anne, a talented artist responsible for the Celtic designs on the Roundstone bodhráns, and mother to his daughter Roma.

'I found it very hard,' says Malachy simply. 'It would be worse in the winter; the loneliness and the regret.'

But once again, that 'sense of bewilderment' brought Malachy Kearns somewhere he never expected.

At Christmas 2000, he was volunteering as Santa at a local centre for asylum seekers ('Santa Claus is a big fella like me!') when he noticed a young Ghanian boy called Jason.

'He was kind of lonely and lost, and I was too,' says Malachy. The child's mother, Gifty, was in her room, still coming to terms with the upheaval of moving from the west of Africa to the west of Ireland. When she was

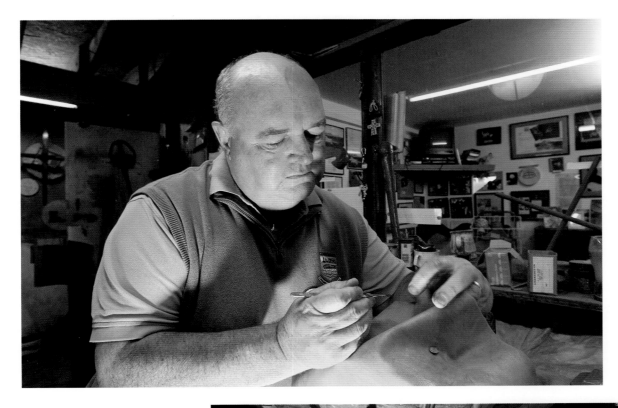

Malachy uses the old traditional techniques for bodhrán making. The goatskins are soaked for seven to ten days in a solution of lime sulphide, which softens the skin, de-hairs it and dissolves the fatty tissue. Sometimes the skin is buried in manure. It is finally stretched under tension onto a birch frame. It is also glued on – this is important for bodhráns being sent abroad. It thus cannot 'rip off' at the tack, traditionally the weakest part of the bodhrán – when exposed to excess heat. The skin is stretched tight when new to give room for residual stretch.

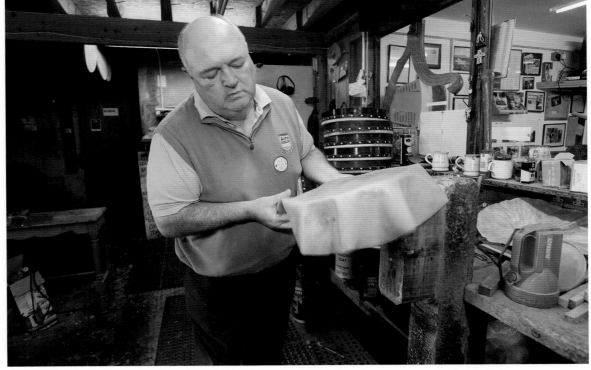

eventually persuaded to join the party, she put on a brave face and her most colourful traditional attire. And that was that for Malachy.

'I fancied Gifty straight away, but I couldn't say much because Santy is under obligation to Mrs Claus,' he says. 'So I had to find an excuse to go back another day.'

The opportunity arose when the BBC children's programme, *The Tweenies*, came to film at the bodhrán workshop. Malachy invited local families along, including Jason and his mother.

They fell in love, 'genuinely, slowly, not rushing into anything' and married in 2005. Malachy describes his wife, who now runs the shop, as 'a rare gift from God', possessing the patience and calmness he feels he lacks; she speaks of his integrity and kindness.

The bodhrán business has not been without its challenges in recent years; whereas in 2004, 'anything that was €50 and would fit in a bag, you could sell it easily', now it is €5. Going part-guarantor for a community marina for Roundstone that never got off the ground has had its stresses too. Malachy is generous to a fault and you get the feeling that he has been hurt by people who have taken advantage of this in the past.

Yet, for all that, Malachy says that the dream that brought him to the end of the last tarmac lane in Western Europe is finally coming true. And the call of the sea is more urgent than ever.

'I think I'll have to work 'til I'm a hundred, but I'm happy,' he says. 'Jason has the school holidays and all he says is, "Daddy, are we going fishing for mackies today?" And they're pulling out life jackets and rods and talking about flies like little expert fishermen.

'I often say to Jason and his friends that there's people in Frankfurt today who never saw or smelt the sea, or never touched a boat or never even heard of a mackerel. And here we are, another day with bags and nets.'

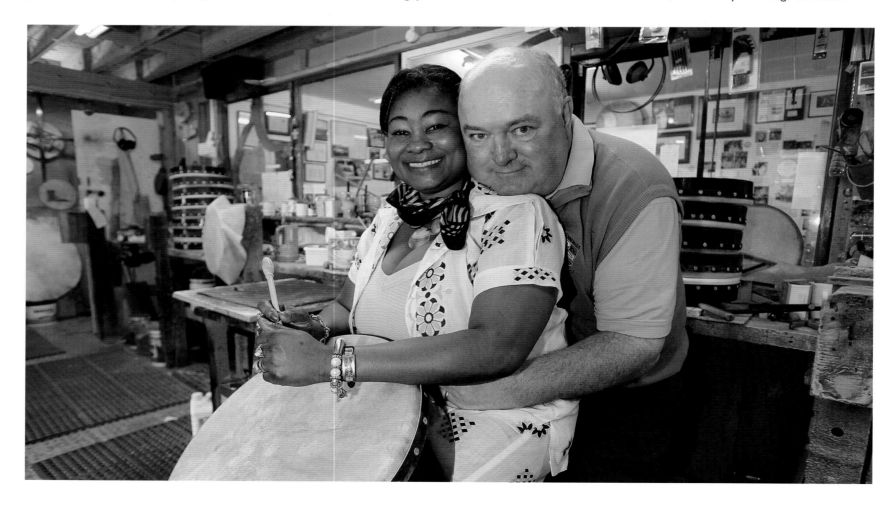

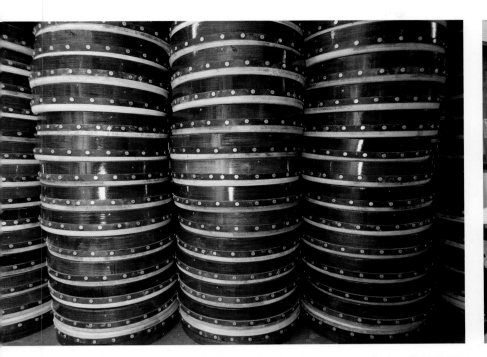

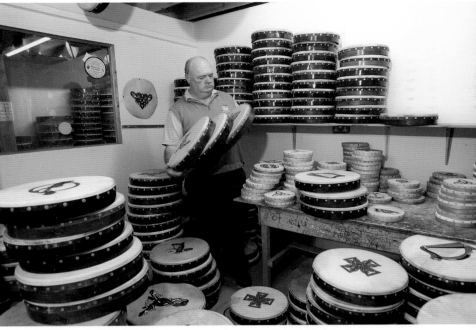

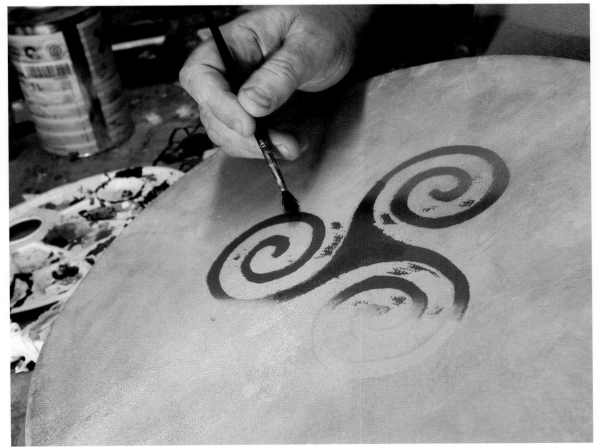

Top left: Malachy exports his bodhráns all over the world and he notes that in the hands of a skilled player the bodhrán can be a subtle and exciting instrument – striking the skin in a variety of ways, one hand tucked in behind the skin, pressing and moving to vary the colour and intensity of the sound.

Top right: Malachy Kearns has been a respected bodhrán maker for over thirty years.

Left: Malachy is a master craftsman, and the only full-time bodhrán maker in the world. He paints each goatskin with a typical Celtic symbol.

Opposite: Malachy Bodhrán with his wife Gifty in his workshop in Roundstone, County Galway.

KILLARY HARBOUR

Killary Harbour is one of three glacial fjords in Ireland, the others being Carlingford Lough and Lough Swilly. This magnificent 16km/10-mile harbour in Connemara forms a natural border between the neighbouring counties of Mayo and Galway that magically and endlessly meanders to the open sea.

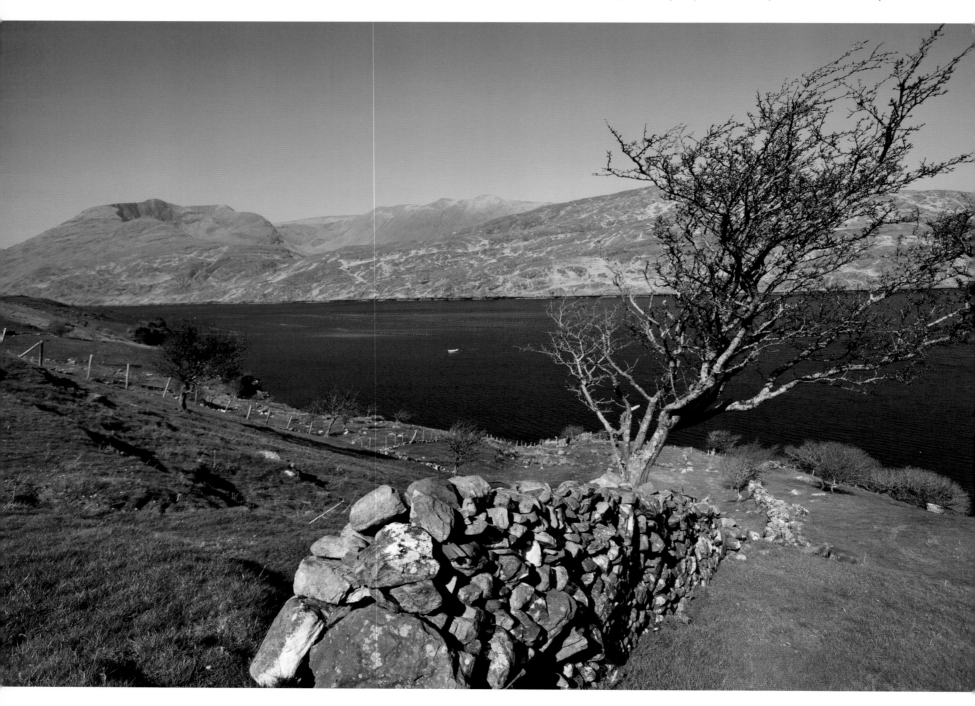

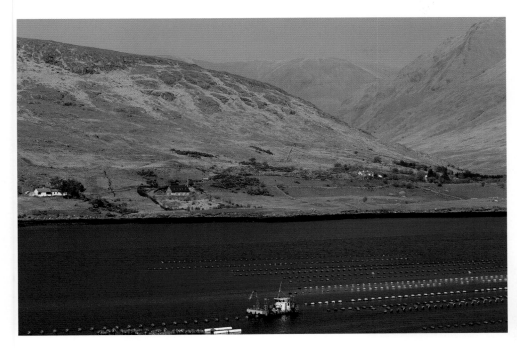

Left: 'The Killary', as it is known locally, has its own distinct environs, different from any other landscape or seascape in Ireland. On the northern shores lie the mountains of Mweelrea, the highest mountains in Connemara; to the southern shores lie the Maumturk Mountains and the famous Twelve Pins. Its rugged coastline is secluded and sheltered by these natural protectors.

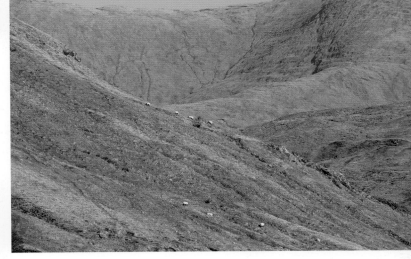

Right: Sheep graze freely on the mountains and coastline at Killary.

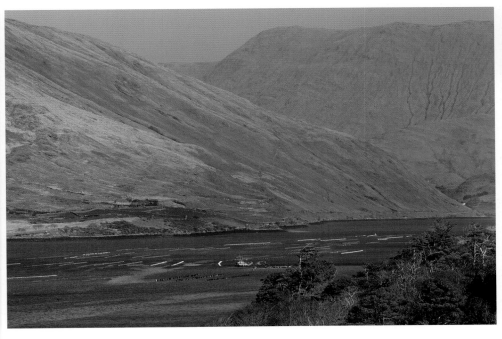

Left: Aquaculture is another industry important to the economy of Killary Harbour. A salmon farm is based in Rossroe and mussel rafts are dotted along the eastern side of Killary.

LEENANE

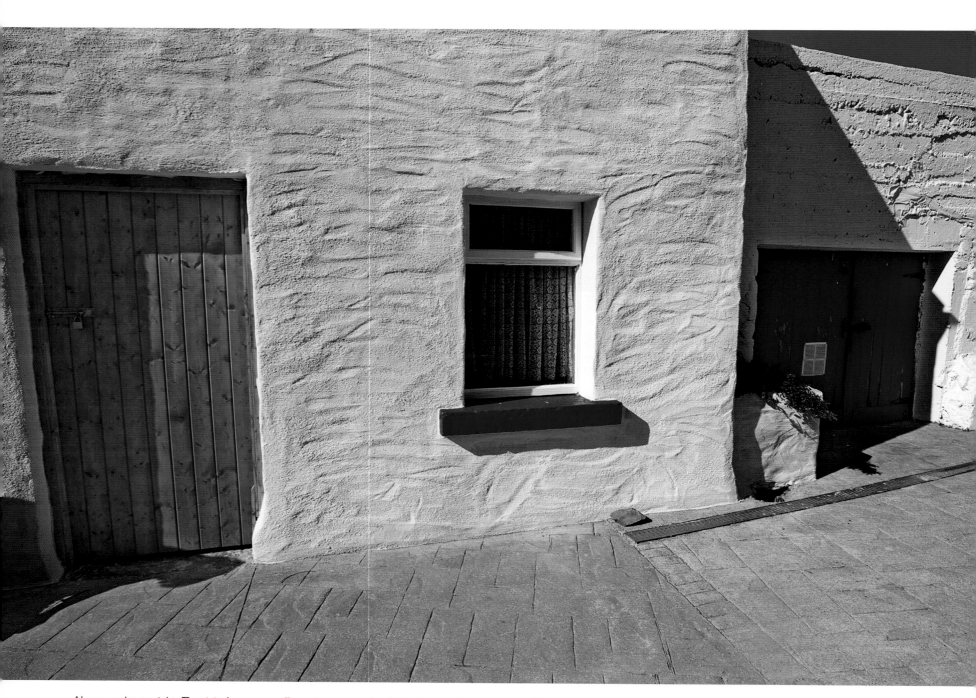

Above and top right: To visit Leenane village is to step back in time and to enter a Connemara 'paradise lost'. Because of its location at the crossroads of Connemara, it is a meeting point for locals and tourists, and a great anchor point for trekkers taking to the nearby Mweelrea, Twelve Pins and Ben Gorm mountains. Leenane serves as a backdrop to Killary Harbour, a lovely quaint village to stop for food and enjoy the scenery.

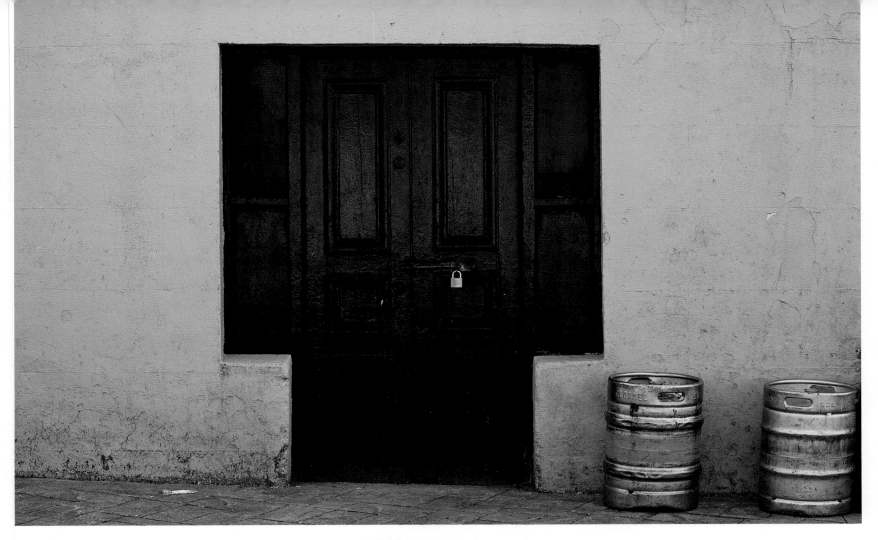

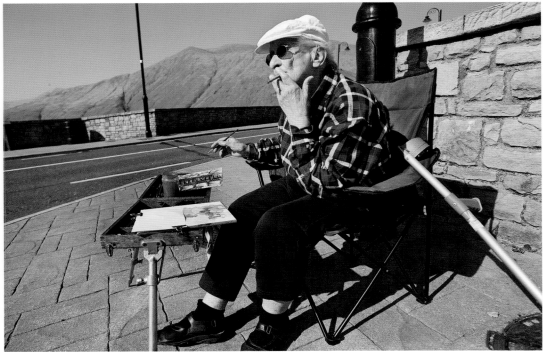

Left: Artist Helga Kaffke paints a scene at Leenane. Helga has been living in nearby Ballycoyle for the past eight years, and is originally from East Germany. Leenane has a long been a haven for playwrights and artists. Martin McDonagh's play *The Beauty Queen of Leenane* is set in the village of Leenane in the early 1900s. It was premiered by the Druid Theatre Company, Galway, and enjoyed successful runs on London's West End and on Broadway. Graynor's pub is featured in John B. Keane's play and film *The Field*, which received worldwide success.

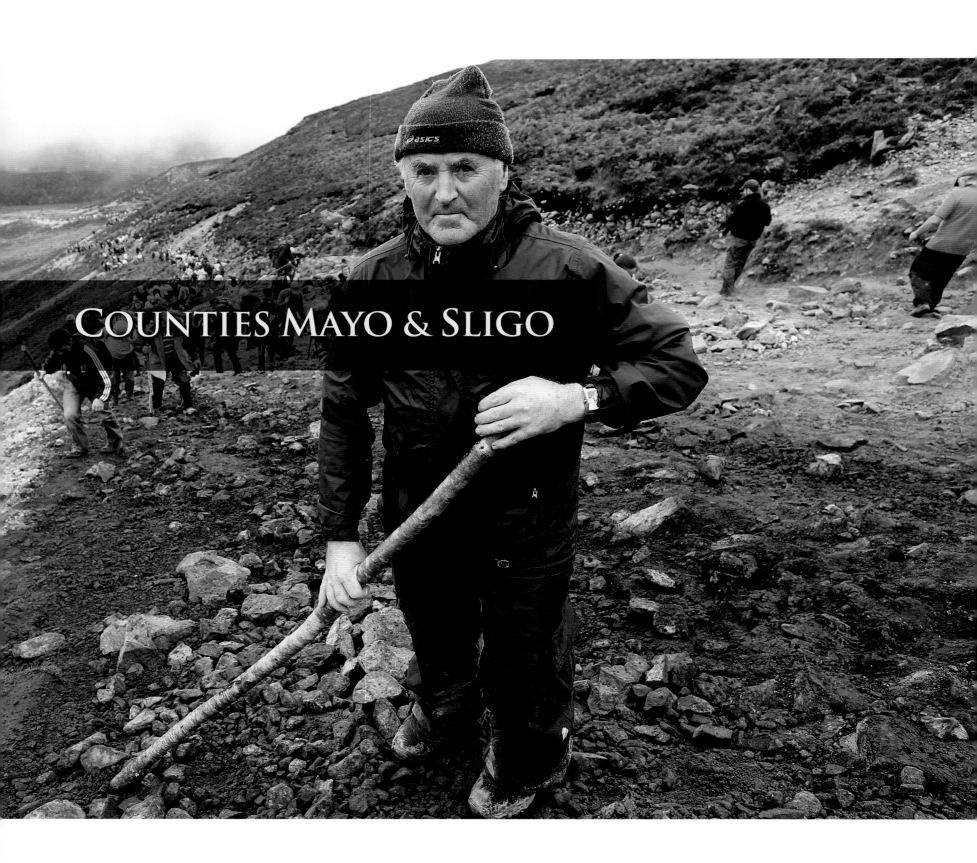

COUNTIES MAYO & SLIGO

CROAGH PATRICK

Named in honour of Patrick, Ireland's patron saint, Croagh Patrick in County Mayo is a 764m (2,507ft) mountain, 8km from Westport, close to Murrisk village. It is the most important Patrician pilgrimage site in Ireland. Each year on the last Sunday in July, over 25,000 pilgrims take to 'The Reek' (Reek Sunday) to make the ascent, people from all walks of life, of every age and creed.

Every GAA jersey in Ireland is represented, the annual raincoat for the Reek is taken out. Refilled bottles of water and sandwiches are the order of the day. Designer gear is not a fashion on this mountain. Even though the mountain is covered in grey mist, the essence of pilgrimage prevails: people stop and chat, everyone has a word for each other. Those who dare to walk in bare feet are encouraged along the path and applauded for their courage. There are three pilgrimage stations on the way to the summit of Croagh Patrick, each of which has a sign with instructions for the proper rituals and prayers. The last thirty minutes of the ascent – the scree slope to the summit – can be dangerous. It is very steep and has resulted in many injuries, especially in poor weather conditions. At the summit, Mass is celebrated throughout the day and confessions are heard in the chapel, which is over a hundred years old.

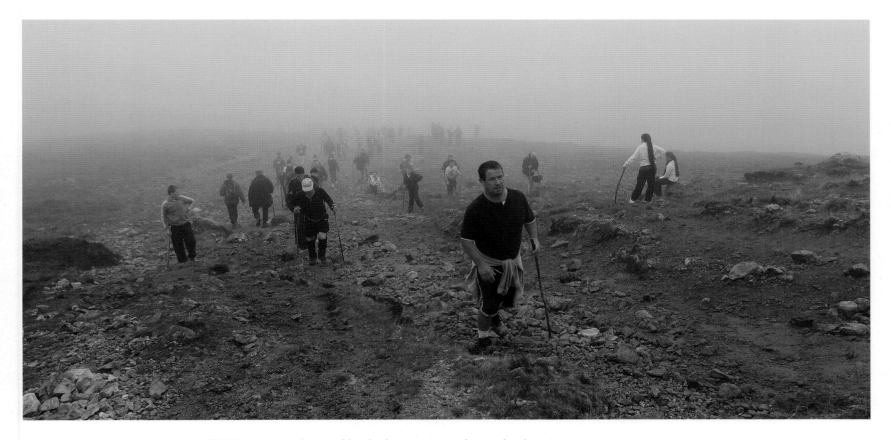

Above: A typical Irish summer's day? Walkers are undeterred by the heavy mist as they make their ascent.

Opposite: Paddy Ward from Newbridge, County Kildare.

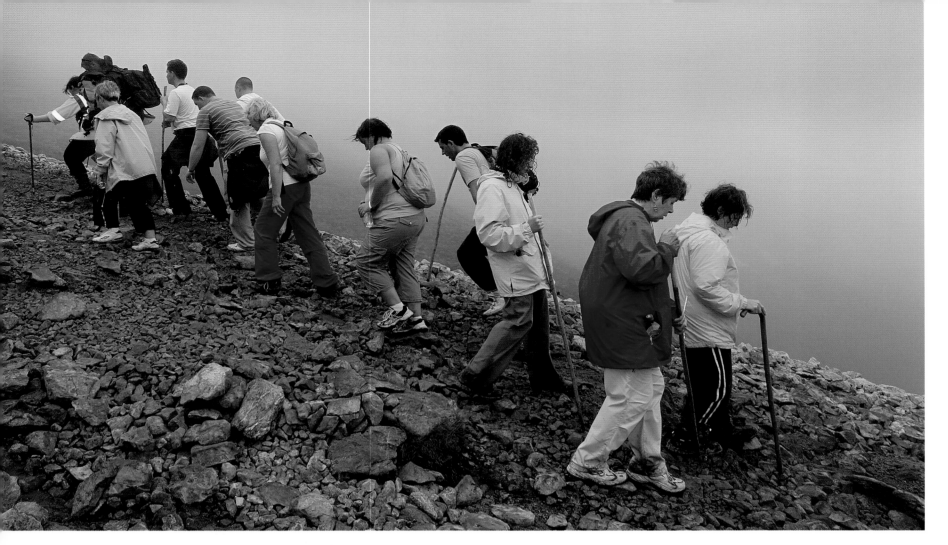

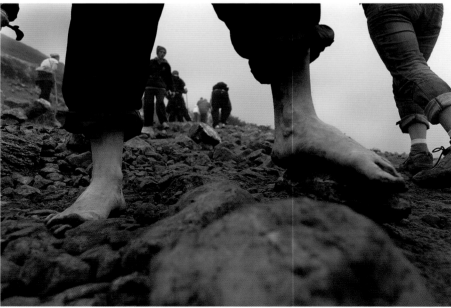

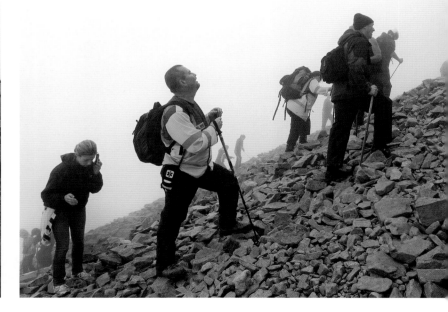

Opposite, clockwise from top: Pilgrims' Path: making the annual journey on Croagh Patrick;

Mike Brigdale, Shannon Order of Malta, ascends the cone, a sheer incline of endurance;

Many pilgrims make the ascent in the traditional fashion: barefoot.

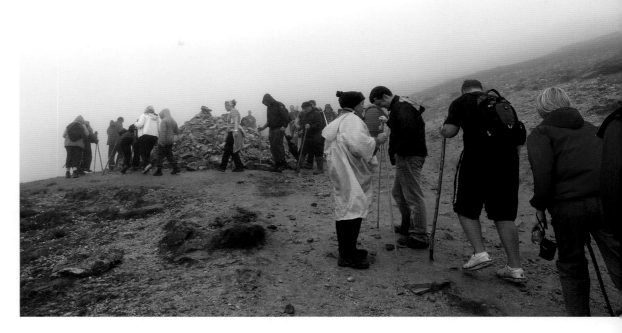

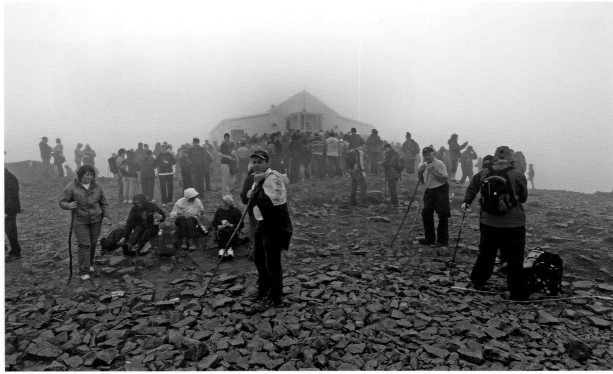

Above: Pilgrims take their place to recite prayers at the third station, *Roilig Mhuire* ('Cemetery of the Blessed Virgin Mary') on the western side of the mountain.

Left: The summit.

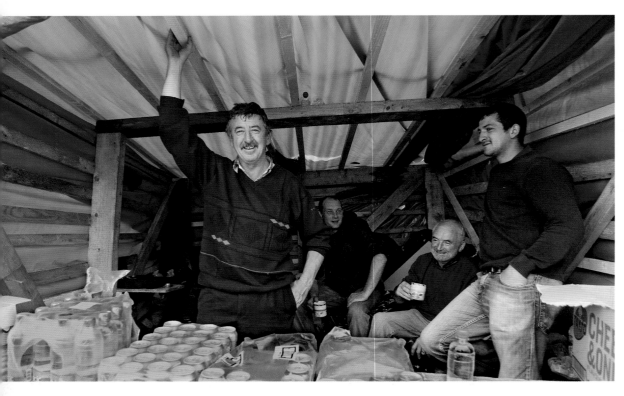

Left: Gerard Herrity of Tiernacroagha, Westport, and friends. The Herrity family have had a shop near the summit of Croagh Patrick for almost a hundred years.

Opposite: The descent of the cone can be treacherous: care with footing and concentration are required.

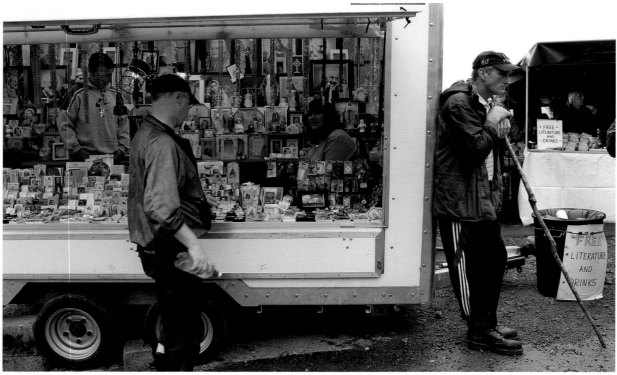

Right: As with all places of pilgrimage, religious trinkets and relics can be found on sale. Walking sticks and water are the most popular purchases at Croagh Patrick.

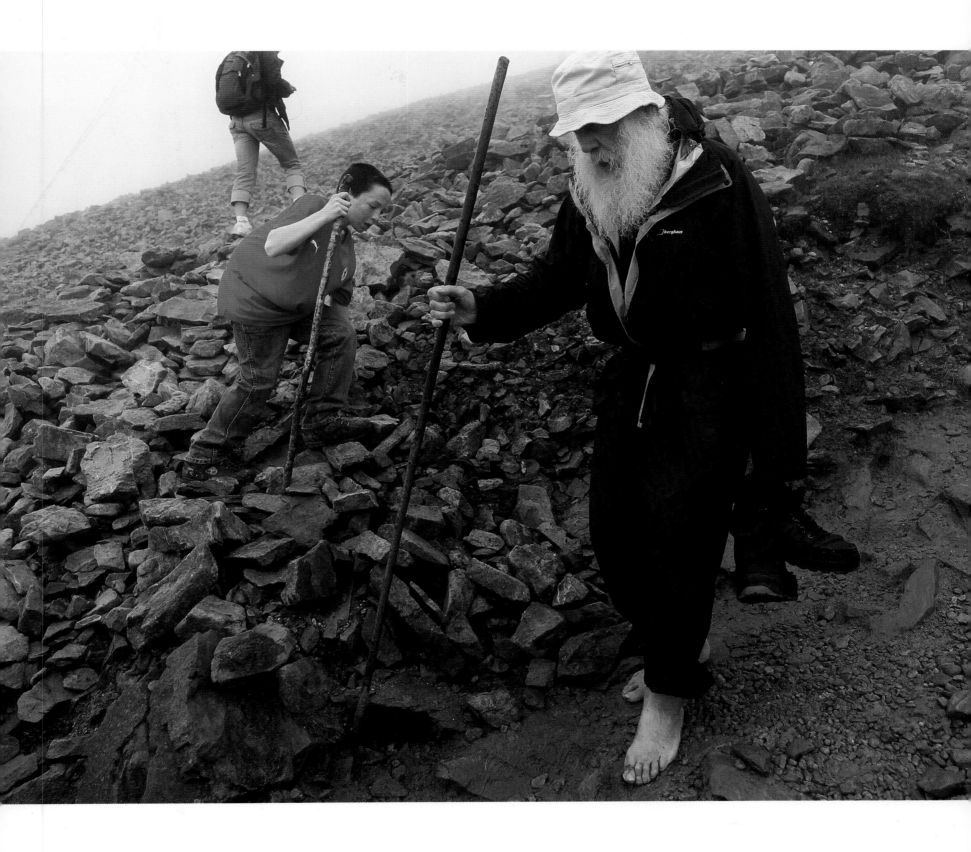

ACHILL ISLAND

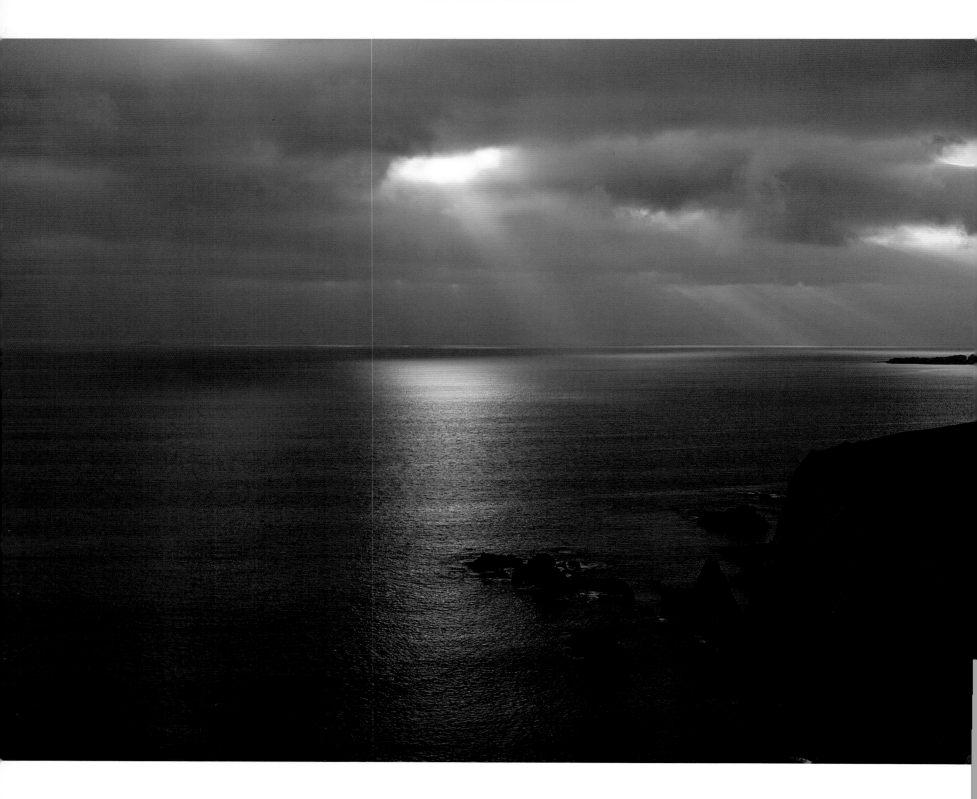

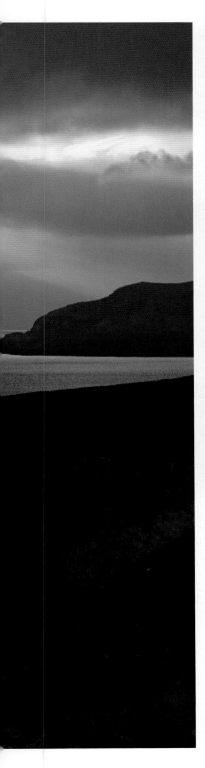

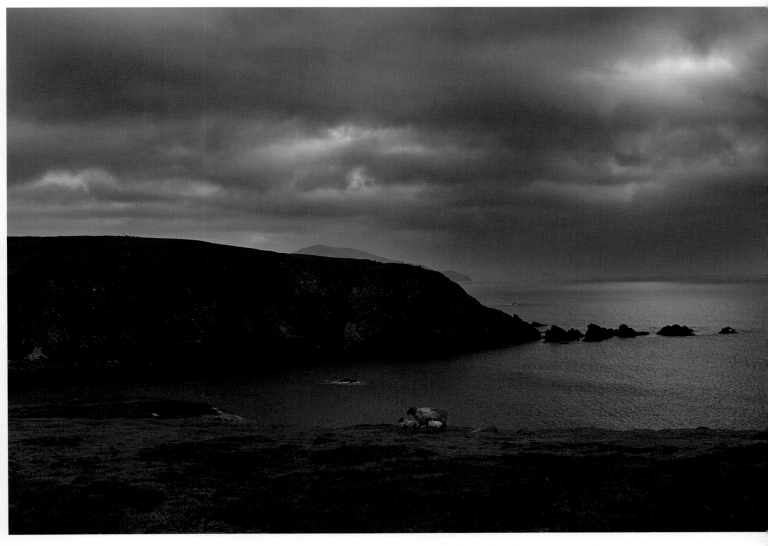

Above: A sheep and her lambs passing by at Ashleam.

Left: Achill Island, County Mayo, is the largest island off the Irish coast. It is attached to the mainland by the Michael Davitt Bridge, and has a population of over 2,700. Tourism is important to this beautiful, unspoiled area, especially outdoor activity holidays.

BLACKSOD LIGHTHOUSE

The information board at the entrance to the Blacksod Lighthouse tells a fascinating story: 'At fifteen minutes after midnight on 6 June 1944, Operation Overlord, the Allied invasion of Hitler's Fortress Europe, became a reality. More than 17,000 paratroopers, 7,000 ships, 3,000 planes and almost 250,000 sailors and fighting men crossed the English Channel to liberate Europe. The D-Day Landings in Normandy were the climax of almost two years of meticulous planning, and Blacksod Lighthouse and weather station played a pivotal role in their success.'

It was from Blacksod that the observation, which finally determined the date of the D-Day Landings in June 1944, emanated. The station is regarded as being particularly important because of its location on the western fringe of Europe. Ted and Maureen Sweeney filed weather reports on the hour to London intelligence, and, because a storm was moving eastwards, the invasion was delayed by thirty-six hours and thousands of lives were saved.

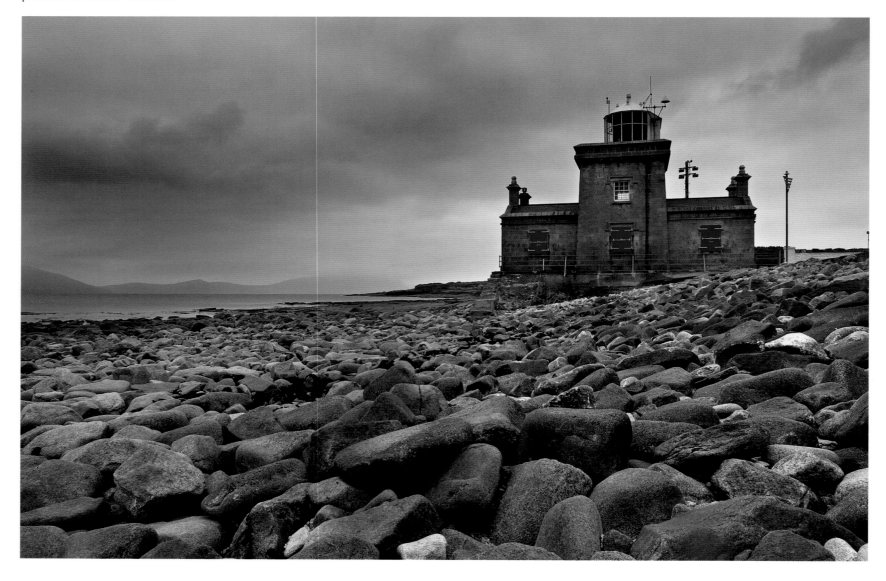

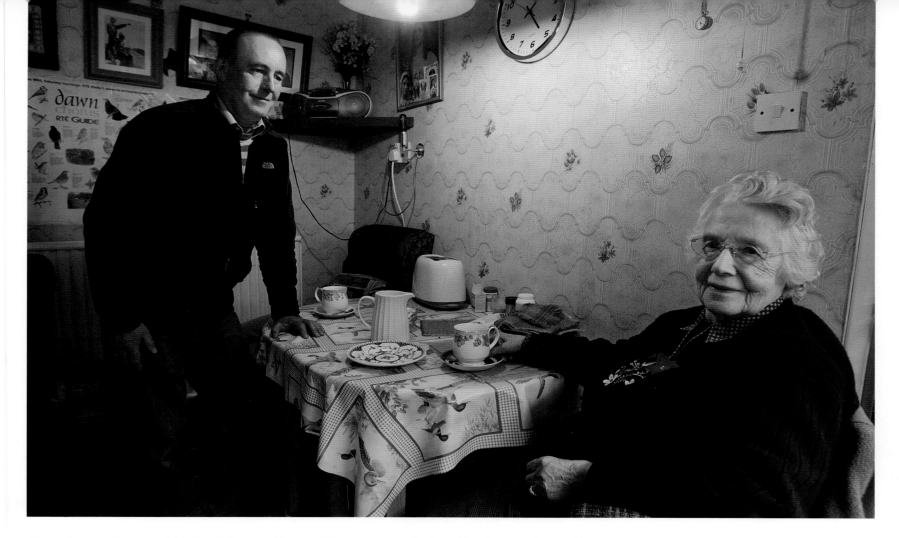

Above: Maureen Sweeney (right) with her son, Vincent. Maureen, originally from Knockanore, County Kerry, read an advertisement in the newspaper in 1942 for the job of postmistress at Blacksod Post Office. After a two-and-a-half-day journey from Kerry, she took up her post at Blacksod. Her husband-to-be, Ted Sweeney, was lighthouse keeper there and, after a time, Maureen was 'roped into sending out the weather reports'. Neither of them was aware of the importance of their hourly weather reports from Blacksod. As Maureen says, 'we were the only weather station with the particular report that meant a cold front had crossed the northwest coast of Ireland, with heavy rain and gale force 7 winds which would be over the English Channel by 5 June, which was the original date of the Normandy invasion and would have proved disastrous'. A break in the weather was predicted by Blacksod on 6 June.

Even when Ted was asked to 'check and repeat' his report three times to London, they both discounted its importance. Maureen continues: 'Of course, General Eisenhower was demanding clear skies, full moon and a low tide at dawn, as if you could get that by ordering it.' Ted and Maureen's weather reports proved critical to the success of the Normandy Landings and changed the course of world history.

Maureen's son and present lighthouse keeper, Vincent, carries on the story: 'It was years later by complete accident we learnt of the importance of the weather reports from Blacksod. A Mr Dixon, who was head of the Meteorological Services, wrote his memoirs after retiring and mentioned Ted Sweeney and the reports from Blacksod that delayed the operation by 36 hours.'

Opposite: Located on the southern end of the Mullet Peninsula, Erris, County Mayo, the Blacksod Lighthouse was established in 1864, and was built from local granite. The first light was an oil lamp, which was replaced by acetylene burner in 1931. The optic remained. Initially unmanned, a lighthouse attendant, Ted Sweeney, was appointed in 1933. The light was electrified in 1967. Today the lighthouse is one of four along the Erris coast.

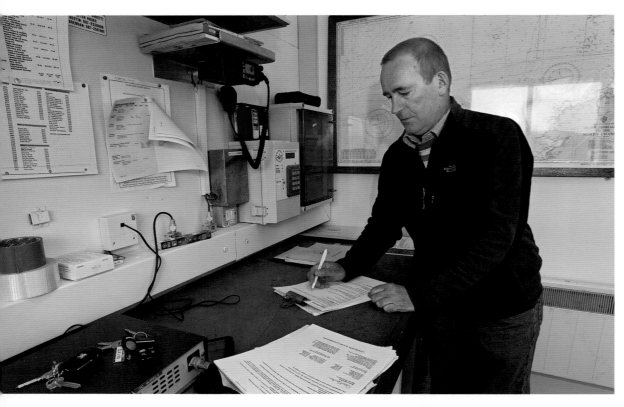

Left: Vincent took over as keeper of the light at Blacksod from his father, Ted, in 1981. As well as maintaining the lighthouse, he controls essential and emergency airlifts at Blacksod in the event of bad weather. A keen angler, Vincent has a great fondness for military history, especially from the Second World War.

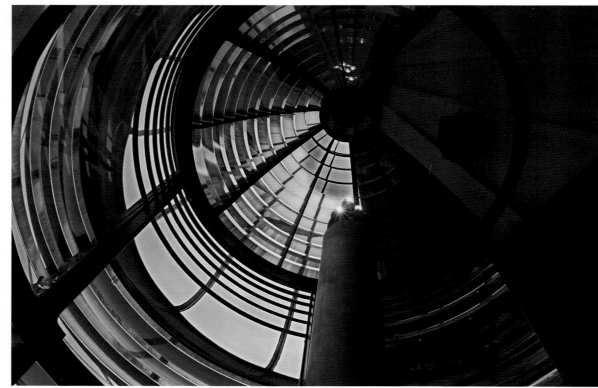

Right: The light range of the lighthouse is white, 12 nautical miles, red 9 nautical miles. The height of the light is 13m.

DOMINIC KEOGH – THE MAN WHO READS STONE

By Breda Joy

The word 'stonescape' might be more accurate than 'landscape' when describing the surroundings of the rocky corner of Mayo where Dominic Keogh washed up after making a start in life on the plains of Kildare and, later, the streets of Birmingham.

The stonemason's home address is monumental in itself: Cashellahenny, Kilmovee, County Mayo. The original Gaelic name of the townland is *Caiseal Laithinne,* which translates as 'Lahinny's stone fort'. Given the sandstone-studded terrain, Lahinny's stonemasons did not have to trawl very widely to source their materials.

The manner in which Dominic Keogh came to follow in their line and work the same materials could be summed up in the phrase from *Hamlet:* 'By indirections find directions out.' He set out on a FÁS to become not a stonemason but a thatcher, and found himself working on the construction of the Coleman Traditional Irish Music Centre in Gurteen, County Sligo.

'I ended up getting fascinated with stone,' he says. 'Cashellahenny is notoriously stony. The sandstone comes in flagstones. It's beautiful stone to work with. There's a lovely grain in it.

'The walls around the fields are fascinating. Some of them are up to three metres tall and about two metres wide at the bottom. It's because the ground is so stony,' he explains. 'They just had to get them off the fields. Clearance pillars standing in the fields were built for the same reason. They are a kind of small shed but just full of stones.'

Progressively and inescapably, Dominic became 'stone mad' as a passion for his accidental vocation consumed him. Apprenticed to Padraig McGoldrick, he began his initiation into the secrets of coaxing form from stone.

'I picked it up through perseverance and practice and a lot of sweat,' he says. Side by side with his new trade emerged a love of traditional Irish music, which, like the stonemasonry, originated from his time working on the Coleman Centre, which commemorates the great Michael Coleman, known for his south Sligo style of fiddle playing. Dominic plays flute and bodhrán and performs regularly on the continent, giving himself a 'break from breaking stones'. But it is the day job that absorbs his creativity. For the most part, Dominic prefers hand tools over power tools, and traditional techniques of dressing the stone.

When he is restoring old buildings, he is conscious of the fact that the exposed stone his eyes rest on was last held in the vision of the craftsmen who built the walls a century or more before. He has learned as much from their shaping and cutting of stone as he has from any living masters of the trade. 'It's almost like a window into the past,' he says. 'When you are holding a stone which has been in place for a hundred and fifty or two hundred

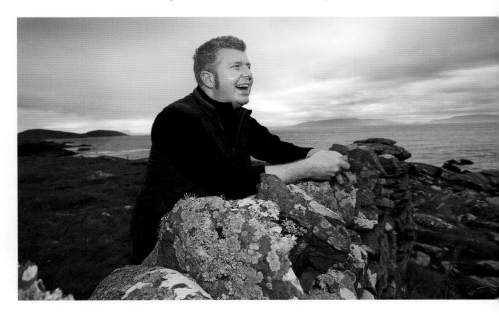

Dominic Keogh is a traditional stonemason; his love of stone and his passion for the craft are impressive. Here he is working on a traditional stone wall in Murrisk, Westport.

years, you wonder about the last person who held that stone and the life they led. It's almost like a personal signature the way they used the tools. 'If you have your eyes open, you can read a building,' he says. 'There is so much information from the way a stone is cut.

'When it comes to choosing an example of craftwork he most admires, Dominic speaks about Rosslyn Chapel in Midlothian, Scotland, with a kind of awe. The church took forty years to build in the 1400s. Its popularity as a tourist destination escalated because of its inclusion in the novel *The Da Vinci Code,* but it has long been a Mecca for stoneworkers because of its intricate carvings. But a building does not have to have the grandiosity of Rosslyn to take Dominic's eye. He can lose himself in the vernacular of simple farm buildings with small details worked into the design for practical purposes – little outshoots incorporated into a wall to hang a scythe, for example. He enjoys the local style and the personality of the men who gathered the

stone from nearby fields to build houses. There is much 'reading' in the lines of the old cottage he now calls home. Recorded in the Ordnance Survey of 1839, the dwelling has had several makeovers in the intervening years. The original line of the roof is still visible in the attic along with clumps of thatch stubbornly wedged between the stones. Along the eaves, a line of flagstones juts out past the wall so that rainwater could be shot away from the house before the advent of gutters. To Dominic, this is another example of the locals knowing their stone and finding a use for it.

One of his treasures is an old millstone, a large piece of conglomerate sandstone that had been used by a local blacksmith for forming cast iron rings for cartwheels. The millstone is prized by Dominic along with some other pieces of old kerbstone. Each has its own individual story for the man who reads stone.

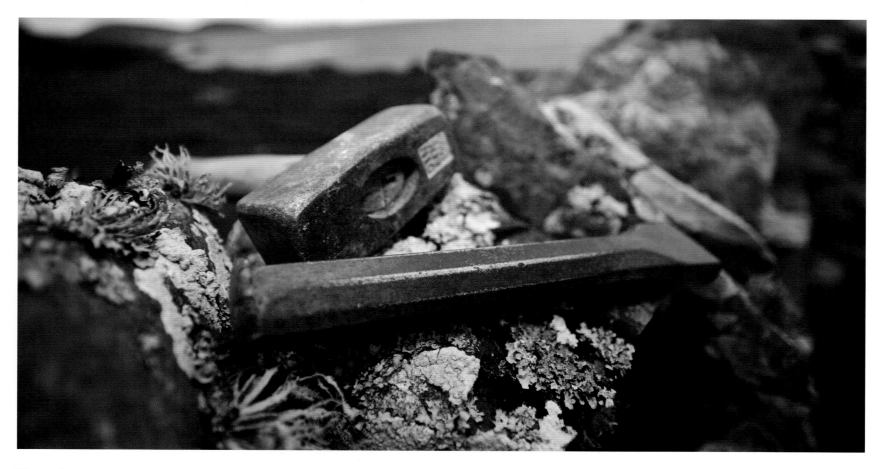

The traditional tools of the trade for stonemason and gifted bodhrán player Dominic Keogh.

FISHERS OF MEN – STEPHEN McHALE

By Lorna Siggins

It looks for all the world like a ship rising out of the ocean – one of many fantastical geomorphological creations cut from the cliffs of north Mayo. Located just below Benwee Head (272m/892ft), this particular prow of exposed bedrock tells a story of tectonic tumult, long before the inner border of this Atlantic rim was carpeted in blanket bog.

And if the seascape, with its stacks and reefs and arches and caves, seems stunning from shore, the Erris landscape is captivating from sea. Here, the footprint of the first Neolithic farmers is celebrated at the Céide Fields near Ballycastle, marked by poet Seamus Heaney's immortal *Belderg,* and here live some of the toughest small fishermen on the west coast. Not that

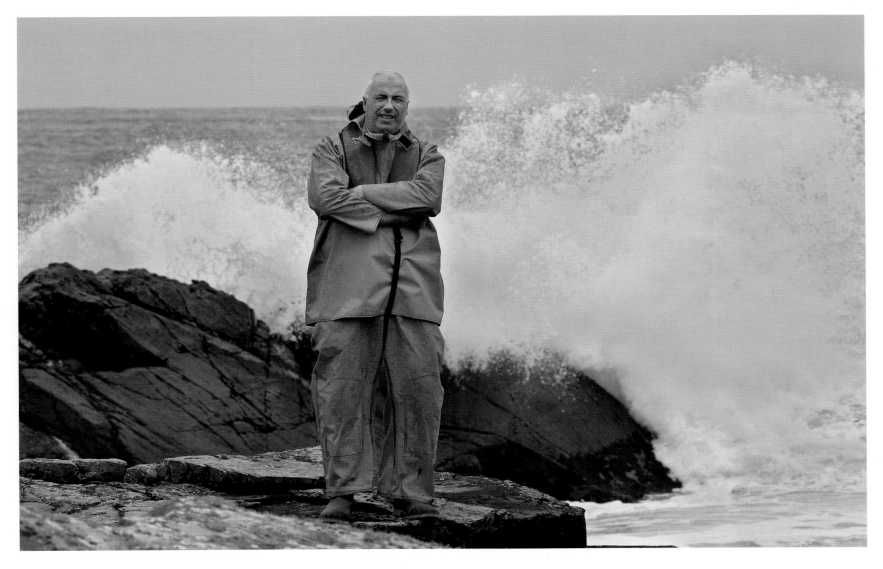

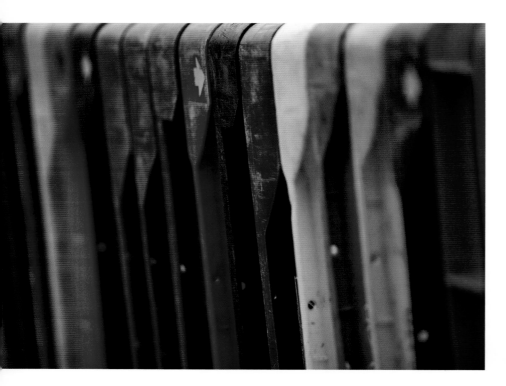

October. We go out at 4.30 a.m., and we set up the jigging machines, which catch the fish individually. It is low impact, and I don't suppose we'd put any big supertrawlers out of business.

'It is one of the roughest stretches of the northwest coast here, with no all-weather harbour between Galway and Killybegs, and we are governed by the tide,' McHale explains. 'We are permitted to land only 500kg, which is about fourteen boxes, so we are in and out every couple of hours. It makes it a bit difficult when you are trying to arrange transport as the vans will only come for a minimum of thirty to forty boxes.'

Often, he has to travel to meet the buyers. 'It would be so much easier if you could sell your fish straight after landing, but coming into the pier is really only half the trip. That's the way it is up here.'

McHale's boat is among a number of vessels submitted for assessment by BIM as a certified passive fishery, with built-in traceability. BIM has been

skippers like Stephen McHale have much time to dwell on it, as he tends his crab pots and hand-lines for migratory mackerel. McHale works from the tiny Belderrig harbour – the 'big red mouth' or *Béal Deirg* – to the west of the Céide Fields. The horseshoe-shaped inlet was sculpted by the relentless erosion of wind and wave, and there was a time not many generations back when the sea took a constant toll, even as hide currachs were replaced by canvas cloth hulls.

The seasonal Erris inshore fleet has depended on wild salmon and shellfish, but that changed when drift netting for salmon was banned under pressure from Europe in 2007. After almost forty years at sea, McHale found himself with an uncertain future. Small enough compensation was awarded at that time to drift-net licence holders, who were subject to tax on the full amount, and who had little alternative employment.

With advice from Bord Iascaigh Mhara (BIM), the state sea fisheries board, McHale opted to develop a sustainable mackerel fishery on his 9m (30ft) boat, *Eileen's Pride*. The vessel, named after his wife, Eileen, is fitted to hand-line for the migratory stock.

'It's a lovely fishery,' he says. 'The mackerel swims half a mile from shore at times, and the quality is great. The season starts in May and continues till

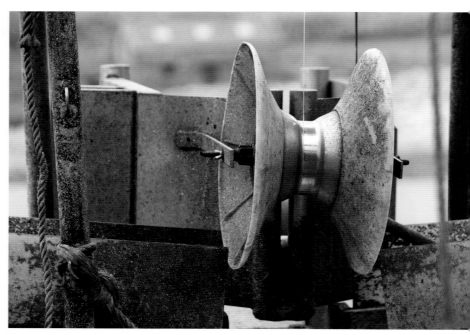

Above: Traditional line for hooking mackerel.

Above left: A colourful stack of fish boxes.

Previous page: Traditional fisherman, Stephen McHale.

working with fishermen in all sizes of boats and ports to develop quality-assurance schemes based on the ISO 65 standard, similar to the United Nations Food and Agricultural Organisation code for responsible fisheries. McHale's wife, Eileen, also depends on his catch, for she serves evening meals at her bed and breakfast, The Yellow Rose, and has done for over twenty years. Archaeologist Dr Seamus Caulfield, whose father first discovered the signs of 5,000-year-old cultivation at Behy, persuaded her initially to consider opening a guesthouse. 'At the time that the Céide Fields interpretative centre opened,' she recalls, 'there was not a bed to be hired between Belmullet and Ballina.'

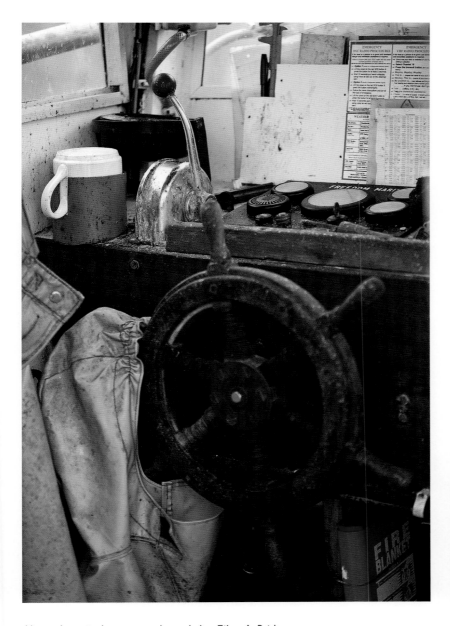

Above: A typical scene on board the *Eileen's Pride.*

Right: The boat's lines are tied up until needed.

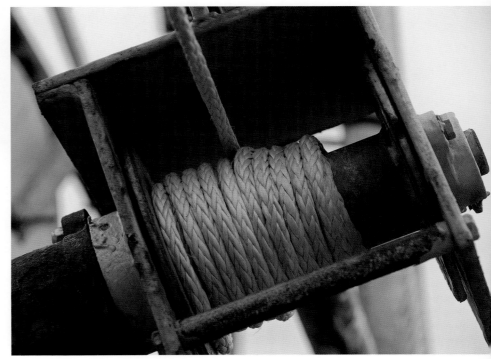

THE CÉIDE FIELDS

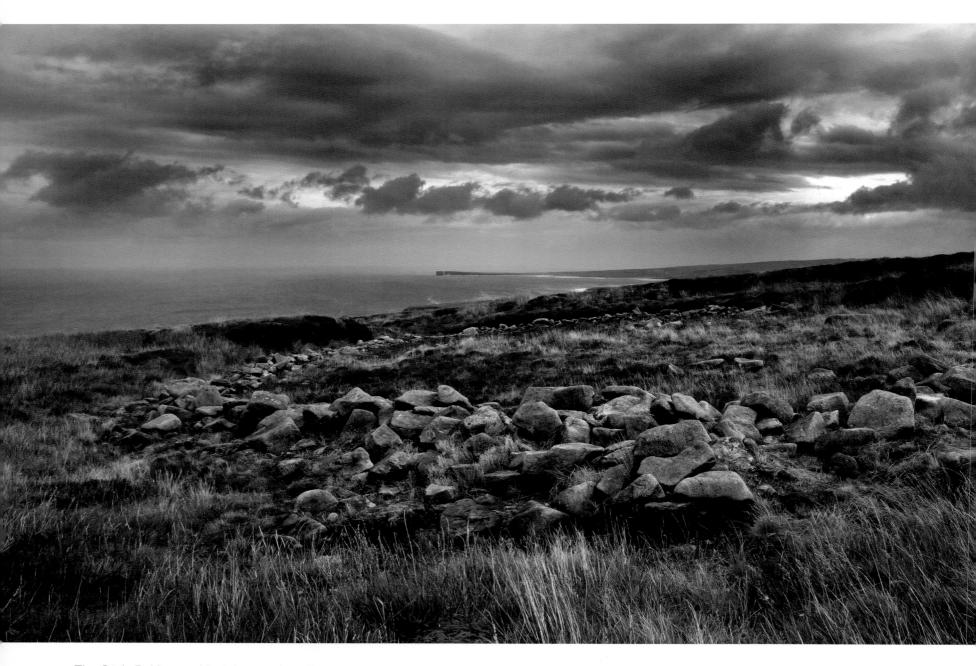

The Céide Fields are a Neolithic site, 8km (5 miles) west of Ballycastle, north County Mayo, consisting of stone-walled fields, the oldest known in the world. The origin of this complex site goes back 6,000 years, when Neolithic settlers arrived in Ireland and brought with them the practice of farming, introducing wheat, barley and farm animals to Ireland. They set about clearing forests and developed areas for this new farming system, building dwellings for the farming community, gardens and field systems, the remains of which lie preserved under rich natural bog.

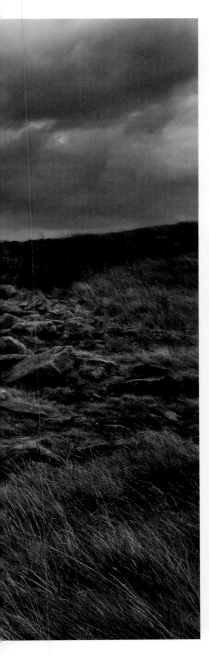
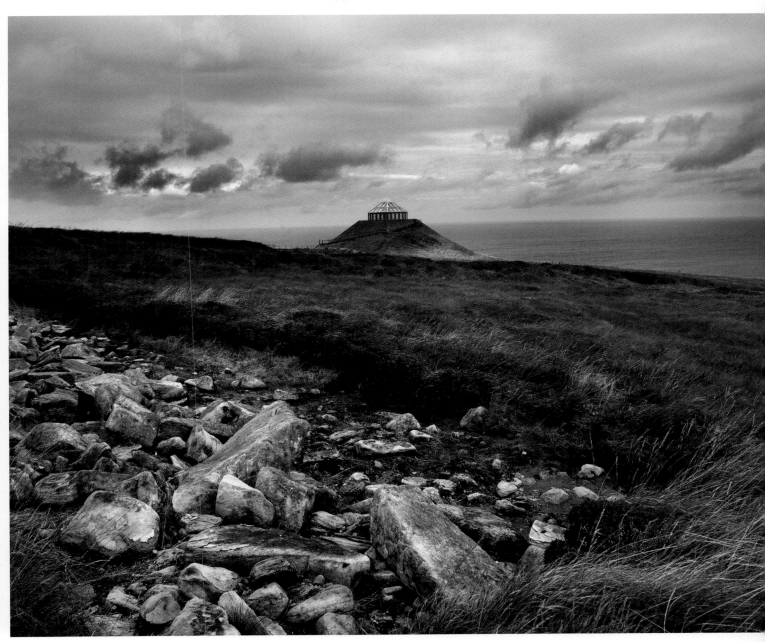

The award-winning Céide Fields interpretative centre was built with sensitivity. The interior was constructed from natural materials – sandstone, oak and glass – and was a combination of local work and resources spearheaded by local archaeologist Dr Seamus Caulfield and the Office of Public Works in Dublin. The centre today is run by archaeological specialist Gretta Byrne.

KILCULLEN'S EDWARDIAN SEAWEED BATHS, ENNISCRONE

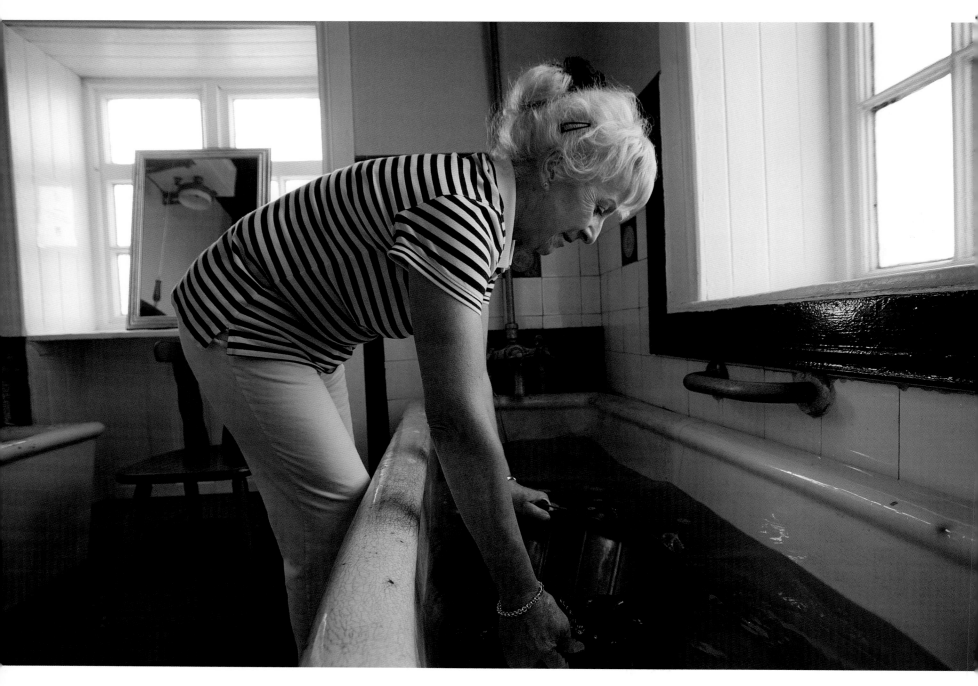

Christine Kilcullen adds a bucket of seaweed freshly gathered from Enniscrone beach into the hot, steamy Atlantic seawater. The amber tint in the water is caused by the extraction of iodine from the seaweed, one of the richest sources of this therapeutic element, which is essential for the body's metabolism. It has a high mineral content and vitamins A, B, C and E. A seaweed bath can give relief from rheumatism and arthritis.

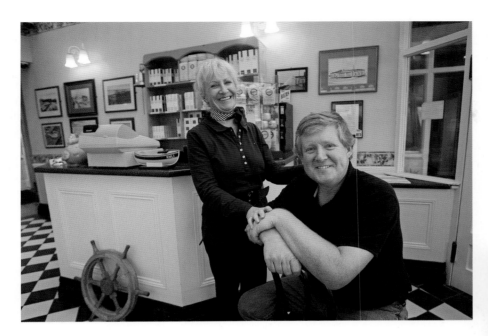

Left: Edward and Christine, Kilcullen's Seaweed Baths, keeping the Edwardian tradition of the therapeutic seaweed bath alive in Ireland.

Right: Odette Casey, Enniscrone, immerses herself in one of nature's most natural therapies.

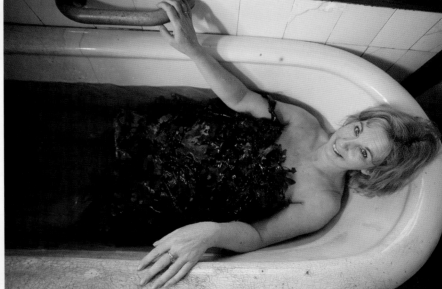

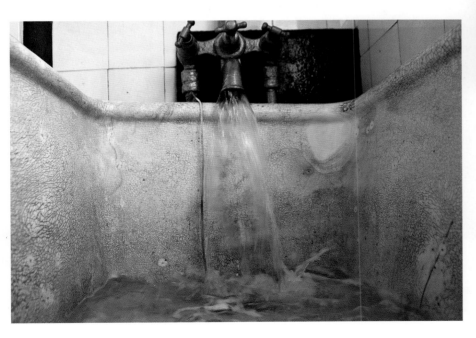

Left: Seawater is pumped in from Enniscrone beach, practically outside the door of the Kilcullen's Edwardian Seaweed Baths, heated to perfection without losing any of its Atlantic quality. The original glazed porcelain baths, solid brass taps and wood-panelled shower cisterns add to the old-world charm that the Kilcullens have embraced for a hundred years.

CAIN KILCULLEN, SURFER

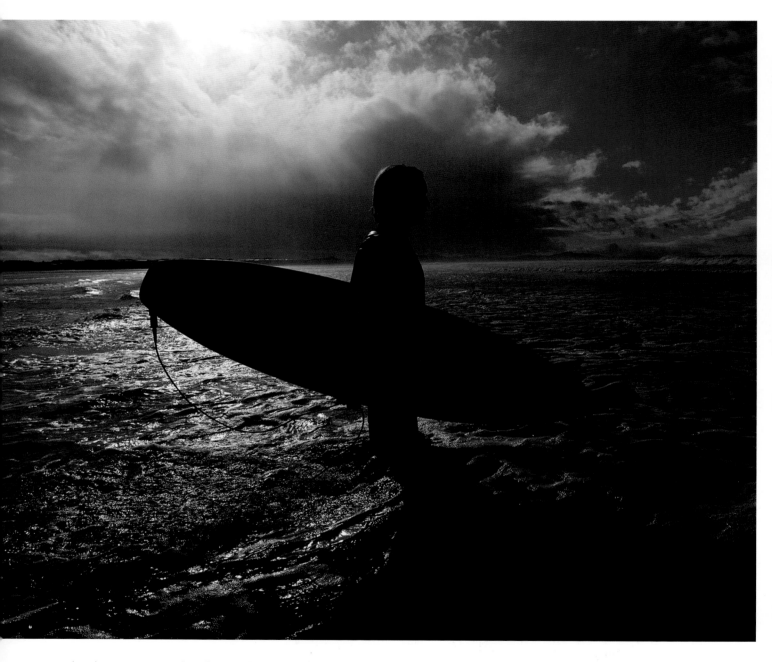
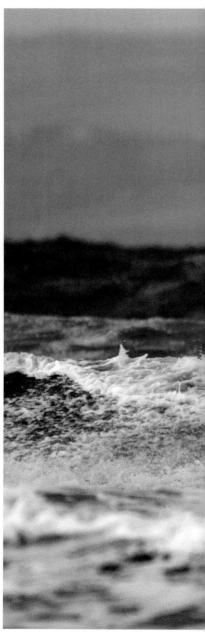

Leading international surfer and Enniscrone native Cain Kilcullen is undoubtedly the best surfer in Ireland and rated third in Europe. His father, Edward, bought him his first surfboard at the tender age of seven. Cain's talent developed quickly. His instinct for free-style surfing is legendary. Cain has won the Irish National Surfing Championships many times, and represented Ireland and won numerous competitions aboard. He is a member of West Sligo Surf Club.

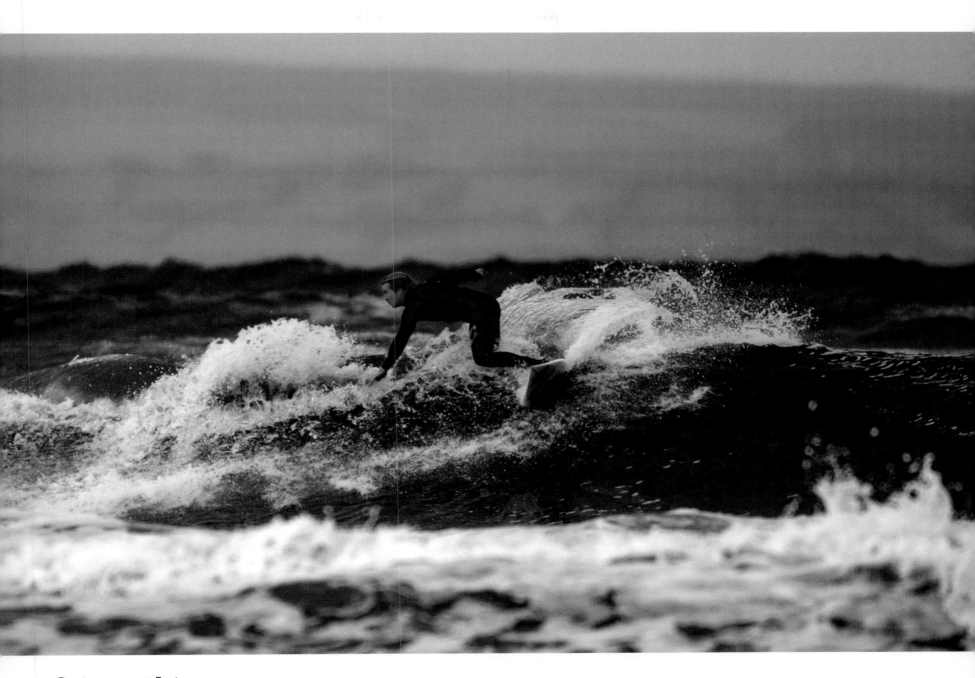

Carving a wave at Enniscrone.

ROSSES POINT

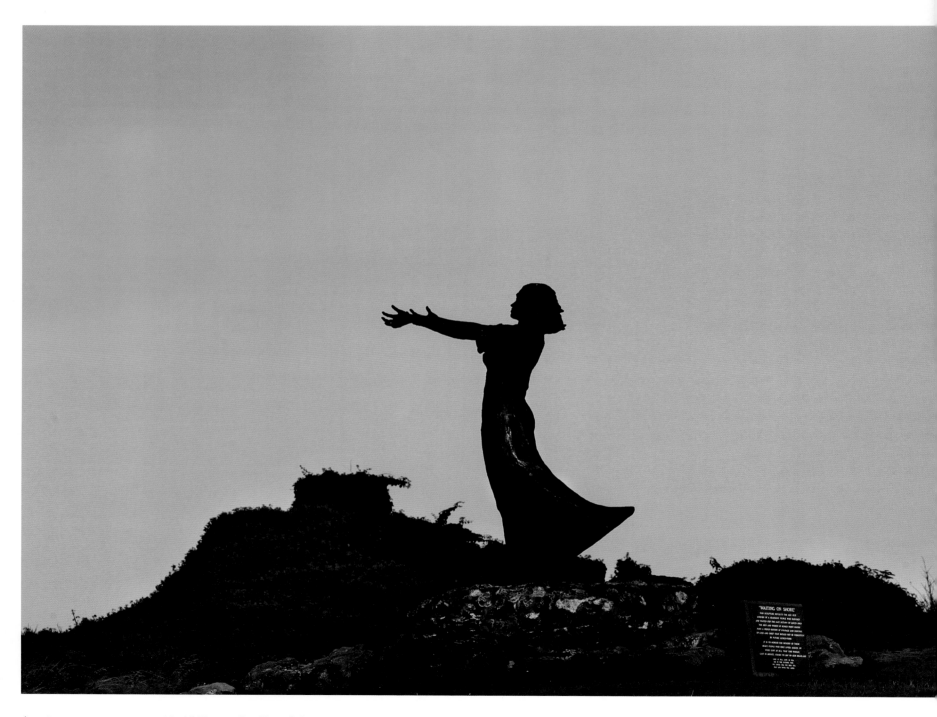

A poignant monument entitled 'Waiting On Shore' depicts a woman with her arms outstretched, a reminder of anxious villagers waiting for news of their loved ones at sea.

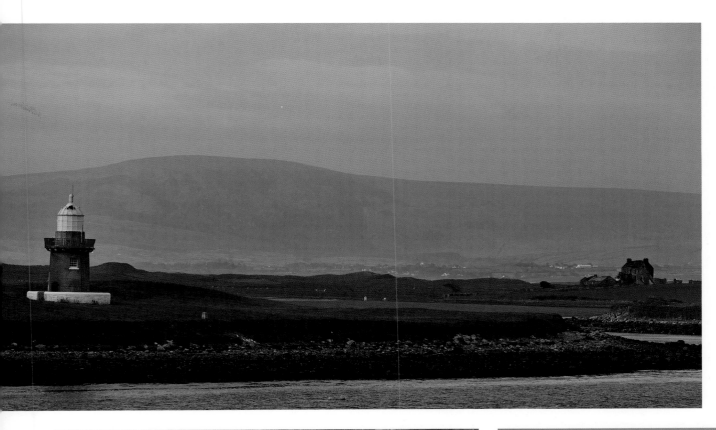

Left: Oyster Island Lighthouse near the old seafaring village of Rosses Point. Built in 1893, the tower is 13m (32ft) high. The light has a range of 10 nautical miles.

Below left: Two brave swimmers race to the waves at Rosses Point.

Below right: Leigh Dunne enjoys an evening's kitesurfing at Rosses Point, Sligo.

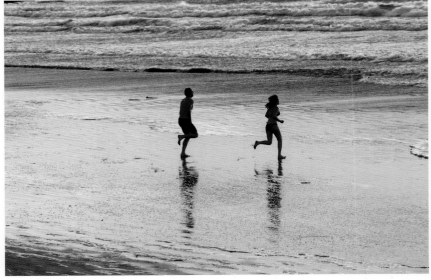

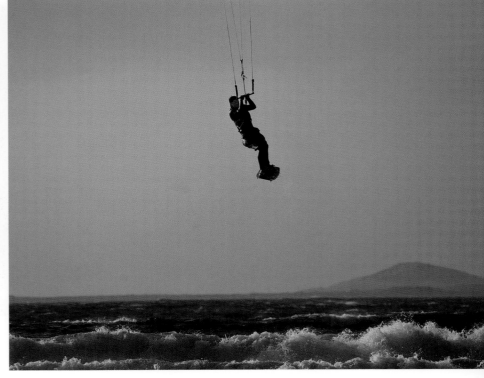

BLACKROCK LIGHTHOUSE

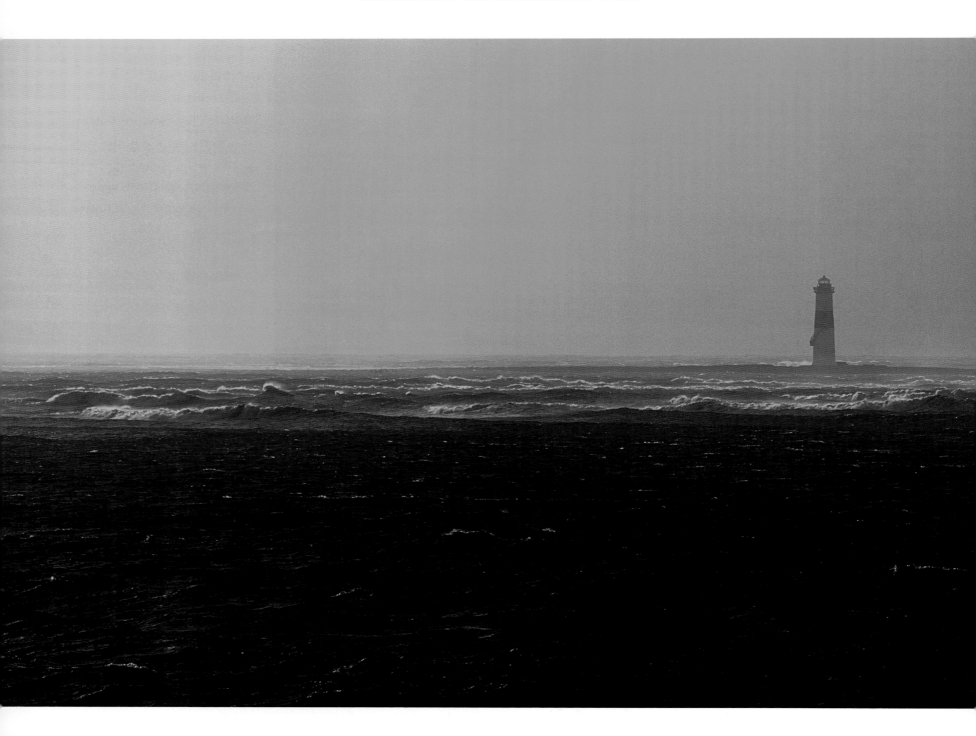

Blackrock Lighthouse on Sligo Bay is an impressive limestone structure overlooking Coney Island. It was established as a navigation beacon in the eighteenth century and converted into a lighthouse in 1834, after a storm in 1819 washed away the first beacon. One of eighty-two lighthouses that guard our coast and mind our mariners, Blackrock Lighthouse has its own unique signature:

Name	Blackrock Sligo
Latitude	54°18.460' North
Longitude	008°37.059' West
Character	Fl WR 5s
Sectors	W130°–107° (337°), R107°–130° (23°)
Light Range	White 10 nautical miles, Red 8 nautical miles
Height of tower	25m
Height of light above MHWS	24m

Technical data courtesy of Commissioners of Irish Lights

PRANNIE RHATIGAN: A GIFT FROM THE SEA

Prannie Rhatigan is a medical doctor who has been harvesting and cooking with seaweed and gardening organically all her life. Born and raised in the northwest of Ireland, she has a keen interest in the connections between food and health. *Irish Seaweed Kitchen* is her first cookbook and it has become the ultimate bible for cooking with seaweeds.

A member of the Slow Food movement, Prannie has represented Ireland's finest food abroad on several occasions and regularly gives workshops and lectures on seaweeds and cooking. Her most recent personal work includes exploring the links between genetics, the environment and the benefits of live foods on health and well being.

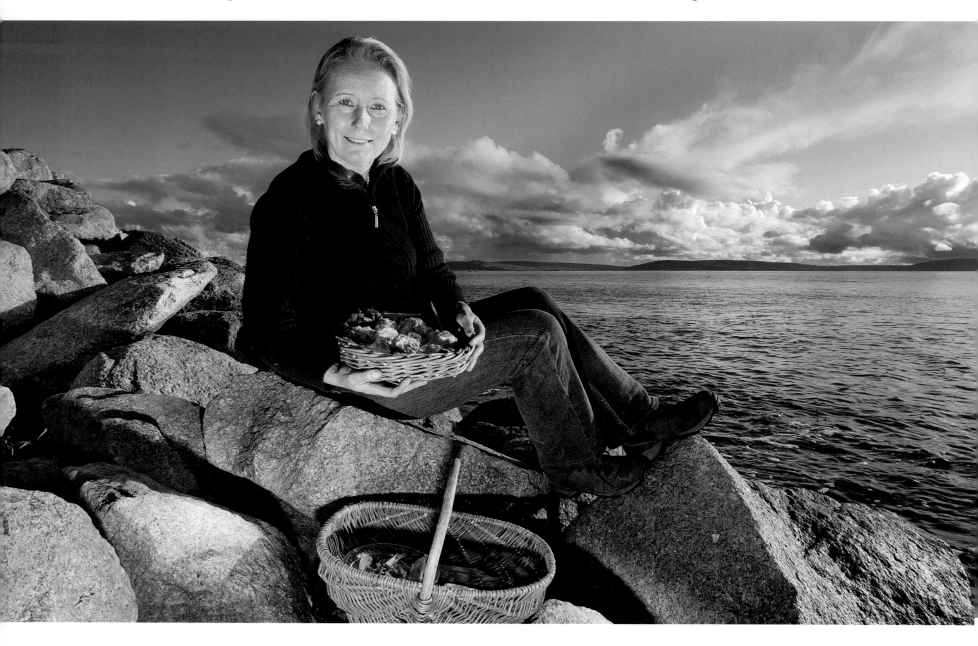

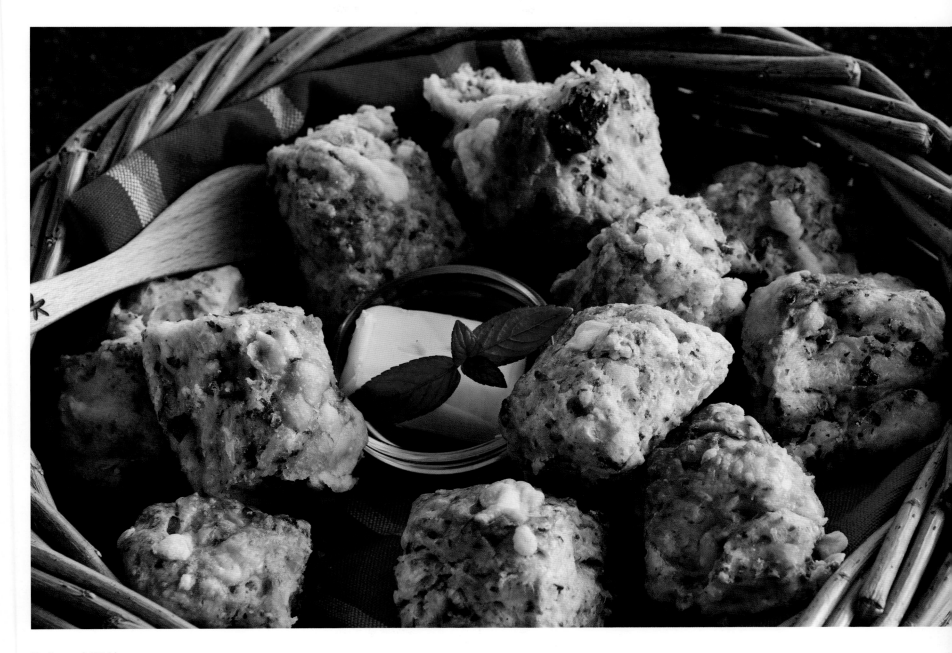

Duileasc (dillisk) scones

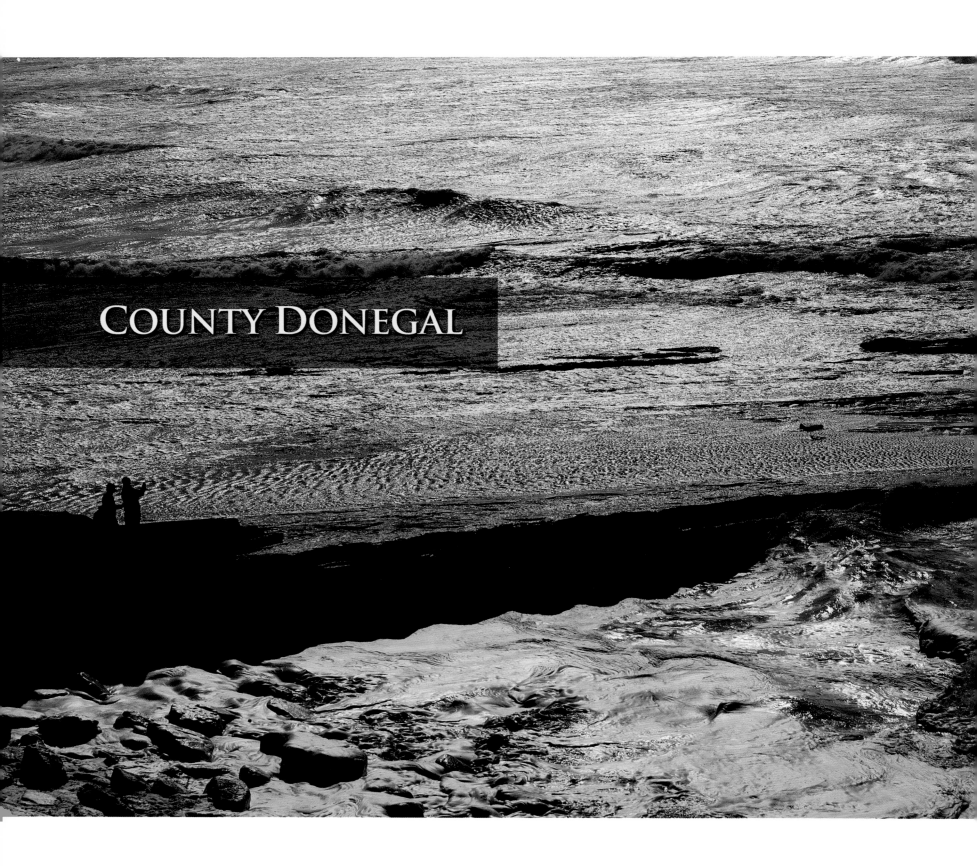

COUNTY DONEGAL

BUNDORAN BEACH

Bundoran Beach (Bundoran meaning 'foot of the little water') is a sandy beach facing Donegal Bay and the Atlantic. It is located north of the resort town of the same name, which has been a popular seaside destination for over 200 years.

The beach is revered among the surfing community as one of the best surfing spots in Europe, and the prestigious Euro Surf championships were held here in 2011.

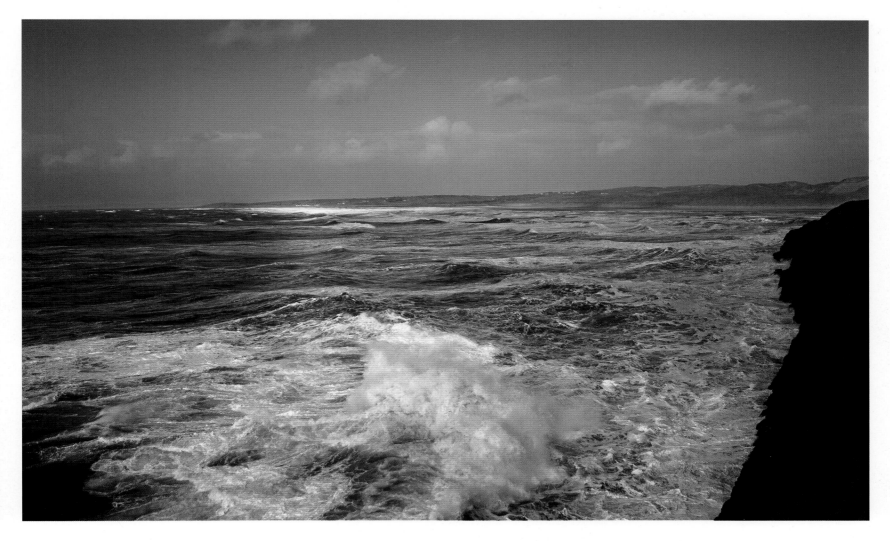

Above: 'The surface of the sea is at the interface of several different worlds. No two waves in millions of years ever curl up the same way.'
John O'Donoghue, 'Tears of the Earth' (from *The Four Elements* (Transworld Ireland 2010))

Opposite: Late evening on Bundoran Beach.

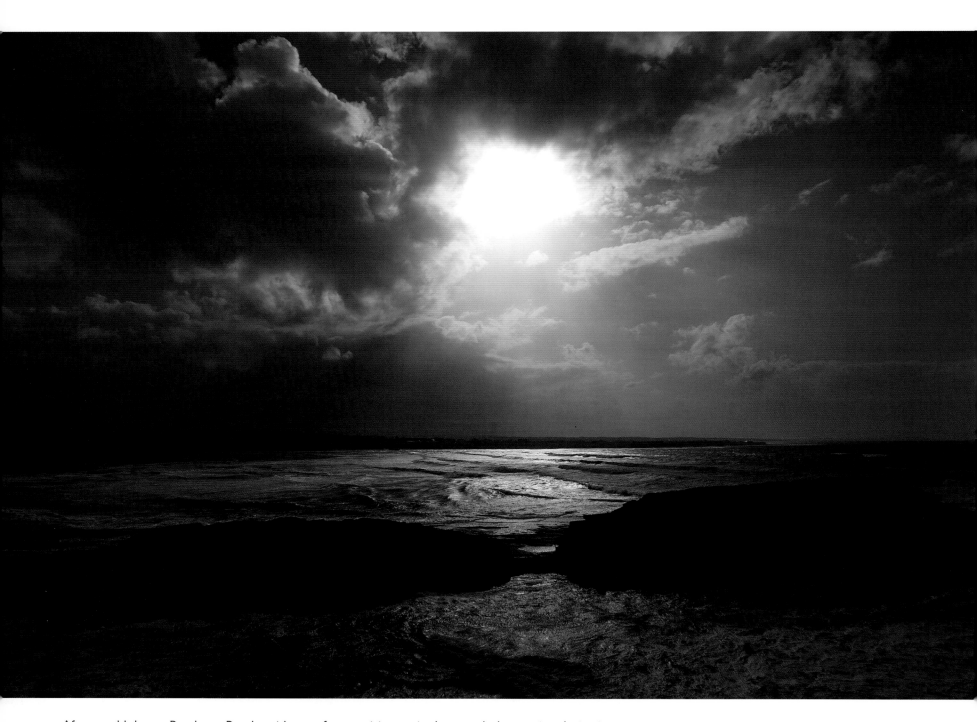

After a cold day on Bundoran Beach, neither surfer nor visitor waited to watch the evening closing in.

KILLYBEGS HARBOUR

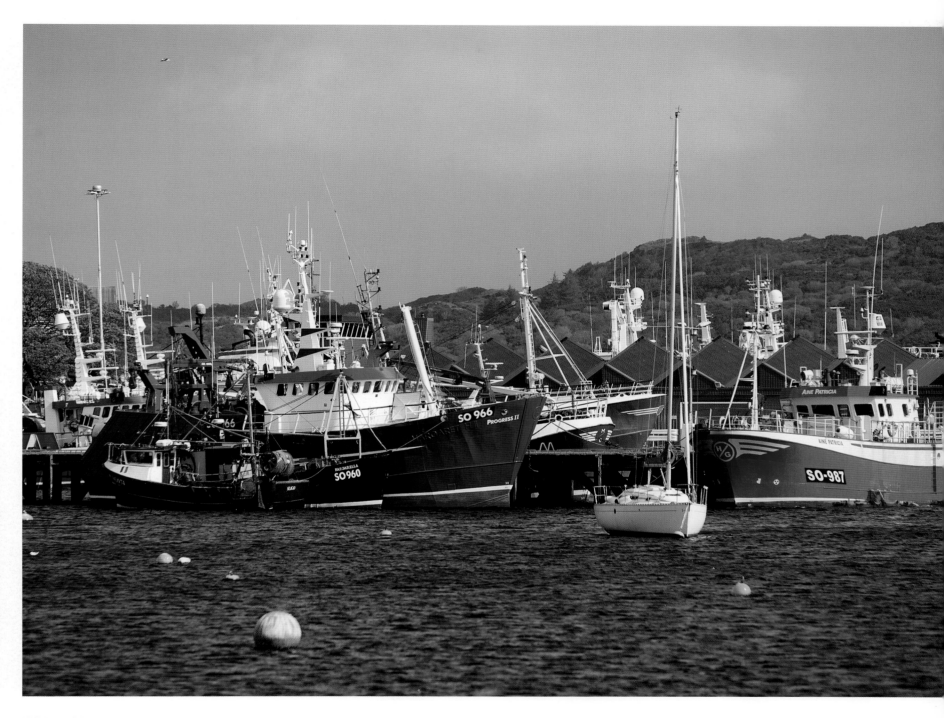

Killybegs Harbour.

In 1588, the Spanish Armada vessel *La Girona* anchored in Killybegs Harbour for repairs. The chieftain of the day, MacSweeney Bannagh, insisted that the locals provide food and shelter for the *Girona*'s crew. The vessel was repaired, before they set sail for Scotland. However, as with many of the Spanish Armada vessels it was shipwrecked, off the Antrim coast, with a loss of 1,300 lives. Over 2,000 Spaniards from other Armada vessels remained in Killybegs, thus adding to the vibrancy and colour of the fishing town.

The nineteenth century saw great changes: the town survived the Great Famine better than most, as fish were in plentiful supply. In 1891 the Congested Districts Board was established, paving the way for the fishing port to be improved with the construction of a new pier, investment in fishing vessels and production. The introduction of the railway line secured a quick delivery of fish to nearby counties. The first training academy to train fishermen in the art of net making, boatbuilding and fishing was set up in 1891.

Killybegs has always been ahead of its time: by 1963, there were twenty-eight boats operating out of the harbour, making it the largest in Ireland at the time. The world's largest fishing vessel, the *Atlantic Dawn*, docks in the harbour.

A new pier was built in 2004 at a cost of €50 million. The development meant not only could it handle the largest midwater pelagic trawlers, but it could also accommodate passenger cruise liners, the specialised importation of wind turbines, and be a service port for offshore drilling rigs. Crews from all over the world use these facilities.

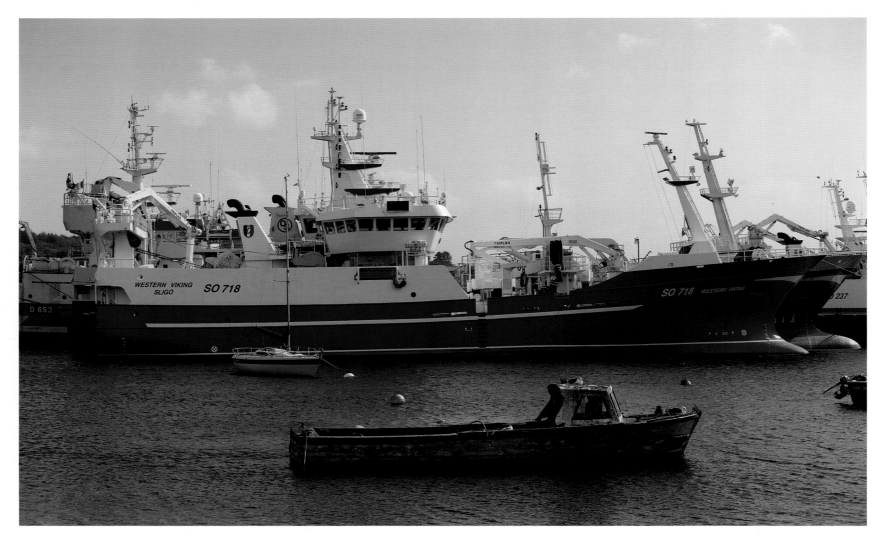

Above: Killybegs, located on the south coast of Donegal, is Ireland's largest fishing port, blessed with a sheltered, fjord-like inlet, which makes it one of the safest deep-water harbours in Ireland. Evidence suggests the tradition of fishing in Killybegs dates back to early Christian times, with a number of nearby monastic cells, from which the name is derived (*Na Cealla Beaga* meaning 'the little cells').

Opposite: The old and the new: Killybegs has ever been a place of contrasts.

ROTTEN ISLAND LIGHTHOUSE

The lighthouse situated on Rotten Island, a small island near Killybegs Harbour, was established in 1838. It provides a harbour light for the passage from St John's Point to the inner channel and past the rocks to the anchorage within Killybegs Harbour. The lighthouse and dwellings were designed by George Halpin. The conical masonry tower of cut granite was painted white and has an identifiable red gallery.

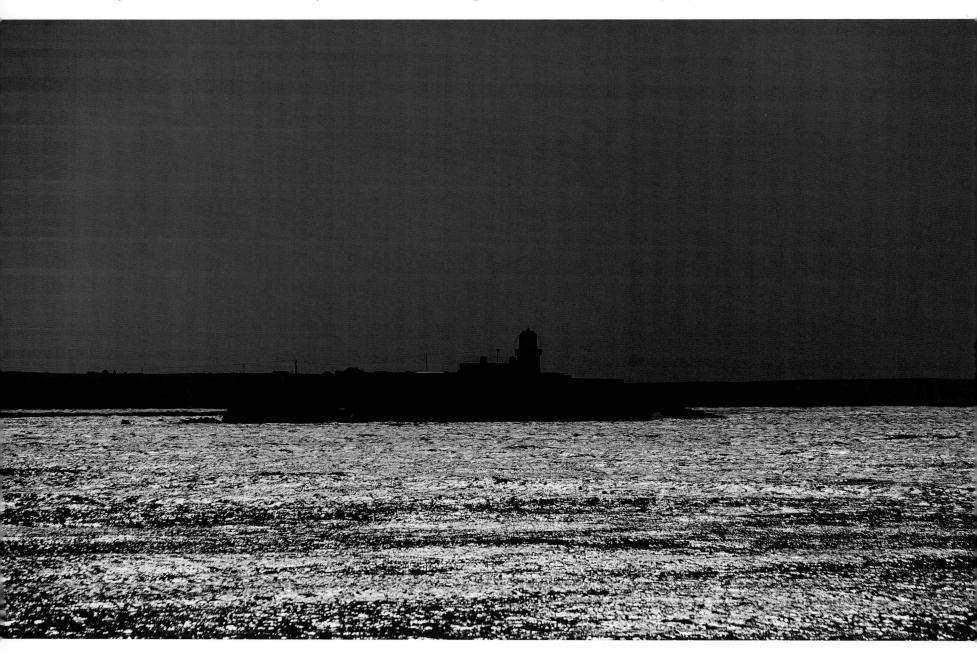

BURTONPORT

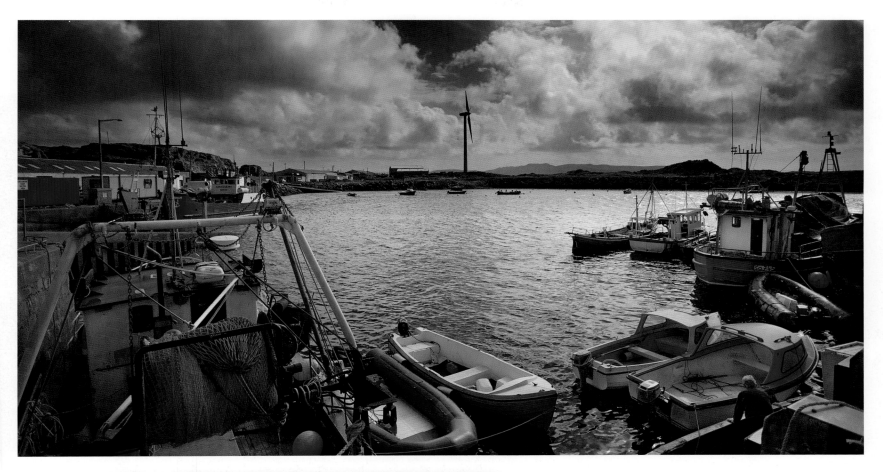

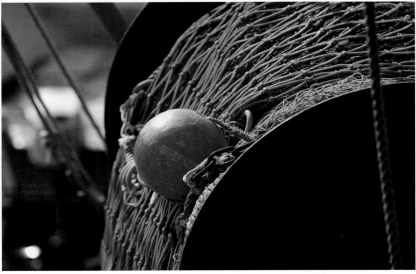

Burtonport (*Ailt an Chorráinn,* or 'ravine of the hook') is a small fishing village on the northwest coast of Donegal. It is in the Gaeltacht region and is an important ferry terminal for nearby Arranmore, Rutland and Innisfree Islands. Its name in English is derived from the landowner Lord Burton Conyngham who established the port and fishing amenities for the inhabitants. Around the time of the plantations in 1609, Ulster was a hive of activity and Burtonport flourished commercially.

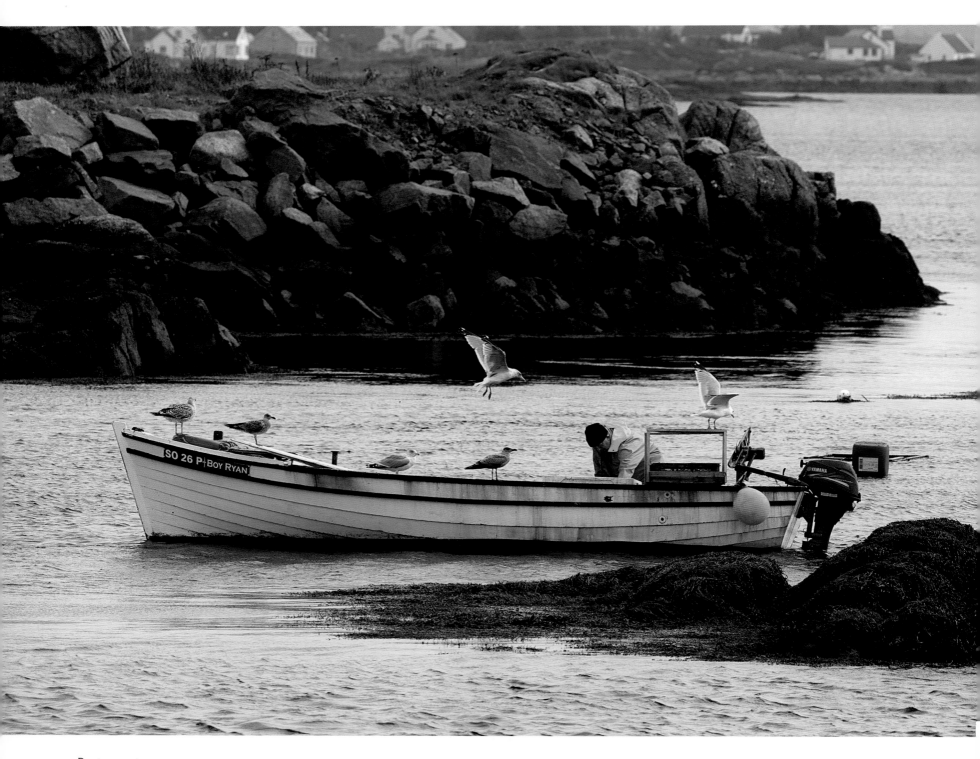

Burtonport.

RUTLAND ISLAND

Rutland Island *(Inis Mhic an Doirn)* is situated about 1km (0.5 miles) from Burtonport Harbour in the Rosses in west Donegal. Rutland was once a thriving colonial island, when English settlers established new roots during the Plantation of Ulster in 1609. Rutland Island holds its own place in history when the Irish rebel James Napper Tandy took hold of the island with French forces at the beginning of the 1798 Rising.

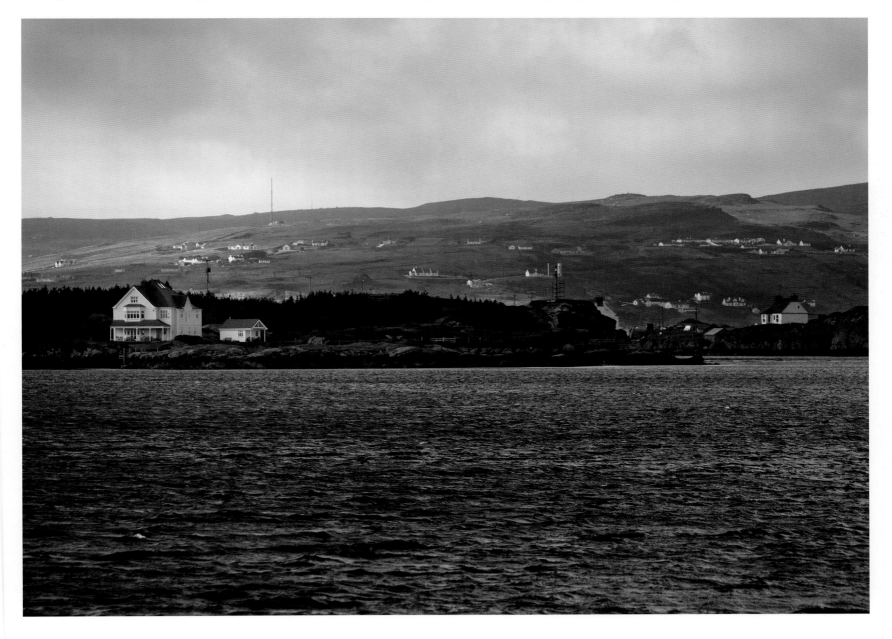

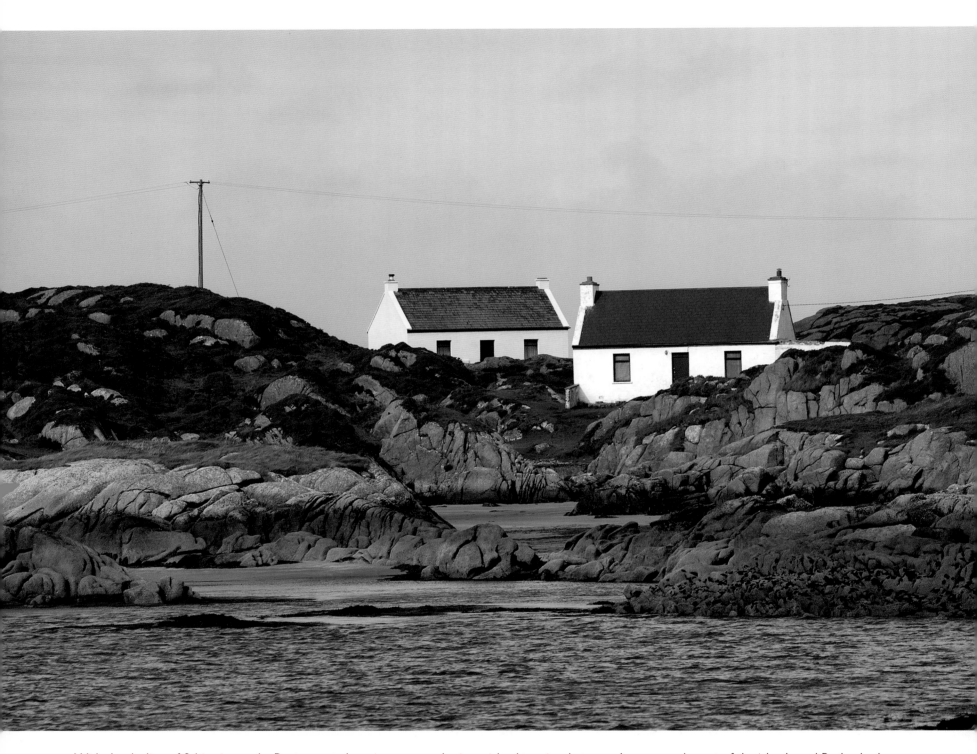

With the decline of fishing in nearby Burtonport, there is more emphasis on island tourism between Arranmore, largest of the islands, and Rutland, whose population consists mainly of original islanders and their families, many of whom have recently renovated their homes. The renovations are in keeping with the island environment.

Right: The remains of Conyngham's fishing complex on Rutland Island. In the eighteenth century local landowner William Burton Conyngham built a fishing station here to harness the plentiful supply of herring off the islands. This successful venture led to the establishment of a 'new town' with streets, a post office, shops and a public house. However, by the 1800s, the herring shoals had disappeared, and soon after the town and the fishing station were abandoned.

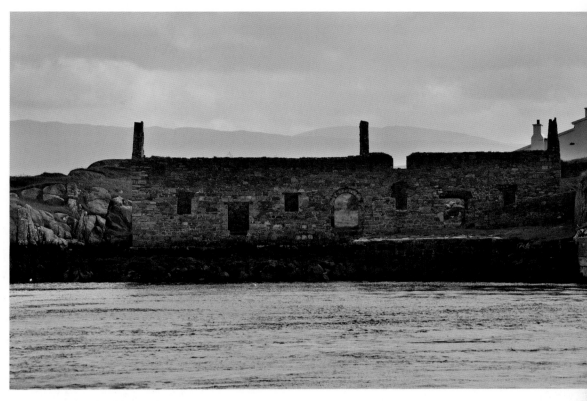

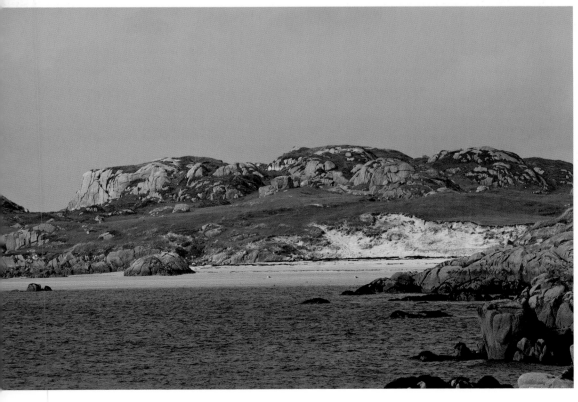

Left: Rutland Island is an idyllic and peaceful setting.

ARRANMORE RNLI

By Lorna Siggins

WHEN NORA FLANAGAN campaigned for a dedicated ambulance service on Donegal's Arranmore island, she never expected that she would become its first patient. Ms Flanagan, a nurse, mother and grandmother, had developed anaphylactic shock as a result of an allergic reaction to an unidentified substance. It occurred just days after an emergency vehicle had been delivered by the Health Service Executive (HSE) to the island.

The campaign for it had lasted four years, and under the deal finally agreed with the HSE, Ms Flanagan volunteered to become a responder with colleague Jane Murphy. Both women attended the National Ambulance Training College in Ballinasloe, County Galway. The island's roll-on roll-off ferry became an essential part of the improved emergency network, as it was equipped to transport the vehicle to the mainland at Burtonport.

When Flanagan collapsed in 2009, however, time was of the essence, and the lifeboat was tasked for the sea leg. She knew the lifeboat crew, naturally, but not just as an island resident. It was while attending a first aid training course at the lifeboat station that she decided to volunteer. When she enlisted in January 1996, she became Arranmore's first female member of the crew panel.

Then a mother of two teenage girls, she was conscious of the sense of history. The first lifeboat had been deployed to Arranmore in 1883, thanks to a donation made by Rev. Richard Vandeleur of Merrion Square, Dublin.

Born in Scotland of Arranmore parents, Nora was three years old when her family returned and lived for a time in a converted lifeboat house. She was one of six children, and left school after primary to work in Scotland, training latterly as a nurse in Edinburgh and moving to London where she worked in hospital theatre. When she and her husband started their own family, she was keen to rear their two girls back home.

She was involved in the island's campaign for a secondary school – a protracted affair: 'Fine Gael's education minister Gemma Hussey had approved the building, and then her government fell. Fianna Fáil reneged on the commitment. Eventually, it came good, and now it is one of the most successful in the small schools category.'

She had a good family support network when she opted to marry the lifeboat – for, in a sense, that's the commitment that an RNLI pager requires. Her first call-out was at 10.30 p.m. on a February night, and the wind had been northwesterly for several days. A crewman who had been assisting in the airlift of an injured colleague off a fishing vessel was swept off the deck,' she said. 'I remember feeling very helpless that night, but the next day when the pager went off it was for an accident on the island. The casualty was going blue and I noticed that his airway was becoming obstructed, so I tilted his head up which relieved and cleared it. It was then that I realised there is a role for everyone on a lifeboat crew. And if you can't tie knots, you can't tie knots – but I can tie a suture.'

Flanagan came ashore in 2003 and became the Arranmore station's press officer. She was as pleased as any of the crew when it they received several awards for the 21-hour-rescue of a single-handed yachtsman, Keith White, in July 2005; White, a Londoner, was sailing around Britain and Ireland to raise funds for various charities, including the RNLI, and was 60 miles northwest of Arranmore when he ran into a storm. His boat capsized several times and he lost power. An RAF aircraft from Kinloss spotted him several miles from his last issued position, and directed the lifeboat to him.

Dawn was breaking in very challenging sea conditions when he was located. 'The boat capsized again, they thought he was gone, and then they saw a hand come up on the hull – it was incredible,' Flanagan says. Coxswain Anton Kavanagh and crew managed to secure a tow rope; seas were too

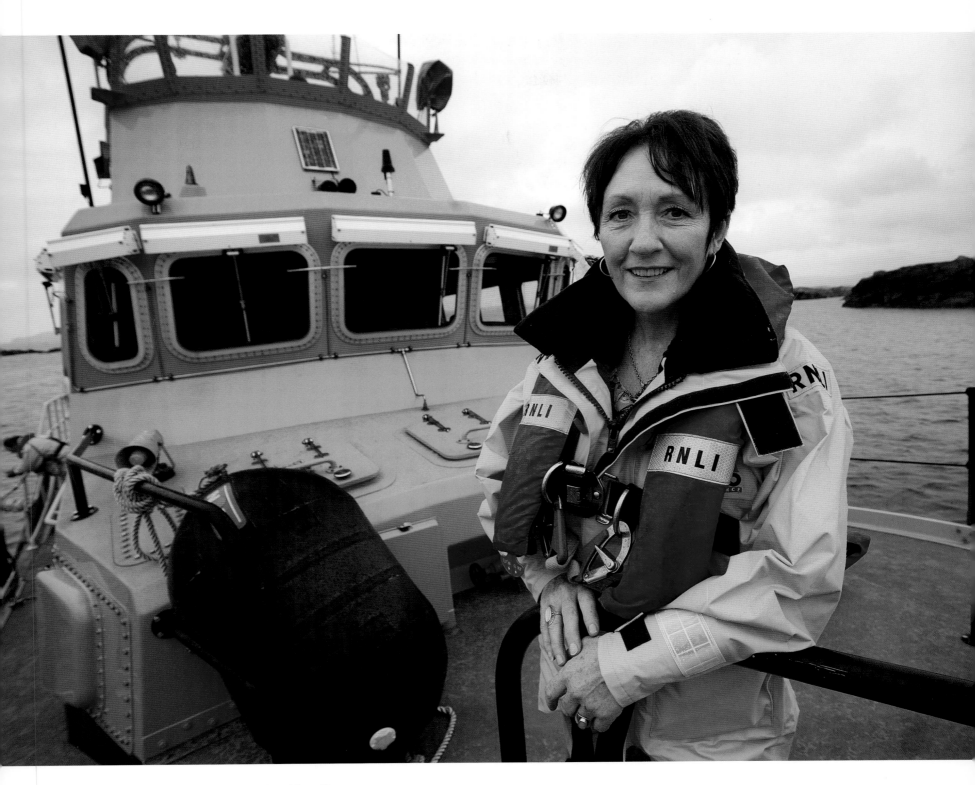

Island campaigner and RNLI crew member Nora Flanagan.

rough to risk coming alongside. White was transferred onto the lifeboat in calmer waters and taken to Letterkenny hospital, where he was treated for cuts and broken ribs. 'He stayed in touch and came back to the island to visit us,' Flanagan recalls. The RNLI honoured Flanagan in 2009, along with the Arranmore lifeboat's tireless medical officer, Dr Marion Broderick. 'The RNLI is like one big family, even though we are physically separated by miles of coast,' Flanagan says. 'You're one of the crew, wherever you are, and wherever you may be.'

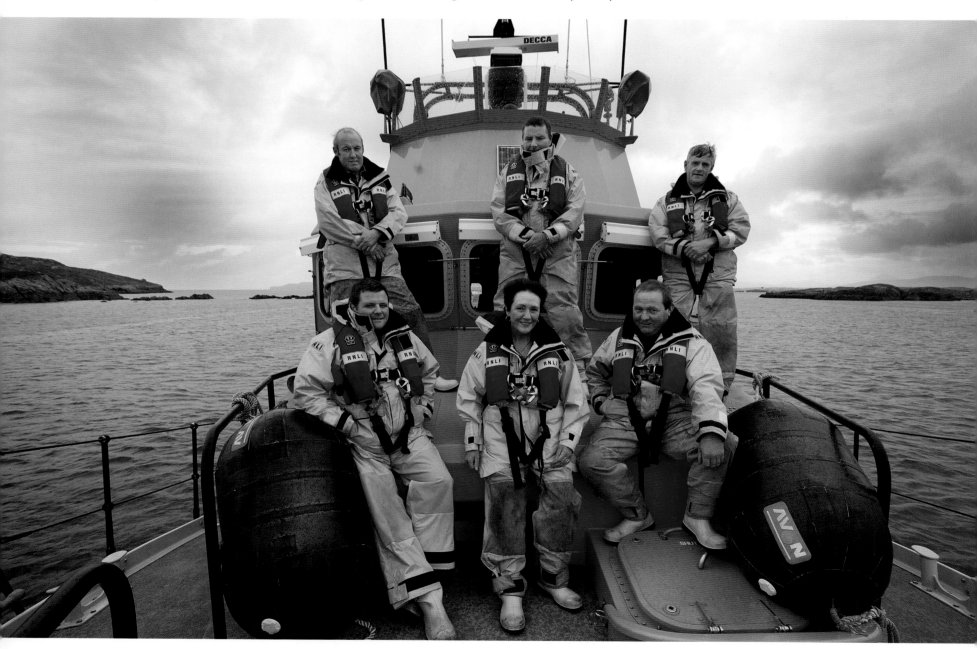

Aranmore RNLI crew members: front (l–r) Philip McAuley, mechanic; Nora Flanagan, crew; Anthony Kavanagh, coxswain; back (l–r) Sean O'Connell, crew; Finbarr Gallagher, crew; Jimmy Early, second coxswain.

MALLAGH BEACON

The locals on Arranmore Island call it 'Mallagh Beacon'. Ballagh Rock (*Carraig an Bealach,* meaning 'the rock road') is located on a open channel of water between Arranmore and Burtonport. There is a large group of exposed and dangerous rocks in this area of the Atlantic for vessels to negotiate. A beacon was established on Ballagh by Irish Lights in 1875 and was considered by mariners to be of great assistance to navigation. The conical-shaped stone beacon is approximately 4.5m (15ft) diameter at the base and 9m (30ft) high. It was electrified in 1983.

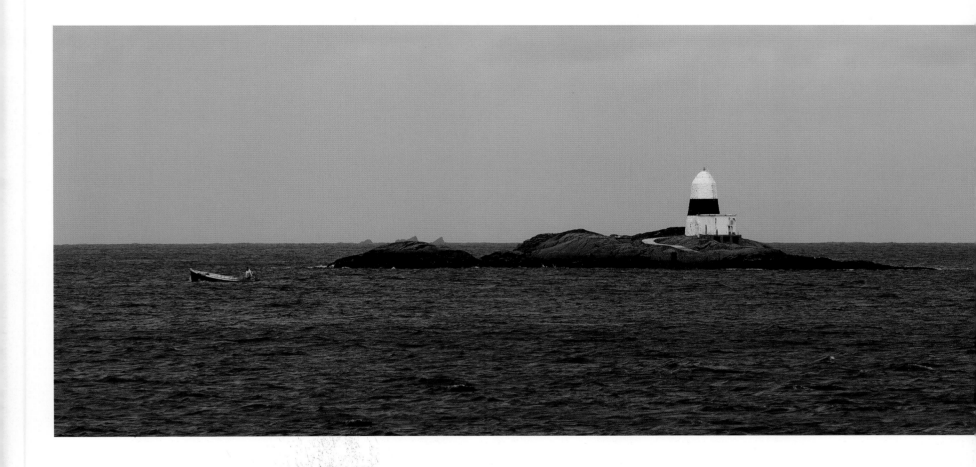

FORT DUNREE

Fort Dunree, located to the west of Inishowen Peninsula overlooking Lough Swilly, is today a military museum.

Fort Dunree Military Museum has a special emphasis on coastal artillery and the military history of the northwest. The maritime defensive site was established towards the end of the eighteenth century during the Napoleonic Wars and up to recently remained as a fort.

The original fort is on the point where the museum stands today. The armaments at the fort included two cannons from the French warship *La Hoche*, which had been captured at the entrance to Lough Swilly in 1798. Aboard *La Hoche* was leading Irish rebel Theobald Wolfe Tone and a French invasion force. During the Second World War, Irish forces were stationed here, to prevent warring nations violating the country's neutrality.

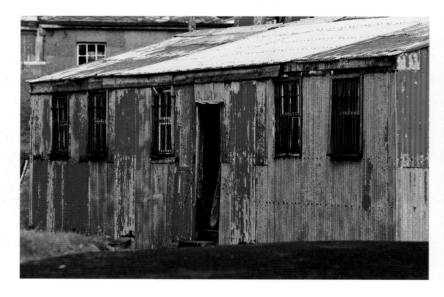

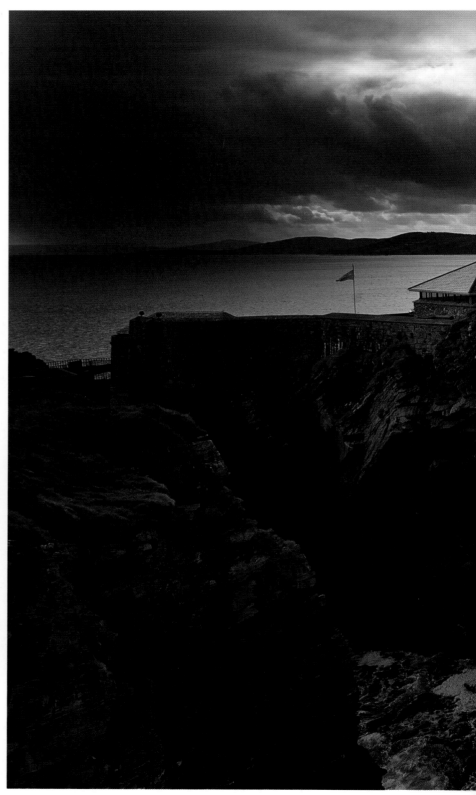

Above: A series of signposted footpaths pass the large number of abandoned military buildings and old bunkers, empty and rusting.

Right: The name Dunree (*Dún Fhraoigh* meaning 'fort of the heather') gives an indication of the wild landscape in which Fort Dunree is located.

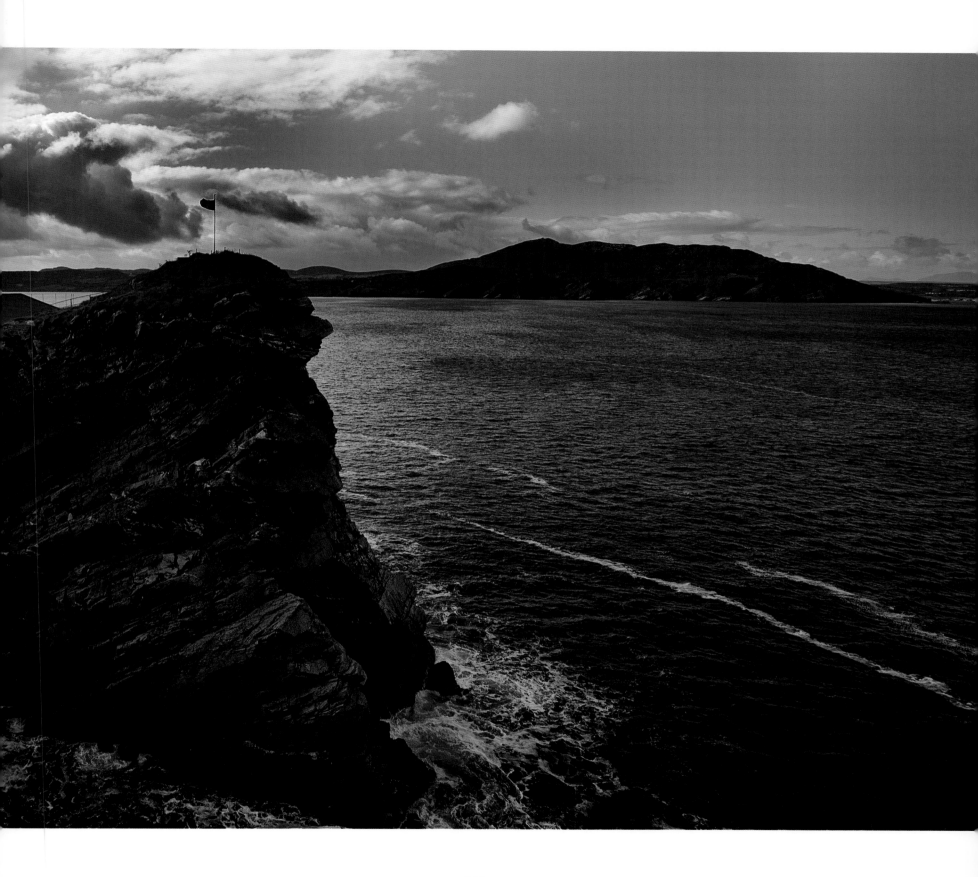

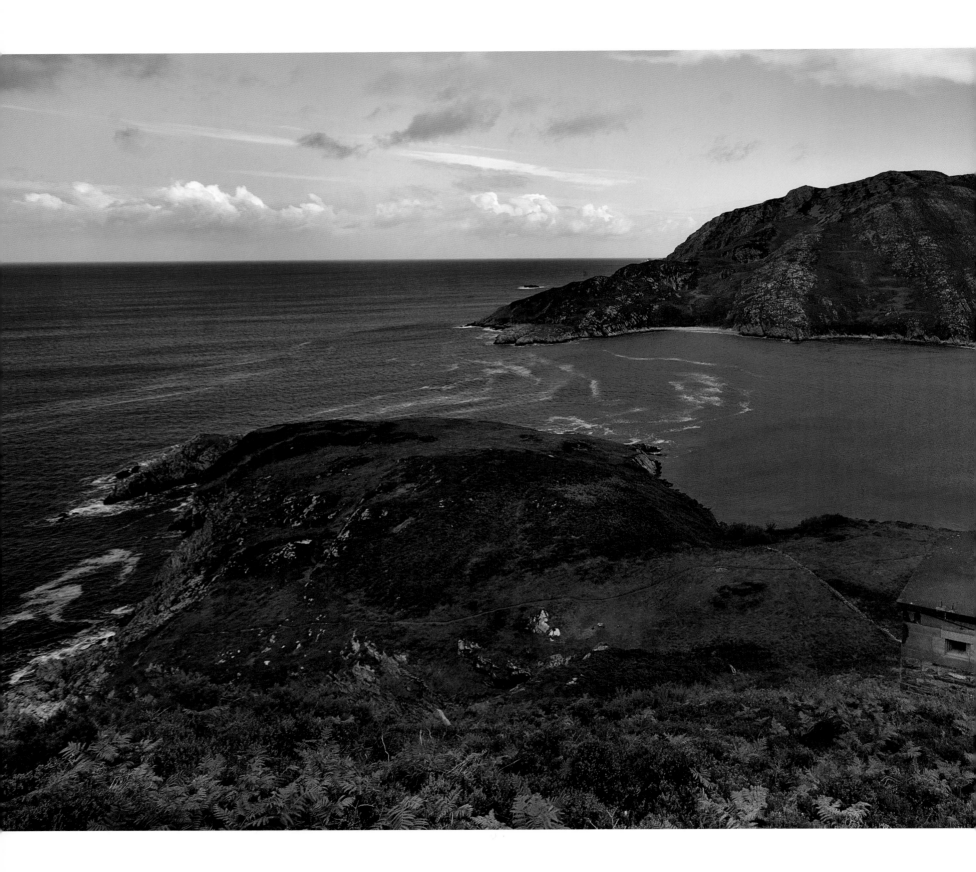

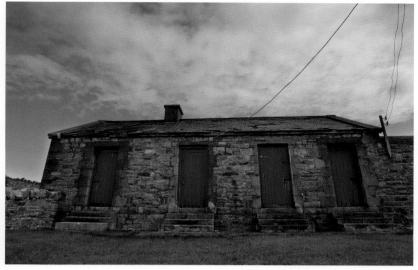

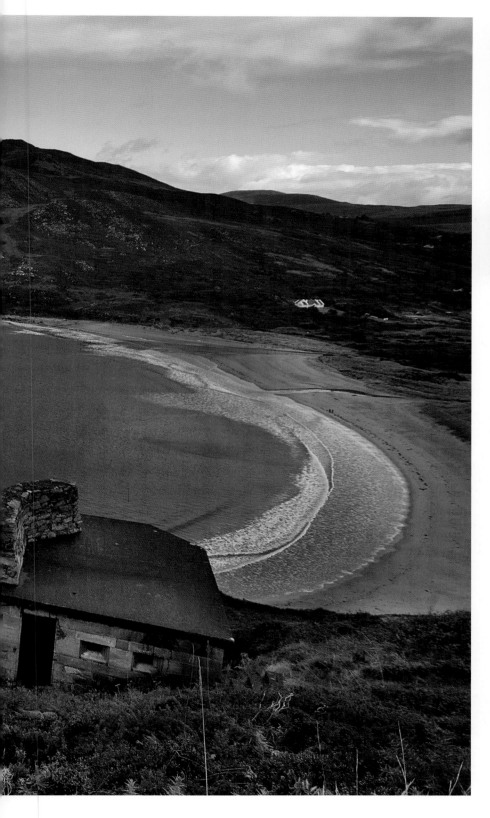

Above: One of many abandoned buildings that serve as a reminder of Dunree's importance as a military base in times past.

Left: Along the Military Trail, a peaceful quiet beach comes into view, with the remains of a military lookout post guarding its shores.

SEA ROVERS FOOTBALL CLUB

Sea Rovers Football Club, at Gortnamullin, on the Inishowen Peninsula, Malin Head, is the most northerly soccer club in Ireland. The club was formed in Malin Head in the late 1920s and remained in existence throughout the 1930s and 1940s, operating without any proper playing facilities. With the expansion of the Inishowen League, the Sea Rovers were re-formed. A community co-operative was set up to purchase a proper sports field and facilities. The entire community became involved, levelling the land, building changing chalets and a spectator chalet and erecting training lights.

Further funding was needed as the soccer club grew in popularity and, in 2009, a new clubhouse was opened with state-of-the-art facilities. The club has almost 100 members, 51 of whom are youth members from Malin Head, aged between six and eighteen years.

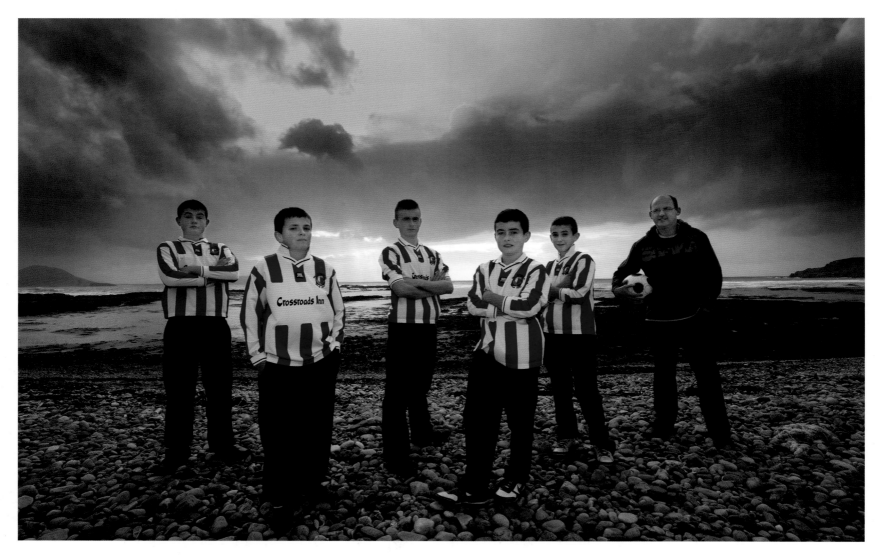

Proud players: (l–r) Cian Stevens, Joseph Doherty, Eamonn Hegarty, Tiarnán Stevens and Christopher Doherty, with Brendan Monagle, club secretary, Sea Rovers Football Club.

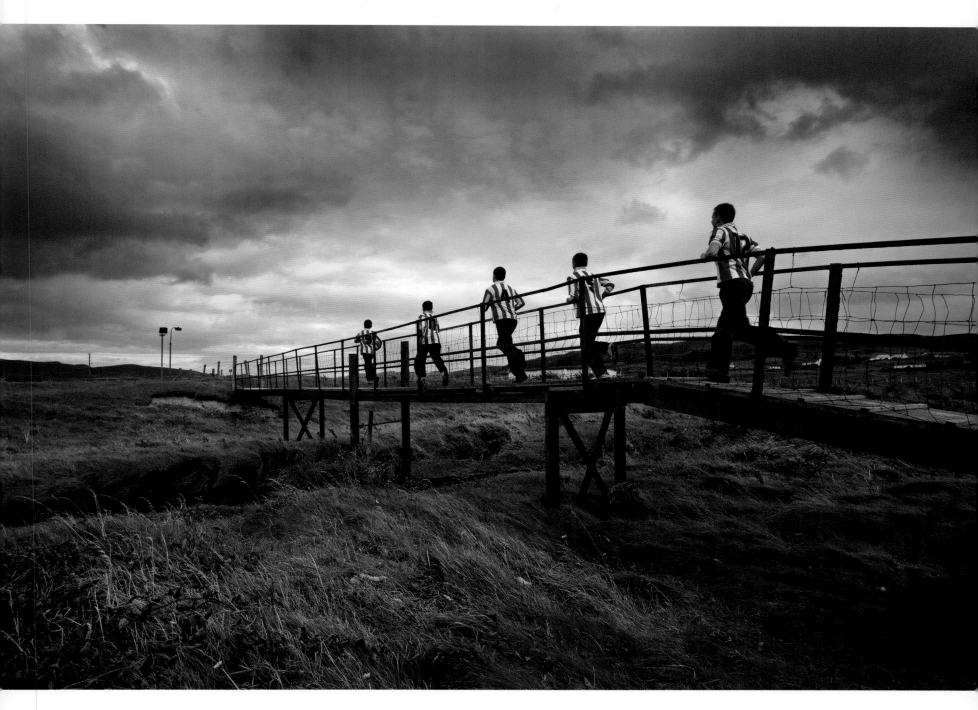

Members of the Sea Rovers boys' team, making their way to the pitch at Gortnamullin.

PETER MCAVENUE, MALIN HEAD

Peter McAvenue runs the most northerly of all shops in Ireland. The Curiosity Shop overlooking Esky Head, Gavan Isles, Inishtrahull lighthouse and Banba's Crown. Peter is a wealth of information and fun. He has lived on Malin Head for thirty years and is married to Susan McAvenue.

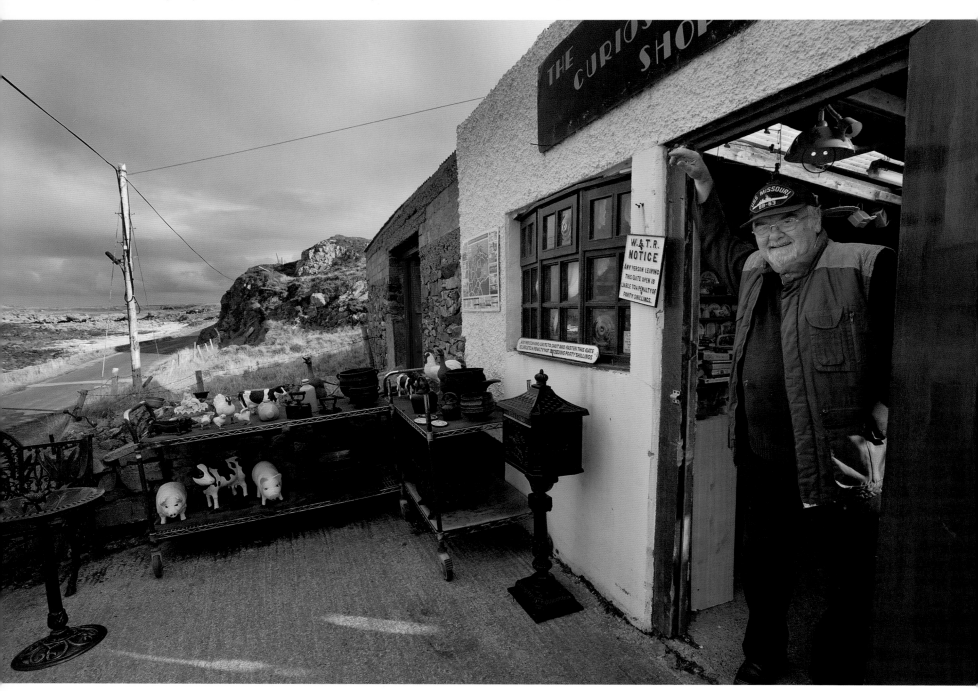

INISHTRAHULL LIGHTHOUSE

Inishtrahull lighthouse, located on the island of the same name, 10km (6 miles) northeast of Malin Head, is home to the most northerly lighthouse in Ireland. It is an important light for international shipping on the north coast of Ireland and a navigation aid for local shipping and fishermen.

The original lighthouse was established in 1813, largely as a result of the increased number of British navy ships using Lough Foyle. In 1958 a new lighthouse was established and the old one was taken out of service. The station was automated and the last of the lighthouse keepers left the station on 30 April 1987. In the same year the haunting Inishtrahull fog horn was silenced. The last inhabitants left Inishtrahull in 1979.

Today the ruins of houses, a school, a graveyard, the old lighthouse and signal station can still be seen. The island is a designated nature reserve managed by the National Parks and Wildlife Service (NPWS) with its resident deer, sea birds and grey seals. Landing on the island can be difficult as Atlantic waves swell up around Inishtrahull Sound. Centuries of old shipwrecks are all part of the nautical history of Malin Head.

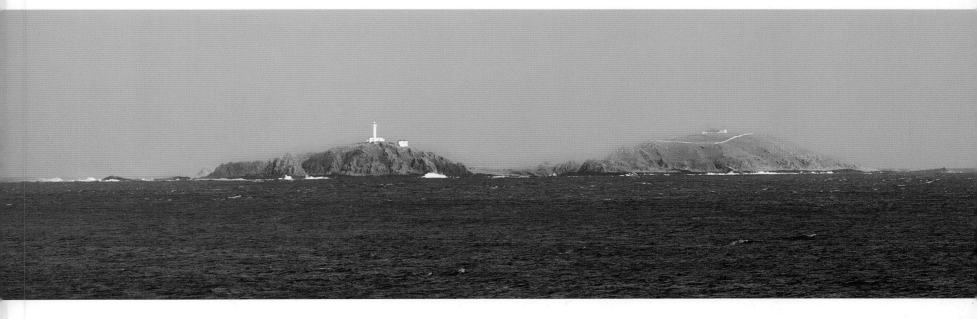

WHITESTRAND BAY

Following pages: Late autumn and an ebbing tide on Whitestrand Bay on the Inishowen Peninsula: the certainty of the tides is predictable, unlike our seasons of late.

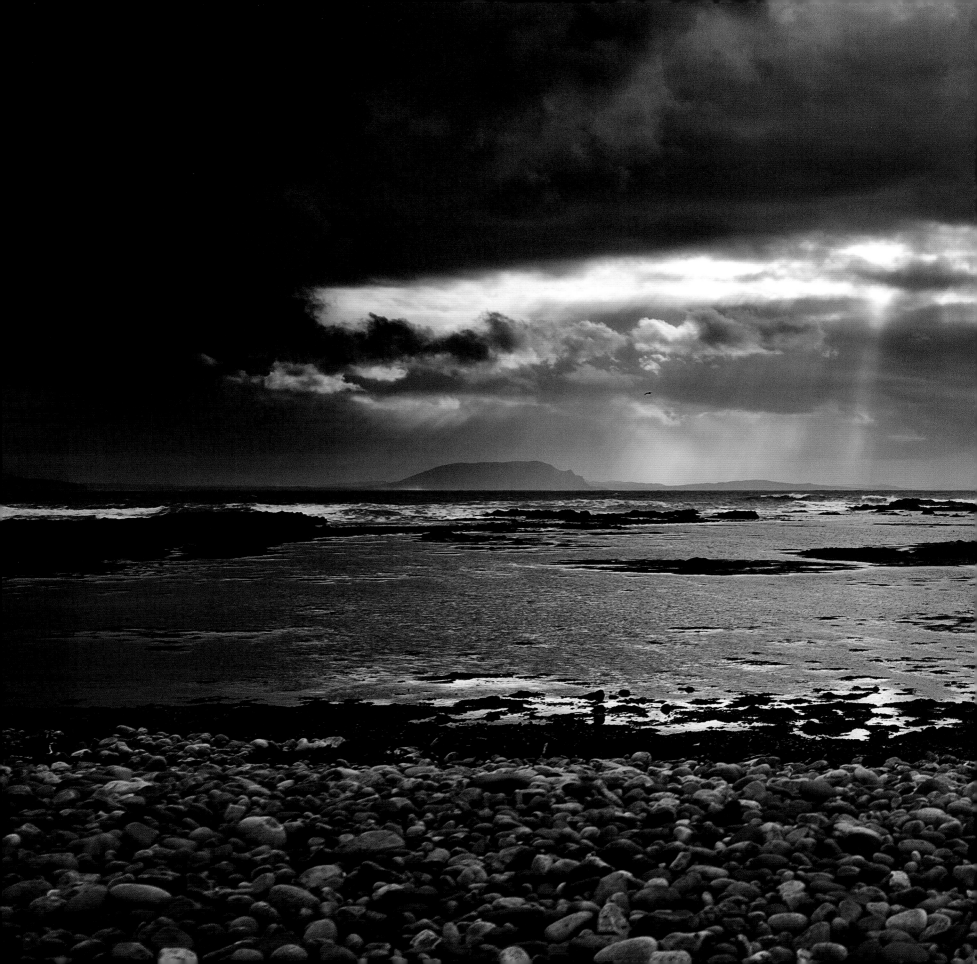

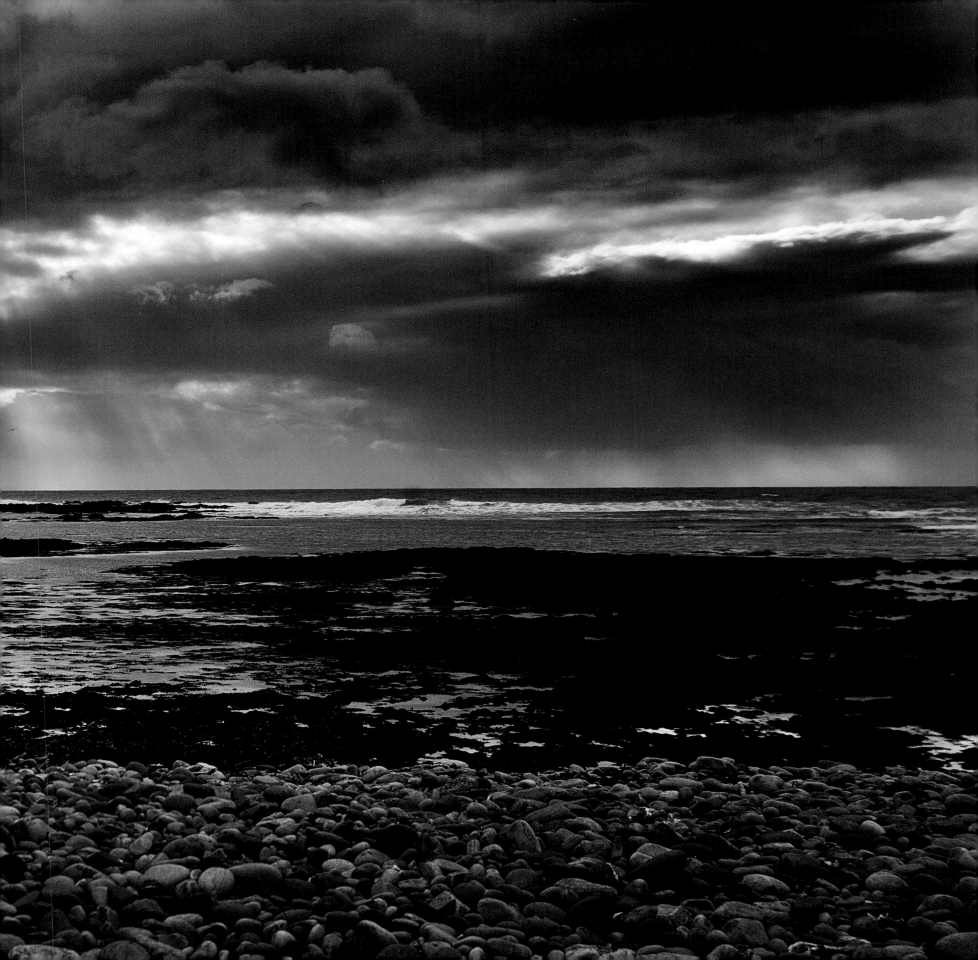

BANBA'S CROWN

Banba's Crown on Malin Head is the most northerly headland of the mainland of Ireland. Banba, the patron goddess of Ireland, was the daughter of Ernmas of the Tuatha Dé Danann. Banba's Crown is 16km (10 miles) from the village of Malin.

A Martello tower, of which only a shell remains, was constructed here during the Napoleonic Wars to guard against a French invasion. In 1805 the British admiralty built a weather tower, because of the importance of recording shipping forecasts both locally and internationally. It then became a signal tower for Lloyd's of London, connecting all ships at sea.

In 1902 the Marconi Company succeeded in sending the first commercial message by wireless from Malin Head to the SS *Lake Ontario*, establishing Malin Head as an important staging post for transatlantic communication, until the Post Office took over from the Marconi Company in 1910.

The military used the lookout tower at Banba's Crown during both World Wars. The concrete bunkers date from the Second World War.

Although all that is left of Banba's Crown is a husk, its lore and history are a reminder of the importance of Ireland's past record in radio communications at sea.

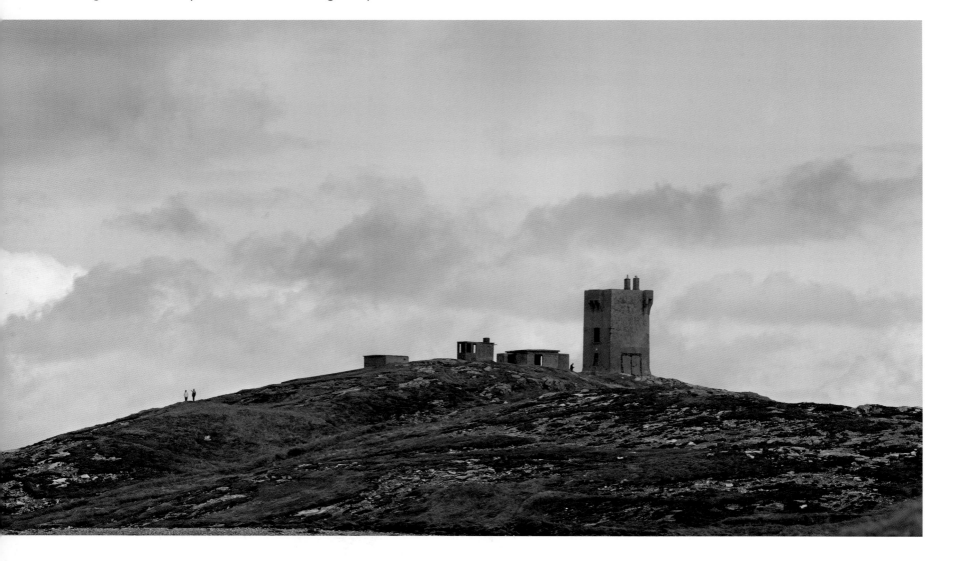

MALIN HEAD

Malin Head on the Inishowen Peninsula in County Donegal is the most northerly point in Ireland. The headland stretches from Lough Swilly in the west to Lough Foyle in the east. Its remoteness and near desolation make it a wonder of untouched landscape. Malin Head, *Cionn Mhálanna* in Irish, gives its name to the Malin sea area and those who listen to the Irish weather forecast are familiar with the weather reports from the nearby weather station.

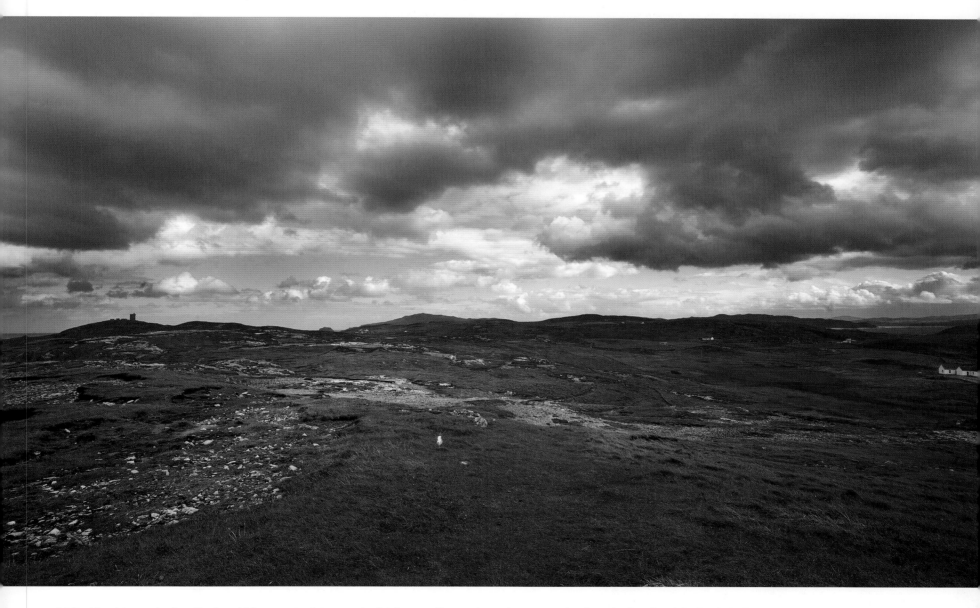

Malin Head is on the Inis Eoghan 100, a scenic drive on the Inishowen Peninsula, and signposts lead to the headland. At Banba's Crown, the word 'Eire' appears in stone, a notice for passing aircraft. The area is isolated by its geography and it remains a haven of peace, untouched by recent tourism development.

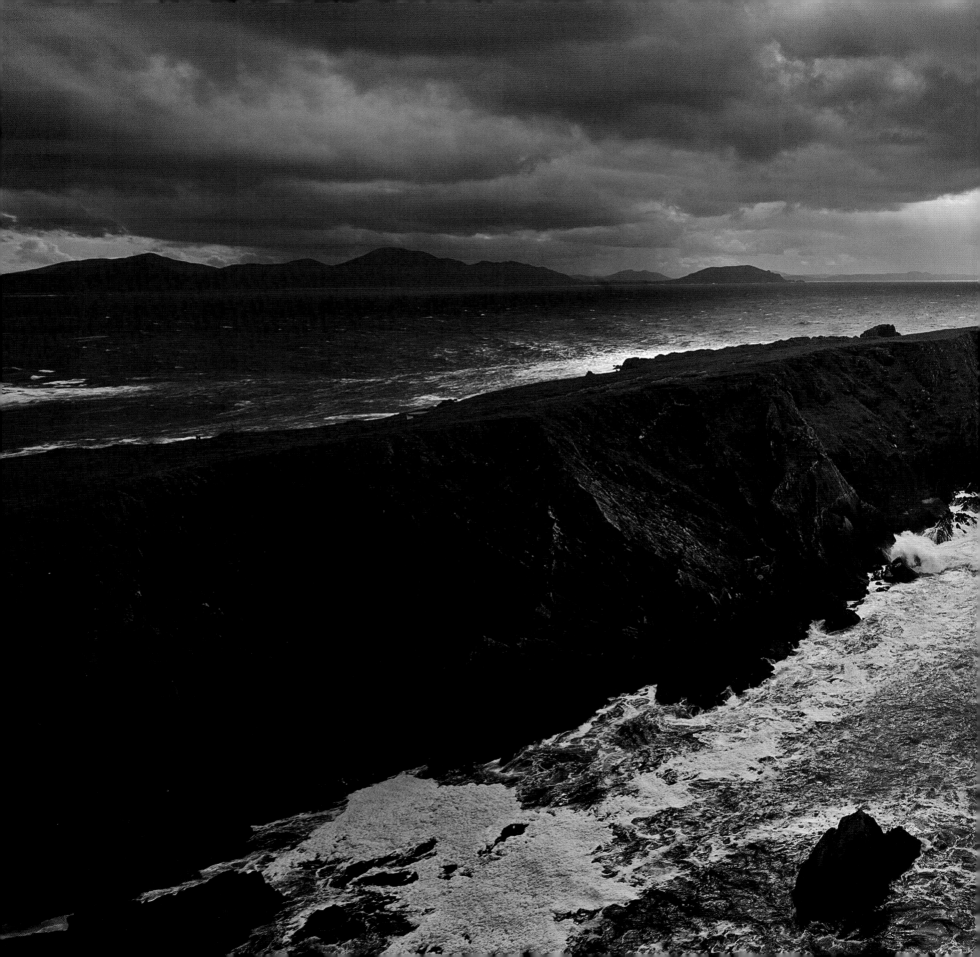

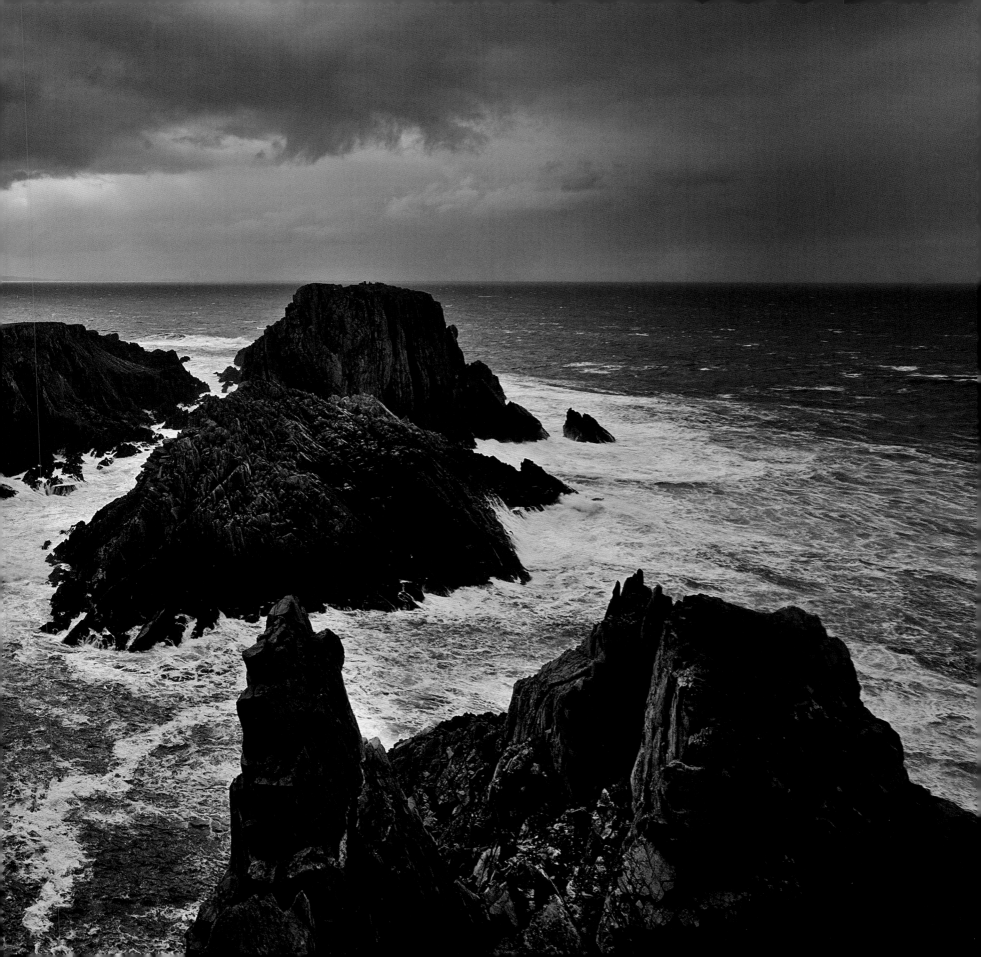

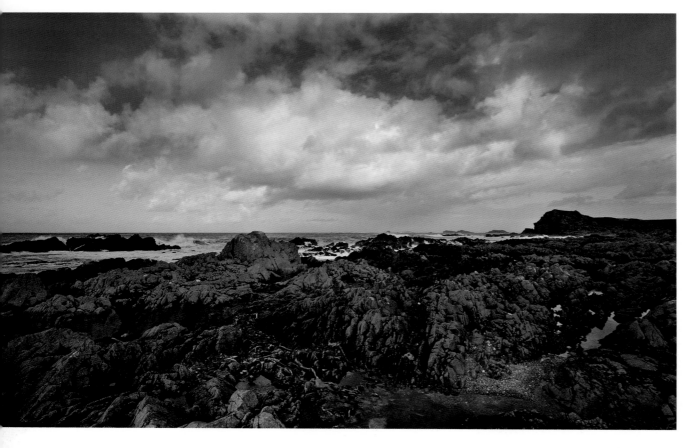

Left: Esky Bay is one of the oldest preserved late-glacial fossil coasts in Ireland. The distinctive feature is a raised beach system, with unique rock formations and crevices. It is of international importance because of its state of preservation.

Right Scéir Dubh, which translates as 'black reef', is an impressive outcrop, with great whirlpools at its base.

Previous pages: Breisle View on the Malin Head Trail lies battered and bruised by the North Atlantic.

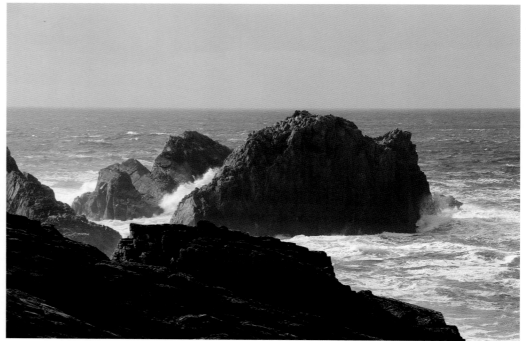

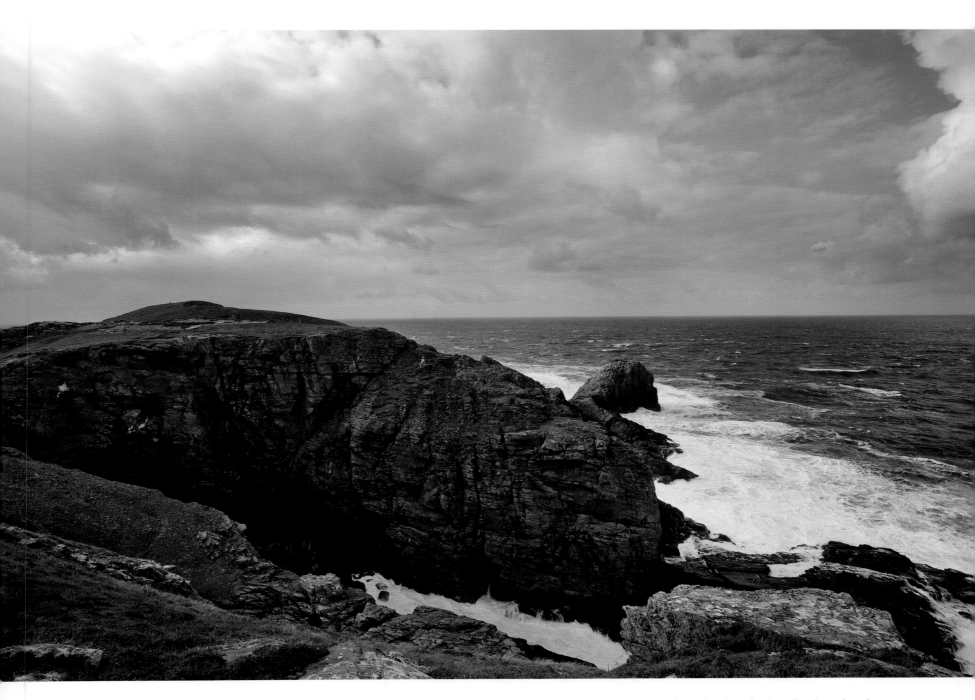

To the left of Banba's Crown is a trail of rugged cliffs, giant sea stacks and storm surges. The North Atlantic has not been kind to this headland; its thunderous waves have shaped a unique landscape with fearsome 'ogrooes', deep and dangerously narrow channels between cliff faces, which provided deep-water hiding places to ships during the Second World War. Tory Island and Glashedy can be viewed from here on a perfect Malin Head day. The cliffs also have a thriving population of nesting seagulls.

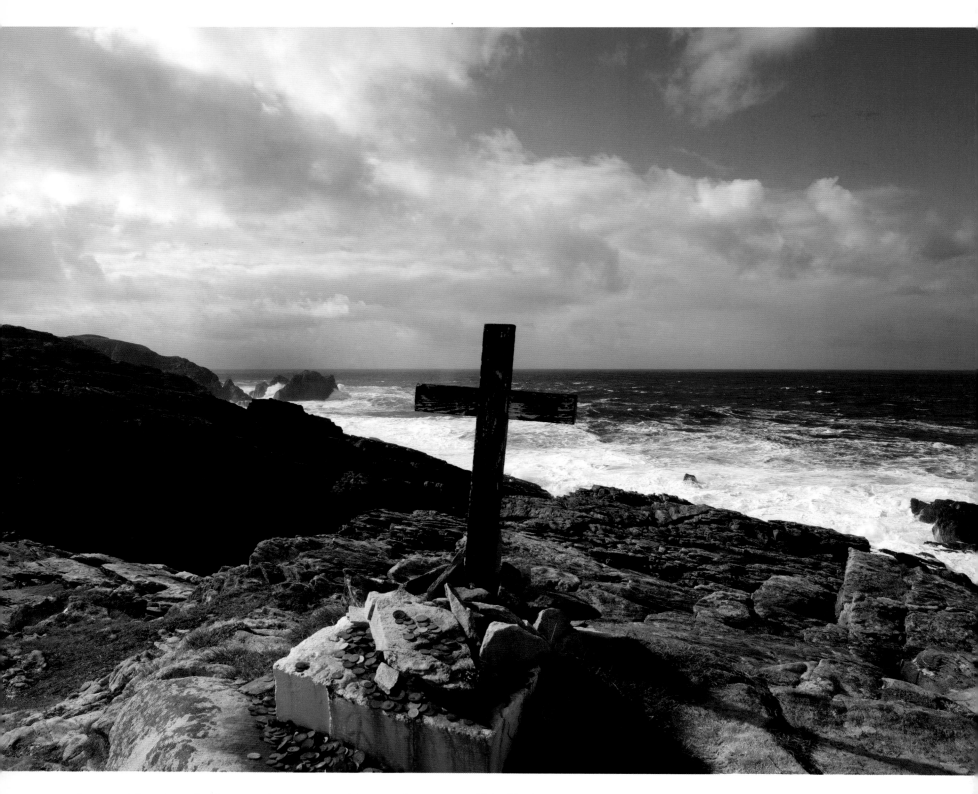

A memorial cross marks the area where a young visitor was lost at sea at Malin Head.